Matthias Bauer, Sigrid Beck, Susanne Riecker, Saskia Brockmann,
Angelika Zirker, Nadine Bade, Carmen Dörge, Julia Braun
Linguistics Meets Literature

Trends in Linguistics
Studies and Monographs

Editors
Chiara Gianollo
Daniël Van Olmen

Editorial Board
Walter Bisang
Tine Breban
Volker Gast
Hans Henrich Hock
Karen Lahousse
Natalia Levshina
Caterina Mauri
Heiko Narrog
Salvador Pons
Niina Ning Zhang
Amir Zeldes

Editor responsible for this volume
Volker Gast

Volume 329

Matthias Bauer, Sigrid Beck, Susanne Riecker,
Saskia Brockmann, Angelika Zirker, Nadine Bade,
Carmen Dörge, Julia Braun

Linguistics Meets Literature

More on the Grammar of Emily Dickinson

DE GRUYTER
MOUTON

ISBN 978-3-11-077747-5
e-ISBN (PDF) 978-3-11-064682-5
e-ISBN (EPUB) 978-3-11-064281-0

Library of Congress Control Number: 2020936378

Bibliographic information published by the Deutsche Nationalbibliothek
The Deutsche Nationalbibliothek lists this publication in the Deutsche Nationalbibliografie;
detailed bibliographic data are available on the Internet at http://dnb.dnb.de.

© 2021 Walter de Gruyter GmbH, Berlin/Boston
This volume is text- and page-identical with the hardback published in 2020.
Printing and binding: CPI books GmbH, Leck

www.degruyter.com

Foreword

This book is the fruit of linguists and literary scholars working together in the project A2 "Interpretability in Context" of the Collaborative Research Center 833 "The Construction of Meaning" at the University of Tübingen. It is a book on language and a book on the poetry of Emily Dickinson, premised on the idea that expert knowledge about language will improve our understanding of literature, and studying literature will lead us to insights about language. It builds on a number of detailed analyses with the aim to inspire a more general interest in combining the methodologies employed by both disciplines.

We hope that our book will be of interest to everyone who wants to broaden the evidential basis for linguistic investigation: we show that poetry is a fascinating source of linguistic phenomena that has often been overlooked by linguists though literary experts are at hand to explain their contexts and pragmatic meaning. We hope that our book will also be of interest to everyone who wants to learn about language as the basis of any meaning of literary texts: they will find precise explanations of phenomena that have often been overlooked or treated inadequately by literary scholars though linguistic experts are at hand to explain how they work.

Although the group of authors is a large one, there are still others to whom we are grateful for ideas, expertise, and support: in the first place, we would like to thank the German Research Foundation (DFG) itself, whose support made our project possible (via the grant of the Deutsche Forschungsgemeinschaft DFG to the SFB 833: 75650358 which is here gratefully acknowledged). Then there are the colleagues in the Collaborative Research Center, the many guests in our workshops over the years, reviewers acting on behalf of the German Research Foundation, and the other project members that have been involved: Giuliano Armenante, Markus Bauer, Julia Chant, Burkhard von Eckartsberg, Nina Fritz, Leonie Kirchhoff, Janina Niefer, Wanda Rothe, Daniel Schrimpf, and Fanni Weber. Last but not least, we would like to thank the editorial team of DeGruyter for their support. Very special thanks are due to Volker Gast for extremely helpful feedback and for noticing blunders in time. They would have been, like those that remain, entirely ours.

Table of Contents

Foreword —— V

Introduction —— 1

Part I: **Individual Analyses**

I.1   "To pile like Thunder": Lexical Ambiguity —— 15

I.2   "You said that I 'was Great'": Scales and Contextual Parameters —— 26

I.3   "I'm Nobody!": Interpreting Quantifiers —— 41

I.4   "This was a Poet": Identifying Referents – Definites and Demonstratives —— 54

I.5   "If it had no pencil": Identifying Referents – Pronouns —— 79

I.6   "My Life had stood – a Loaded Gun": Semantic Mismatches and Coercion —— 99

Part II: **Emily Dickinson: The Poet as Linguist, and the Linguist as Poet**

II.1   The Poet as Linguist —— 133

II.2   The Linguist as Poet —— 158

Part III: **Benefits of Interdisciplinary Work**

III.1   Poetry as a Data Source for Formal Linguistics —— 179

III.2   Formal Linguistics as a Tool in Literary Studies —— 199

Appendix —— 221

Bibliography —— 239

Index —— 249

Introduction

Emily Dickinson is one of the most mysterious poets in the English language. She devoted her life to "the Vision / the Word applied to fill" (J1126/Fr1243); in other words, to having language do the most challenging job conceivable: make us see at least "a Portion" (J1126/Fr1243) of what she saw and imagined. In pursuing that aim, she wrote, as Cristanne Miller puts it, "cryptically elusive poems that baffle even sophisticated readers" (Miller 1987, 1). If readers do not just remain baffled, however, but actively engage in understanding what Emily Dickinson's poems mean, the rewards are manifold. Not only do we learn to share her vision, we also realize how much the poems tell us about language. What is cryptic and elusive is combined with the greatest possible awareness of how language works. Accordingly, this book hopes to show how not to remain bewildered by Emily Dickinson's poetry and how to learn more about language by understanding some of the ways in which Dickinson uses it.

Our study is the outcome of a research project in which semanticists and literary scholars have worked together on the topic of "interpretability in context."[1] This is why, in this chapter, we will introduce our specific contribution to the linguistics-literary scholarship interface (section 0.1), explain in more depth why we think Emily Dickinson's use of language is especially fit for our purposes (section 0.2), and address the question of who our intended audience is (section 0.3).

0.1 The Combination of Linguistics and Literary Studies

We favour a text-centred approach to literary studies, and draw on descriptive and theoretical linguistics, especially formal semantics and pragmatics. From the viewpoint of literary studies, the methods of linguistics serve as a tool in reaching a better understanding of a literary text: linguistics will give a very precise and detailed analysis of a text, unaffected by arbitrary interpretations or conjectures. From the point of view of linguistics, a literary text can be seen as a tool for reaching a better understanding of linguistic mechanisms: a literary text as a complex form of utterance serves as a touchstone to test the accuracy and viability of linguistic theories and analyses.

---

[1] Our interdisciplinary work has been pursued within the Collaborative Research Centre "The Construction of Meaning" (funded by the DFG) at the University of Tübingen since 2009.

In the following subsections we will introduce the respective traditions our work in linguistics and literature is embedded in (sections 0.1.1 to 0.1.3), and state our assumptions about the pragmatics of fiction (section 0.1.4).

0.1.1 The Literature-Linguistics Interface

The approach to analysing literary texts by means of linguistic structures, mechanisms, and methodology is not new; since literary texts tend to show virtually every possible feature of language (Coseriu 1988, 292) they have frequently been the object of linguistic analysis. Especially since Roman Jakobson's influential essay on "Linguistics and Poetics" (1960), many attempts have been made to integrate modern linguistic approaches with literary studies.[2] Milestones on that road include Jakobson's notion of a poetic function of language (Waugh 1980) and John Searle's application of speech act theory to fictional discourse (1975).[3] Deirdre Wilson's and Dan Sperber's model of communication proposed in Relevance (1986) and the linguistic analysis of style promoted by Geoffrey Leech and others have had a similarly pervasive impact on literary studies.[4] The specific focus of our project, however, namely to apply the tools of formal linguistics, in particular formal semantics and pragmatics, is a fairly recent development.[5]

---

[2] For a survey, see especially the rich volume *Linguistics and Literary Studies: Interfaces, Encounters, Transfers* (2014), edited by Monika Fludernik, and the framing contributions "Sprach- und Literaturwissenschaft: Zuständigkeiten und Begegnungen" by Daniel Jacob as well as Fludernik's own "Closing Statement: Revisiting Jakobson." See also the more recent *Literary Analysis and Linguistics* by Ekkehard König and Manfred Pfister (2017).

[3] Importantly, Searle has pointed out that "[a]lmost any important work of fiction conveys a 'message' or 'messages' which are conveyed *by* the text but are not *in* the text" (1975, 332). This idea of literary texts presenting a means of communication and thus "a message" to the reader beyond what is literally communicated within the text itself between a speaker and addressee is an integral part of our research as well.

[4] Leech's *Linguistic Guide to English Poetry* (1969) is a thorough examination of the ways in which linguistic analysis can be applied to literary texts as regards stylistics. We moreover find in Leech another proponent of the idea that fictional and non-fictional discourse should be considered under the same terms and not as two distinct kinds of language: "Just as there is no firm dividing line between 'poetic' and 'ordinary' language, so it would be artificial to enforce a clear division between the language of poetry, considered as verse literature, and that of other literary kinds" (Leech 1969, 6).

[5] Notably, there has been a special volume of *Poetics* on *Formal Semantics and Literary Theory* in 1979. Its contributions by and large focus on the logical status of fiction rather than a formal linguistic analysis of literary discourse. We refer to a larger sample of approaches that integrate

0.1.2 Formal Semantics within Linguistics

Our approach to linguistics is based on Generative Grammar (Chomsky 1957), which argues that the grammar of a language can be described by a finite set of formal rules that generate the grammatical structures of the language. The goal of modern linguistic theory is thus to provide a formal rule system that models natural language. This book is concerned with the syntactic, semantic and pragmatic components of grammar. Syntactic rules model well-formed sentences. Formal semantics investigates how sentence meanings arise systematically from the meanings of the component parts of the sentence (Montague 1970). We rely on the recent version of compositional semantics elaborated in Heim & Kratzer (1998). Pragmatics is the subfield of linguistics that investigates language use. It is concerned with integrating context information into the semantics, and examines the meaning of a sentence in the context of its use.

One goal we pursue in this book is to arrive at a well-founded understanding of the meaning of texts (lyrical texts by Emily Dickinson). The interpretation of a text is based on the linguistic material used (the sentences in the text). Their interpretation (the semantics of the sentences) is the basis of further investigation of text meaning. Textual interpretation integrates semantics with pragmatic information. We argue, therefore, that the insights that modern linguistic analysis offers in the areas of syntax, semantics and pragmatics are essential for reasoning about the interpretation of a text.

For a more comprehensive overview of the theory of syntax, semantics and pragmatics we adopt, and a short introduction to the formal analysis, we encourage the reader to consider the appendix.

0.1.3 Our Approach to Text Analysis and Interpretation

Our approach in literary scholarship is largely text-oriented, as we argue for plausible interpretations derived from a linguistic analysis of the literary text. On the basis of this analysis, we incorporate extra-linguistic, contextual

---

both linguistics and literary studies in the analysis of fictional texts in chapter III.2, where we discuss the specific benefits that arise when combining literary studies with formal linguistics. Probably the most thorough and useful work on how to combine formal semantics in particular with literary texts is Regine Eckardt's book on *The Semantics of Free Indirect Discourse* (2015). This field has also attracted the attention of other semanticists, such as Emar Maier (2014; 2017) and Yael Sharvit (2008).

knowledge provided by the resources of literary scholarship in order to achieve plausible global interpretations. When analysing Dickinson's poetry from the perspective of literary studies, the main aspects we look at are biographical information, intertextual references and influences as well as textual aspects that are not covered by a strictly semantic analysis.

Considering biographical information in our case does not mean to match statements in her poems to biographical occurrences. Rather, we use our knowledge of Dickinson's biography to substantiate our approach. For example, the special importance we attach to the definitions given by Noah Webster's *An American Dictionary of the English Language* is justified because we know that it was one of Dickinson's most-used books (cf. Benvenuto 1983; Hallen and Harvey 1993), and was a point of reference for the many reflections about words, writing, language and poetry that we find in Dickinson's works (cf. Thackrey 1963). When studying a poet who once said: "for several years, my Lexicon – was my only companion –" (L261, cf. Miller 1987, 154), biographical information to no small extent means information about the words and quotations found in that dictionary. The meaning of particular words (that is, definitions, synonyms, and possible connotations) in Dickinson's time, and especially in Noah Webster's *Dictionary* draws our attention to intertextuality: we look at other instances in which Dickinson uses a word or phrase, that is, we look at those of her poems (and letters) where the word occurs and at how it is used there (in what kind of grammatical construction, in what kind of context) in order to understand her idiolect.

We also look at possible (and plausible) references to other texts. Dickinson's poems abound with biblical allusions, for example, and their recognition and understanding is in many cases essential for a plausible interpretation (cf. McGregor 1987; Bauer 2006). There are also instances where references to other literary works are manifest and influential on the meaning of a poem (cf. Pollack 1974; Cuddy 1978). Without aligning us with a specifically labelled approach, such as New Criticism, Reader-Response Criticism, and New Historicism, we place great emphasis on the close reading of a text, take the position of the reader into account, and bear the poet's cultural context in mind. Generally, we do not use literary texts as examples of extraneous notions but start as readers of the text first and foremost. In doing so, however, one assumption is made: We regard poetry (unless it is clearly marked otherwise) as a fictional genre (**fictional** denoting a specific relationship to the actual world unlike a prose narrative).⁶ This means that the speaker is not identical with the author and whatever references are made to the actual world, the truth of the speaker's utterance does not depend on their being factually correct. The next section elaborates on this.

0.1.4 Pragmatics of Fiction

> Attention: This subsection presupposes familiarity with possible world semantics and speech act operations. For an explanation of these concepts in the framework we adopt, see the appendix.

This section introduces our linguistic analysis of the pragmatics of a fictional utterance. While hearers or readers generally take non-fictional statements to make direct claims about reality, this is not the case in a parallel way for fictional texts. This makes necessary a pragmatic theory of fictional utterances.

In non-fictional discourse, hearers or readers typically take a statement uttered to be an assertion. The effect of a successful assertion is that the participants in the discourse add the content of the statement to the set of joint beliefs in the conversation. In more technical terms, the **common ground** of the discourse (the set of shared assumptions of the participants, speaker and hearer) is updated with the content of the utterance. We call this "the pragmatic step" and model it (after Krifka 2014) with the speech act operator Assert. The pragmatic step relates the semantics of a linguistic expression to the context of the hearer/reader. See the appendix for definitions.

In the pragmatic interpretation of fictional texts, the operator Assert cannot apply. A fictional text is not meant to be a literal description of actual facts. Often it is incompatible with our world knowledge. However, we still take the text to have a meaning that is relevant to the actual hearer/reader.

Intuitively, we establish a different relation between the text and the actual world. This captures that the text retains its relevance for us, albeit it being implied that the text is not actually "true." We model this pragmatic step with the speech act operator FictionalAssert. To see how it operates, first consider the following fable:

---

6 For an elaboration of this point, see also chapter III.2, "Formal Linguistics as a Tool in Literary Studies."

(1)   The Crow and the Pitcher
        A Crow perishing with thirst saw a pitcher, and hoping to find water, flew to it with delight. When he reached it, he discovered to his grief that it contained so little water that he could not possibly get at it. He tried everything he could think of to reach the water, but all his efforts were in vain. At last he collected as many stones as he could carry and dropped them one by one with his beak into the pitcher, until he brought the water within his reach and thus saved his life.— Necessity is the mother of invention.
        (*Aesop's Fables*, trans. George Fyler Townsend, 2012)

The text offers elements that the reader can relate to their own experience. In the example above, it is the crow and its inventive behaviour. Establishing a relation between the text and us could lead us to approach a difficulty with inventiveness, just like the crow that finds a creative way to quench its thirst.
The speech act operator FictionalAssert models how this happens. Let us start with its definition given in (2) below (cf. Bauer and Beck 2014):

(2) $[\![\text{FictionalAssert}]\!] = \lambda T. [\lambda w. \forall w' [T(w') \ \& \ w'$ is maximally similar to w otherwise $\rightarrow R(w)(w')]]$
        "Worlds in which everything the text says is the case and which are maximally similar to the actual world otherwise, are worlds that stand in relation R to the actual world."

FictionalAssert relates the worlds in which what the text says is true to the evaluation world of the reader via the relation R. The relation R is a free variable in (2) and models the inference that the reader draws from the text. Applying FictionalAssert to a text results in a conditional meaning. In our example, this meaning can be paraphrased as in (3) (see the appendix on modals and conditionals).

(3)   If everything the text says is the case, then I should be inventive and persistent in solving my problems.

As (3) indicates, the relation R is based on a mapping between elements of the fictional worlds and parts of the real world. In the fable, the crow is the counterpart of the reader. The thirst represents a problem, the low water level a complication and so on. The relation R that the intuitive pragmatic interpretation of the fable is based on is given in (4) (where w' are the text worlds and w the actual context, cf. the definition in (2)).

(4)   R(w)(w') iff the crow in w' is the reader in w and the thirst in w' is a problem of the reader in w and as the crow is inventive in w', so is (or should be) the reader in w, ...

The pragmatic step that is modelled by FictionalAssert is thus an inference that the reader draws from the semantics of the text that allows them to relate the fictional text to their actual situation. The example of the fable is a fairly clear case, since it has an intended message – a way in which the reader is supposed to relate the fable to themselves. In other fictional texts, establishing a plausible relation R may be less obvious and may rely on other cues. A first-person narrative, for example, may be an invitation to identify with the fictional speaker. We will encounter examples later. See Bauer & Beck (2014) for discussion.

The way the operator is defined in (2) shows how interpretation proceeds: FictionalAssert operates on the meaning of the text (T in (2), a proposition). This is the semantics or literal meaning of all the sentences in the text taken together. The pragmatic step is performed by FictionalAssert on the basis of this text meaning. This entails that the text meaning is arrived at by the regular mechanisms of the grammar of the language that the text is written in. The semantic interpretation of the text is specific, not arbitrary or subjective. Much of what is subjective about the interpretation of fictional texts comes about in the pragmatic step, i.e. via FictionalAssert.

The formulation in (2) also entails that the text as a whole is the input to the speech act operator that models the pragmatic step. In other communicative situations, it may be more typical to perform the pragmatic step utterance per utterance, i.e. for smaller linguistic units. We conjecture that fictional texts (especially short poems such as Emily Dickinson's) invite postponing the pragmatic step, and that it may make more sense for a reader to look for the pragmatic interpretation of the text after the semantic interpretation of a large chunk of linguistic material is determined.

The operator FictionalAssert models the way in which a reader derives how the text relates to them, and what the text means for them. This determines the subjective interpretation. By relating the text to ourselves, we perform a transfer from what is the case in the text to what is true in our context and thus discover the text's relevance to ourselves. We will see in the following chapters how FictionalAssert interacts with properties of Emily Dickinson's texts, for example ambiguity and underspecification, leading to several possible readings.

0.2 Dickinson's Special Use of Language

We concentrate on the poetry of Emily Dickinson, since it displays a highly uncommon use of language, which we argue is part of her poetic strategy and gives evidence of a large degree of linguistic competence and awareness. In our view, the reason for Dickinson's apparent non-compliance with linguistic rules is neither ignorance nor eccentricity but the desire to show that, to her, poetry means extending the range of linguistic expression as far as possible and activating complex processes of interpretation. Dickinson's poems thereby reveal the flexibility and potential of grammar. We will see that its rules are not suspended but function differently in her poetry, and in poetry generally. These modified rules are assumed to be systematic deviances from the original grammar, which is why speakers are able to adapt to them. It is this adaptation process that increases speakers' awareness of the rule system underlying language.

Our analyses of selected poems by Emily Dickinson will show that the poet deals with language creatively, bending the rules of grammar, and exploiting a number of phenomena, e.g., reference, ambiguity, ellipsis, quantification and coercion. This repeated use of the same set of phenomena suggests that she does so systematically, and we are interested in identifying their influence on the meaning of her poems. One effect of her use of language is that we are provoked to think about the way language works. Linguistic phenomena are used in a way that differs from non-fictional use in that they serve to trigger a reflection about language in the reader. This presupposes a high command of language, as well as a fine intuition concerning linguistic rules and the processing of language on the part of the poet. Dickinson's intense and systematic occupation with language, discernible in her poetry, indicates that she possessed such an extensive command and intuition.

Dickinson's use of language is rhetorical in so far as she exploits language for a distinct purpose – not to convince the reader of a particular agenda but to cause a process of reflective interpretation and to create an awareness of language and linguistic rules. While a similar strategy can be observed in some other poets as well (for example in metaphysical poets such as John Donne and George Herbert), most poets either generally conform to the rules of language or do not use deviations for the same purposes as Dickinson. This can be seen when considering Dickinson's contemporary Alfred Lord Tennyson. Like Dickinson's poetry, his work is distinguished by a special use of language, yet these peculiarities are not primarily employed to point at special features of the language system or at the mechanisms of understanding utterances. Instead, by giving, for example, a quaint and archaic flavour to his language, Tennyson links his poetry to specific traditions (see Staines 1982). Consider, for instance, the beginning of "The Coming of Arthur" from *Idylls of the King*:

(5) Leodogran, the King of Cameliard,
 Had one fair daughter, and none other child;
 And she was the fairest of all flesh on earth,
 Guinevere, and in her his one delight.

 For many a petty king ere Arthur came
 Ruled in this isle, and ever waging war
 Each upon other, wasted all the land; [...]

 (Tennyson 1908, 4)

Tennyson uses inversions ("for many a petty king ere Arthur came ruled in this isle" instead of "for many a petty king ruled in this isle ere Arthur came"), ungrammatical constructions ("none other child"[7] instead of "no other child"), ellipsis ("in her his one delight" instead of "in her was his one delight") as well as old-fashioned and unusual words ("ere" instead of the more modern "before," "isle" instead of the more common "island") to make his description of King Arthur's time sound like a description from an old historical document. He mainly manipulates those aspects which are relevant for the text's atmosphere, while Dickinson, as we will see, manipulates grammatical aspects which are relevant with regard to a text's meaning, the conscious interpretation of which requires reflection on how language works. The study of Dickinson's poetry is therefore especially worthwhile to deepen an understanding of language.

In our analyses of Emily Dickinson's poems, we look at the language of a poem both at a local level, beginning with single words, phrases and sentences; and at a global level, considering stanzas, the poem as a whole, and extra-textual aspects. Both are interlinked and dependent on each other. Our method is indebted to Cristanne Miller's *Emily Dickinson: A Poet's Grammar* (1987), which is largely concerned with the peculiarities of Dickinson's syntax. Miller's

---

[7] The use of "none" instead of "no" was fully grammatical in the 15th and 16th century, as exemplified by the *OED*: "Beastes..in the acte of generation wyll accompany with none other beast, but suche as is of his owne propre kynde" (*OED* "accompany, v." 3.a.); "Grace seketh nat any temporal thynge: nor it asketh none other thing but god allon for rewarde: nor it asketh no more of temporall thinges" (*OED* "ask, v." II.11.a.); "Lytell Johan toke none other mesure But his bowe tre" (*OED* "bow-tree, n.").

study is the first (and so far only) to attempt a systematic approach and classification of linguistic phenomena in Dickinson's poetry. To her insights into Dickinson's syntax, we add the analysis of semantic phenomena and incorporate the consideration of pragmatic mechanisms. In focusing on Dickinson's systematic approach to establishing meaning, and in consistently and systematically combining literary and linguistic perspectives in our work, our approach is unprecedented, and it has proven to be fruitful during our collaboration.

0.3 Structure of the Book and Intended Readership

We hope that this book will be useful to theoretical linguists and literary scholars alike (and not just those who specialise in Dickinson's poetry). It will be a valuable help in teaching university courses to students of both disciplines, as well as courses focusing on Dickinson's poetry. In addition to exploring specific linguistic phenomena, we provide examples of accurate textual analyses which are useful to scholars and students interested in either a thorough analysis of a certain poem or a demonstration of how Dickinson's poetry works in general. By combining literary scholarship and linguistics, the book will thus provide a foundation and starting point for semanticists wanting to explore an unusual approach to semantics and pragmatics, and for literary scholars interested in a new approach to textual analysis.

The book is divided into three parts: The first part consists of six in-depth analyses of individual poems. These analyses will serve to identify a pattern in Emily Dickinson's work that demonstrates her linguistic intuition. Table 1 below illustrates this pattern: the left column of the table lists the linguistic phenomena she uses frequently to yield a certain semantic-pragmatic effect. These include referential expressions, such as pronouns and demonstratives, presuppositions, but also lexical and structural ambiguities, as well as reinterpretation and different types of quantifiers. In the head of the table we list the poems we discuss in detail in part I of the book. We specify which of the linguistic phenomena are key to the analysis and interpretations of which poem. The table's purpose is thus to help scholars find examples of how these phenomena are analysed semantically within the context of a poem. For linguists, it serves the purpose of providing examples of interesting uses of these phenomena in a special textual setting, which highlights their semantic properties. Furthermore, it summarises the focus of each poem's interpretation given what phenomena we are taking to be central to its analysis. In addition to identifying patterns of how linguistic phenomena are used, the goal of part I is to sharpen our understanding of these phenomena given the special corpus we looked at.

Tab. 1: Linguistic Phenomena Across Chapters

Chapter → Phenomena ↓	Chapter 1 "To pile like Thunder"	Chapter 2 "You said that I 'was Great'"	Chapter 3 "I'm Nobody!"	Chapter 4 "This was a Poet"	Chapter 5 "If it had no pencil"	Chapter 6 "My Life had stood"
Demonstratives	this			This		
Pronouns		you, I	I, you		it	
Presuppositions			too	the Robbing	the Daisy	the Owner
Lexical ambiguity	prove, consume					carry away
Structural ambiguity	crumble			before	now	identified
Ellipsis	either, consume	would that?		harm		longer must
Reinterpretation				distill		stood, speak, reply
Quantifiers			nobody, somebody			modals must, can
Scales		Great				longer

The patterns we discover in these poems show that Emily Dickinson plays with the potential and flexibility of meaning created by linguistic mechanisms. Our analysis shall then serve as the basis for establishing, in the second part of the book, a systematic description of her status as an intuitive linguist. In a subsequent step, we will elaborate on the specific poetic nature of Emily Dickinson's work. We will outline her system of language use by abstracting from the detailed analyses and by offering generalizations regarding the derivation of global meanings in Dickinson's poetry. We find that her poems offer a level of underspecification and flexibility through the mechanisms she employs which oftentimes allows for adopting a meta-level interpretation whose topic is interpretation and language itself. Finally, in the third part of the book, we discuss how the poetry of Emily Dickinson can serve as a valuable data source in the disciplines of linguistics and literary studies. We establish why looking at this particular data source is worthwhile for linguists, especially those interested in the interface of semantics and pragmatics; and we advocate for applying semantic analyses to poetry, since it is a powerful tool offering additional insights into Emily Dickinson's use of language, and poetic language use in general.

Part I: **Individual Analyses**

The six chapters of Part I each offer a detailed analysis of an exemplary poem by Emily Dickinson. We will focus on specific linguistic phenomena in order to show the range and depth of her understanding of language as an intuitive linguist.

The first poem we discuss in detail is J1247/Fr1353, "To pile like Thunder" (chapter I.1). We will see compelling examples of lexical underspecification. These local phenomena create global ambiguity. In J738/Fr736, "You said that I 'was Great'" (chapter I.2), the speaker of the poem herself attempts a playful "linguistic" dissection of what it means to be "great." Emily Dickinson deliberately violates basic combinatory rules in J288/Fr261, "I'm Nobody" (chapter I.3), though this violation itself serves as part of the overall meaning of the text and reveals interesting properties of quantifiers. Moreover, through the particular use of quantifiers in this poem, we see that we have to adapt our notion of the text meaning in order to apprehend that more than one reading of the text is available at the same time. In J448/Fr446A, "This was a Poet" (chapter I.4), we find predominantly structural ambiguities interacting on a syntactic level with referential ambiguities: determining the reference for demonstrative pronouns contributes to the overall meaning. Because of the particular use of demonstratives in this poem, we will need to extend the definition of FictionalAssert. J921/Fr184A, "If it had no pencil" (chapter I.5), in turn, is a poem where the assignment of referents that agree with additional meaning components of the pronouns, like their gender requirement, turns out to be problematic and thus creates a special underspecification which is crucial to its interpretation. The reference in "If it had no Pencil" furthermore interacts with the speech act of the poem, as the poem as a whole poses a question. Thus, a further extension of the theory of speech act operators will become necessary. Finally, in J754/Fr764, "My Life had stood" (chapter I.6), lexical meanings need to be reinterpreted due to combinatory constraints, leading to the availability of two overall readings of the text, similar to "I'm Nobody." Thus, we will broaden our semantic-pragmatic framework where necessary in order to capture the interpretation of the individual poems. The poems chosen each represent different aspects of Emily Dickinson's language use; as such, they are examples of wider tendencies in her poetry, but also exhibit idiosyncrasies unique to each individual poem. We have therefore ordered our analyses in ascending complexity of their pragmatic interpretation.

While some poems make poetry their explicit topic ("To pile like Thunder," "This was a Poet"), others focus on writing ("If it had no pencil") and issues of the self and identity ("I'm Nobody," "You said that I 'was Great,'" "My Life had stood"). From a thematic point of view, it will thus become evident that the poems chosen not only exhibit growing complexity as far as the linguistic interpretation is concerned, but that they also present a meta-reflection about poetry and language use itself, culminating in the two overall readings of "My Life had stood," the complex interplay of which gives rise to a third, self-reflective reading of the poem. Part I will thus lay the groundwork for a more theoretical reflection about the language use and poetics of Emily Dickinson in Part II.

1.1 "To pile like Thunder": Lexical Ambiguity

> Attention: This chapter presupposes familiarity with syntactic and lexical ambiguity, variable assignments, possible world semantics and speech act operations. For an explanation of these concepts in the framework we adopt, see the appendix.

1 To pile like Thunder to its close
2 Then crumble grand away
3 While Everything created hid –
4 This – would be Poetry –

5 Or Love – the two coeval come –
6 We both and neither prove –
7 Experience either and consume –
8 For None see God and live –
(J1247/Fr1353)

1.1 Introduction

"To pile like Thunder," written c. 1875, posits both poetry and love in comparison to the natural phenomenon of thunder, and then proceeds to reflect on the relation between the two as well as their interaction with "us," i.e. a group that the speaker is part of. We find ourselves confronted with underspecified lexical meanings on the one hand and a logical riddle on the other. The interplay of both aspects highlights the reflection process in the poem, and illustrates the difficulty human beings face in comprehending what poetry and love are.

We first discuss the interpretation of stanza one in section 1.2, and then the interpretation of stanza two in section 1.3. Section 1.4 is concerned with the overall text meaning. Conclusions are drawn in section 1.5. We wrap up this chapter and the following ones in a "summary box."

1.2 Stanza One, Lines 1–4

Stanza one introduces the imagery of thunder, which is then compared to poetry and love. The verbs "pile" and "crumble" in this stanza are the key to an understanding of this imagery of thunder.[1] As both verbs are underspecified in their meaning, a first step is to see which meanings of the verbs are intended here and how these meanings interact.

As far as "to pile" is concerned, of the meanings listed by the *OED*, most are in reference to a physical event of piling or stacking something, i.e. "[t]o form into a pile or heap; to heap up" (*OED*, "pile, v." 2.a.). Considering that the agent of piling is thunder, we find it most plausible to define piling as "form[ing] into a heap or mass; [...] increas[ing] in quantity" (*OED*, "pile, v." 3.a.), or "amass[ing], [...] accumulat[ing]" (*OED*, "pile, v." 4.a.). Together with crumbling, i.e. to "fall asunder in [...] particles" (*OED*, "crumble, v." 2.), the image created is a potently physical one: the juxtaposition "To pile like Thunder" and "crumble grand away" suggests either thunderclouds amassing and then dispersing again, or even the attempt to visualize the actual noise that can be heard in thunderstorms. We may also consider the nature of sound when it travels to first grow louder, and then gradually "crumble" away. While thunder can, thus, not literally "pile" or "crumble," a metaphoric reinterpretation allows us to enrich the proposition constructed on the basis of the lexical meaning of either verb and consequently make sense of it. The physicality that is achieved in this way remains with the reader throughout the poem. What is more, Webster's *Dictionary* evokes the religious dimension of earthly existence in its definition of "crumble, v.": "2. *intransitive*. To fall to decay; to perish; as, our flesh shall *crumble* into dust." In our discussion of stanza two, we will come back to the religious motifs present in the poem; as of yet, it is striking that, from the first two lines onwards, both the physical, natural world, as well as its demise in a religious context, are present.[2] The question of how "pile" and "crumble" are related can only be determined by a closer look at the syntactic construction in which they are embedded.

The first stanza is comprised of one sentence that runs on into stanza two. Although the punctuation is unclear, the adverbials "while" and "then" are

---

[1] Ford (1997) discusses this poem in the context of Dickinson's implicit poetics, which she links to the imagery of thunder in the first lines: "Perhaps Dickinson never wrote a poetic treatise because her poetics take shape in the course of her poems and are formulated only as they are enacted. [...] Here again, poetry terrifies and intimidates its listeners, who hide from its thunderous voice. Moreover, in the description of the *process* of the thunder—an initial frightening clap succeeded by a gradual recession of sound—we can recognise the poetic structure identified by Porter: emphatic assertion followed by formal disintegration" (41). On our own view of Dickinson's poetics, see chapter II.2, "The Linguist as Poet."

[2] Cf. Genesis 3:19 ("unto dust shalt thou return"). For the religious contexts evoked, see also McIntosh (2000) and Freedman (2011).

embedded in an infinitival clause ("to pile like thunder to its close while everything created hid then crumble grand away"[3]) which is left adjoined to the matrix clause ("this would be poetry or love"). There is, however, a structural element that is harder to integrate in the syntax of the infinitival clause: the modification "like thunder" can be positioned at various points in the sentence structure. It can be an adjunct of "pile" as well as of the bigger structural element "pile then crumble grand away." In the first case, only the piling is compared to thunder, whereas, in the second case, both piling and crumbling are part of the comparison with thunder. As the second option seems more plausible in the context of the stanza as a whole, which describes the natural phenomenon of thunder and compares this with poetry and love, we will assume the following structure for the sentence:

(1) a. Matrix Sentence: [IP this$_1$ [I' [I would] [VP [V' [v be] [NP poetry or love]]]]]
 b. Infinitival Construction: [IP [IP PRO$_i$ [I' [I to] [VP [VP [V' [v pile]] [PP to its$_1$ close]] [CP then crumble grand away]] [CP while everything created hid]]]] [like thunder]]

Intuitively, the demonstrative "this" seems to refer to the complete infinitival construction given in (1b). We model this in the following way: we interpret the demonstrative as containing a covert definite and a free variable, see (2a). The free variable receives its value from the context (cf. the appendix for the formal implementation). In the poem, the context furnishes the meaning of the infinitival construction as the value, see (2b). The resulting meaning of the demonstrative is (2c).

(2) a. ⟦this$_{<v>}$⟧^{g} = ⟦ [DP DEF [P$_2$ $_{<v,t>}$]] ⟧
 b. ⟦P$_2$⟧^{g} = g(P$_2$) = λe. e is a piling to its close [...]
 c. "this" = the unique event e s.t. e is a piling to its close [...]

Interestingly, we see that here, the demonstrative refers to an event rather than an individual (see also chapter I.4, "This was a Poet").

Looking at the infinitival construction given in (1b) in more detail, we find that a combination of its parts results in the following meaning:

---

[3] For in-text quotations, we adhere to capitalization and punctuation as they are given in the poems when citing their visual form, or the poem's material as such. In those cases where we refer to the linguistic material, however, we ignore Dickinson's punctuation and capitalization.

(3) λe. ∃t [e is a piling to a close at t in w & ∀y [y is an individual in w & y is created in w → y hid at t in w & ∃e' [e' is a crumbling & t < τ(e')]]] and e is in w like thunder

(4) "the set of events e such that e is a piling to a close, while everything created hid, and e is followed by a crumbling grand away, and e is like thunder."

With this semantics, the covert definite in the meaning of the demonstrative (see (2a)) triggers a uniqueness presupposition that there be only one relevant piling event. We accommodate that this is indeed the case: there is a unique piling event and poetry and love are compared to that piling event.

The matrix clause which bridges the gap between stanzas one and two identifies poetry or love with what is expressed in the infinitival construction. It contains the modal "would." This modal indicates that the structure as a whole is a **counterfactual conditional** (see (5)).[4]

(5) $[\![would]\!] = \lambda w. [\lambda R_{<s,<s,t>>}. [\lambda p_{<s,t>}. [\lambda q_{<s,t>}: p(w)=0. \forall w' [R(w)(w') \& p(w') \rightarrow q(w')]]]]$

(6) $[\![R]\!]^g = g(R) = \lambda w_1. [\lambda w_2. w_2 \text{ is maximally similar to } w_1]$

(7) If it were Tuesday, Peter would come.

Consider the example in (7): we take counterfactual conditionals to presuppose that the antecedent is false, i.e. in the actual world it is in fact not Tuesday. The sentence asserts that all worlds in which it is Tuesday and that are maximally similar to the actual world are worlds in which Peter comes. We assume this maximal similarity to come in through the covert accessibility relation R in (6), cf. the appendix.

The analysis of the counterfactual in the poem works parallel to this example: we consider the infinitival construction to be the antecedent and the matrix clause to be the consequent of the conditional. However, in contrast to "would" in (7), "would" in the poem does not relate other possible worlds to the actual world, but to the text worlds. Here, the sentence describes worlds which are maximally similar to the text worlds. In the text worlds, the piling event does

---

4 For convenience, we assume "would" itself to carry the meaning of the counterfactual conditional. See the literature cited in the appendix for conditional semantics.

not occur. However, if there were a piling event in the text worlds, then it would be identified with poetry or love. A simplified meaning of the overall clause is given below.

(8) λw: there is no piling event in w. ∀w' [there is a unique piling event in w' and w' is maximally similar to w → the unique piling event is (like) poetry or love in w']

The notion of **counterfactuality** will become relevant again in the discussion of counterfactual conditionals in chapter I.5, "If it had no pencil," where the same analysis will be employed.

As an interim summary of the first stanza, we find that it reveals a description of a piling event that is compared to the natural phenomenon of thunder. This event is then identified with poetry or love. The counterfactual evoked by "would" says that this event does not occur in the text worlds. Through the demonstrative "this," the image of piling and crumbling which is compared to thunder is integrated into the matrix clause (see (9)).

We thus can paraphrase the combination of the matrix clause with the infinitive as follows:

(9) "The event e, such that e is a piling like thunder piles to its close, while everything created hid, then crumbling grandly away, would be poetry or love."

Though the syntactic structure of stanza one provides us with little challenge in general, what continues to engage our attention is the matrix clause enjambment that connects stanzas one and two with each other.

1.3 Stanza Two, Lines 5–8

The second stanza presents the reader with a logical puzzle that is intertwined with more lexical underspecifications similar to "pile" and "crumble." From a syntactic point of view, the sentence structures are quite straightforward. However, the second stanza concentrates on the possible functions of poetry and love and their interaction, and presents their interplay as a logical riddle. Let us briefly go back to the disjunction that combines poetry and love: What has been described as a phenomenon comparable to thunder in stanza one is said to be "poetry or love." The disjunction "or" can be interpreted either inclusively or exclusively. If we take it to be exclusive, only one, either love or poetry, is like a natural phenomenon. The inclusive "or" means that both love and poetry can be captured by the image of a natural phenomenon. With the latter reading, it is important to note that love and poetry are not read conjunctively – the inclusive "or" allows for both options to be possible, whereas "and" would state that both options have to be true at the same time. In the poem, love and poetry are both likened to thunder. The nature of love and poetry is elaborated on in the second stanza: "the two coeval come" states that both poetry and love are "of the same age or standing in point of time *with* another" (*OED*, "coeval, *adj.* and *n.*" B.1.), that is, contemporaries (see also meanings B.2. and B.3. listed in the *OED*). The temporal co-existence of the two that is expressed here supports the inclusive reading of "or."

In the second sentence of the second stanza, we find a logical riddle that presents us with a contradiction: "We both and neither prove –" can be paraphrased as "we prove both and we prove neither," that is, resolving the N' ellipsis:

(10)   We prove both poetry and love, and we prove neither poetry nor love.

This should be contradictory in the same way as the simpler example (11):

(11)   I called both Robin and Laura and I called neither Robin nor Laura.

It cannot simultaneously be true that I called Laura and that I did not call Laura. Thus, at the semantic level, interpretation should fail. But readers do not stop with their interpretation once they arrive at a contradiction; rather, they look for a resolution, e.g. a reinterpretation that is not contradictory.

Such cases of resolved contradiction can be found outside of poetry:

(12)   A: "Did Hans attend the seminar?" B: "Yes and no." (e.g. he was physically present, but did not pay attention)

In the case of "we both and neither prove," the key to the solution lies in the semantic contribution of the verb "prove" and the possibility of harnessing different lexical entries within the same sentence. The lexical ambiguity of "prove" provides a way to resolve the paradox: in "we both and neither prove," we are thus dealing with a zeugma, i.e. a rhetorical device with which "multiple clauses are governed by a single word, most often a noun or verb" (Moore 2012, 1553), as the verb "prove" takes on different meanings in accordance with the elements of the sentence that it governs. The use of a zeugma in this case is an economical means to emphasise the double nature of "prove":

(13) $[\![\text{prove}_1]\!] = \lambda y. [\lambda x.\ x$ presents logical reasoning for y$]$

(14) $[\![\text{prove}_2]\!] = \lambda y. [\lambda x.\ x$'s existence is (implicit) proof of y$]$

To illustrate the distinction, consider a situation in which the existence of the moon is to be proven:

(15) I prove that the moon exists by providing empirical evidence, for instance because it is visible to the unaided eye.

(16) The oceanic tide proves that the moon exists, because it is a direct consequence of lunar gravitational fields.

To prove the moon's existence, I can either present a logical argument, in which case I am the agent who undertakes the proof, as in (13) and (15); but likewise, it can equally be proven by a circumstance or entity that is concomitant with what is to be proven, as in (14) and (16).

Logically, this lexical ambiguity of "prove" allows for four different readings of the line "We both and neither prove –" overall:

(17) We prove$_1$ both and we prove$_2$ neither.

(18) We prove$_1$ both and we prove$_1$ neither.

(19) We prove$_2$ both and we prove$_1$ neither.

(20) We prove$_2$ both and we prove$_2$ neither.

In the following, we will focus on readings (17) and (19) because they reflect the lexical ambiguity within the zeugmatic structure, whereas (18) and (20) are less plausible readings since they do not resolve the contradiction, but rather underline it. Since we are dealing with intensely abstract concepts in "love" and "poetry," the seeming paradox that results from the zeugmatic construction is stimulus to reflect on the nature of both love and poetry, and our relation to each. The line can thus be paraphrased as one of the following two readings:

(21)   We prove both poetry and love with logical argumentation, but are ourselves proof of neither poetry nor love.

(22)   We are proof of both poetry and love, but prove neither poetry nor love with logical argumentation.

The passage does not suggest which of these two readings is preferable, but we continue reading on and collect more information. The last line of the poem, "For None see God and live," is a close echo of the Exodus verse which states that man cannot look at God: "And he said, Thou canst not see my face: for there shall no man see me, and live" (Exod. 33:20). With this context, the meaning of "consume" in the line beforehand can be paraphrased as "to waste away" (*OED*, "consume v.¹" 3.b.). The speaker equates the experience of poetry or love with the perception of God. This means that they are regarded as transcendental. If we were to experience the perfect idea of poetry or love – that is, the very idea, and not one of its many instantiations in the world – we would have to perish, as it would be beyond our human capacities to grasp the magnificence of those two phenomena. This reading moreover presents an obvious link to the lexical ambiguity of "crumble" as outlined above, where Webster provides a definition that takes heed of the religious connotation in the sense of "to perish." If we were to experience love and poetry as the abstract concepts they are and thus fully understand them, this would qualify as providing evidence for them. However, together with "consume," we would have to die as an effect of that evidence. Instead, we only partially experience them and thus prove that they exist. It would be impossible to prove poetry and love as transcendental, abstract ideas, but we certainly are capable of loving, and reading or writing poetry. Thus, reinterpreting "prove" as providing evidence through grasping the conceptual notions of poetry and love in their entirety would lead the speakers of the poem to perish.

This is the solution of the logical riddle: while we cannot provide evidence for the abstract ideas love or poetry (the meaning of "prove" in (13)), we do prove their existence by experiencing both (the meaning of "prove" in (14)), even if this experience only imperfectly captures the idea. This points back to the beginning of the poem, and the modal "would." The natural phenomenon does not actually exist in the worlds described in the text. The impossibility of identifying poetry and love in a specific manner is indicated at its beginning. In the first stanza, this impossibility is expressed by comparing love and poetry to a natural phenomenon, namely something like thunder; in the second stanza, the theme of impossibility re-emerges, and counterfactuality is explicated through a logical riddle. In the text worlds, poetry and love cannot be a natural phenomenon, but they are in maximally similar worlds. This circumstance can be seen in parallel to the possibility of proving that both exist by experiencing them, and the impossibility of proving them by providing evidence: the evidence is part of worlds not accessible to us human beings, i.e. worlds in which we as human beings could experience the complexity of poetry and love.

1.4 Resulting Interpretation

The local ambiguities interact with each other, which leads to the global text meaning. The poem begins with a comparison: what is compared to thunder is hypothetically identified with love and poetry. The second stanza further explains the complex nature of poetry and love, which is presented in the form of a logical riddle. This logical riddle interacts with different lexical meanings of the individual verbs. On the basis of our analysis, we arrive at the following paraphrase of the overall text meaning:

(23) "Poetry and love are like natural phenomena comparable to thunder. Both are equivalent in their value, as they are contemporaries to each other. By experiencing both, we are living proof of their existence. At the same time, we cannot prove their existence in their complexity by providing evidence because if we experienced both in their entirety, we would perish. This is in parallel to seeing God, since no one may see God and survive."

(23) is a paraphrase of the semantics of the text. What is the pragmatic meaning of the text? How does it relate to the actual reader? At this point, the speech act operator FictionalAssert comes into play.

Applying FictionalAssert to the text meaning in (23) suggests a value for R: the subject of the poem, "we," is not a specific group of people, but most likely interpreted generically as all human beings. The poem thus gives information on the capabilities and limits of humankind in general.

(24) $[\![FictionalAssert_R]\!]((23)) = 1 \text{ iff } \forall w' \, [(23)(w') \rightarrow R(@)(w')]$

(25) "The relation R between the text worlds w' and the actual world @ holds iff w' is exactly like @ except that the counterpart of the speakers in w' are all human beings in @ and like the speakers in w', all human beings in @ can be proof of love and poetry by experiencing them but not by providing evidence."

On the basis of (24) and (25), we formulate the following pragmatic interpretation of the poem:

(26)   "If everything the text says is true, then humankind has only access to a subpart of the essence of poetry and love and they are a basis of our existence at the same time."

In figuring out R, this juxtaposition of poetry and love is all the more remarkable as Emily Dickinson elevates poetry to the same status as love in that both are phenomena beyond human comprehension, and both are essential to humankind. This outstanding role of poetry as one of the great constants of human life, comparable to such ideas as love or indeed faith, often appears in Dickinson's poetry. This recurrence demonstrates the value she assigns to poetry as a constitutive element of the world – one that we also find in our discussions of other poems, which will become especially explicit in chapter II.2, "The Linguist as Poet."

1.5 Conclusion

The poem presents the reader with lexical ambiguities and a logical puzzle. As we have seen, the two are used to establish a complex relation between poetry and love and their role for humans. The resolution of the contradiction in the second stanza shows Emily Dickinson's conscious play with logical properties of language. The riddle and its resolution are based on regular mechanisms of language.

Dickinson deliberately uses underspecification in order to trigger a reflection process about the main topics discussed, which are poetry and love in this poem.

Tab. 1: Chapter Summary

Core Phenomenon

Lexical Ambiguity, Contradiction
⟦prove₁⟧ = λy. [λx. x presents logical reasoning for y]
⟦prove₂⟧ = λy. [λx. x's existence is (implicit) proof of y]

see also *pile, crumble, consume*

Text Interpretation

Meaning of the Text:
T: Poetry and love are like natural phenomena comparable to thunder. Both are equivalent in their value, as they are contemporaries to each other. By experiencing both, we are living proof that they exist. At the same time, we cannot prove their existence in their complexity by providing evidence because if we experienced both in their entirety, we would perish. This is in parallel to seeing God, since no one may see God and survive.

Relation R: "The relation R between the text worlds w' and the actual world @ holds iff w' is exactly like @ except that the counterpart of the speakers in w' are all human beings in @ and like the speakers in w', all human beings in @ can be proof of love and poetry by experiencing them but not by providing evidence."

Pragmatic Interpretation:
"If everything the text says is true, then humankind has only access to a subpart of the essence of poetry and love and they are a basis of our existence at the same time."

Lexical Ambiguity in other Chapters

(In chapter I.6): The Owner passed – identified – // And carried Me away –
⟦carry away₁⟧ = λx. [λy. [λl. y transports x from l]]
⟦carry away₂⟧ = λx. [λy. x overwhelms y emotionally]

Other Phenomena in this Chapter

Demonstratives: This – would be Poetry – // Or Love – the two coeval come –
⟦this₁⟧^{g} = the unique event e such that e is a piling to a close, while everything created hid, and e is followed by a crumbling grand away, and e is like thunder

I.2 "You said that I 'was Great'": Scales and Contextual Parameters

> **!** Attention: This chapter presupposes familiarity with degree semantics, possible world semantics and speech act operations. For an explanation of these concepts in the framework we adopt, see the appendix.

1 You said that I 'was Great' – one Day –
2 Then 'Great' it be – if that please Thee –
3 Or Small – or any size at all –
4 Nay – I'm the size suit Thee –

5 Tall – like the Stag – would that?
6 Or lower – like the Wren –
7 Or other heights of Other Ones
8 I've seen?

9 Tell which – it's dull to guess –
10 And I must be Rhinoceros
11 Or Mouse –
12 At once – for Thee –

13 So say – if Queen it be –
14 Or Page – please Thee –
15 I'm that – or nought –
16 Or other thing – if other thing there be –
17 With just this Stipulus –
18 I suit Thee –

(J738/Fr736)

2.1 Introduction

"You said that I 'was Great,'" c. 1863, presents the process of a speaker's identifying the meaning of an utterance made to her, and it does so in a playful and dexterous manner, revealing insight into the relationship between speaker and addressee.[1] The focus lies on the semantic content of the utterance "you are great," highlighting that the expression is vague and that contextual infor-

---

[1] Parts of the discussion in this chapter are based on Bauer & Beck (2009).

https://doi.org/10.1515/9783110646825-003

mation is necessary in order to fully understand what is meant by being "great." The phenomena that directly contribute to the speaker's analysis of the addressee's utterance are degree constructions and the scales and contextual parameters necessary for their semantic interpretation. We will proceed by considering each stanza in turn and at the end will arrive at an overall interpretation and conclusions.

2.2 Stanza One, Lines 1–4

The first interpretive problem that the reader encounters in stanza one is that the poem seems to start in the middle of things. We have not yet encountered either speaker (S) or addressee (A),[2] but in the first line, the speaker by way of citation presupposes an earlier conversation in which A told S that she[3] is "Great." Since this utterance by A is the topic of the poem, we are inclined to assume that there is a (fictional) conversation[4] that has taken place earlier than the beginning of the poem in which this utterance was made. However, we do not know what exactly the conversation was about. This means that important contextual information about what A could have meant by the utterance quoted is not available to the readers. The lack of contextual information opens up interpretive possibilities which Dickinson deliberately plays with by using a combination of lexical ambiguity and the inherent context-dependency of adjectives.

Concerning the semantics of the predicate "to be great," we need to consider two aspects in order to arrive at a meaning. Firstly, semantic analysis describes "great" as a gradable property (see e.g. Beck 2011 for a recent overview), i.e. it talks about the degree to which something or someone is "great." Degree

---

[2] Kher (1974) identifies the addressee as "her lover" (154) but gives no reference as to why this particular relation must be the case. Phillips (1988) reads it intertextually as a "light-hearted and amusing [...] courtship verse[s]" that goes back to "Jane Eyre's story of her devotion to Rochester and the efforts she made to cheer, to tease, and to 'suit' him" (107). Phillips underlines this by admitting that even though "the poet's own experiences contribute to the brio of the moment, [...] her use of the fictive voice is undeniable" (108).
[3] In order to distinguish more easily between the persons involved, we assume S to be female and A to be male. Apart from the fact that the poem was written by a woman, which may lead to the assumption that S is female, there is no evidence as to the sex of either S or A.
[4] Deppman (2008) considers this poem part of "Dickinson's profoundly conversational, other-dependent conception of poetry" and counts it as one of those that "stage conversations between lovers, friends, spirit and body, the heart and the mind, natural phenomena, and other entities" (28f.). In this context, he also mentions "I'm Nobody"; see chapter I.3.

properties always operate on scales that can be retrieved by the lexical information of the predicate; for instance, the adjective "tall" operates on a scale of height (see (1)), whereas the adjective "fast" operates on a scale of speed.

(1)   a. $[\![tall]\!] = \lambda d. [\lambda x. \text{Height}(x) \geq d]$
      b.   "x reaches the degree d on the height scale."

Secondly, we see that the adjective "great" is notoriously versatile in its lexical meaning when we consider, for instance, that the *OED* lists 23 different lexical entries for the adjective alone (that is, not counting the entries for "great" as noun or adverb), most of which are divided into even smaller units. Webster likewise lists 25 meanings. Central to the word's meaning is that it can be used with reference not only to size but also to rank, power, etc. (see *OED*, "great, *adj.*, *n.*, *adv.*, and *int.*" A.III.16.c.), which is often metaphorical. Dickinson's dictionary told her that "Large in bulk or dimensions" was the first meaning of "GREAT, a. [L. crassus]" (Webster 1828). "Great" in this sense may refer to, for example, "a great house; a great farm." Webster's second meaning of "great," "Being of extended length or breadth," is exemplified by "a great distance; a great lake." None of these meanings are applicable to persons; yet in the poem, the speaker teases the addressee by contrasting "great" with "Small – or any size at all –" and assuming that A actually did refer to her physical size.

The predicate "great" is underspecified, which means that several scales could be meant. In everyday conversation, this predicate can easily be used in order to make a statement about someone's personality, though very often it is also used as a general predicate to distinguish the quality of a thing or a circumstance.[5] Other possibilities of scales on which individuals are arranged when contemplating their "greatness" can be, besides (literal) physical size, also status and (metaphorical) greatness (i.e. rank, power, etc.). Thus, there are several possibilities for the meaning of the property, for instance:

(2) $[\![great_1]\!] = \lambda d. [\lambda x. \text{ physical size}(x) \geq d]$

(3) $[\![great_2]\!] = \lambda d. [\lambda x. \text{ social rank}(x) \geq d]$

---

[5] For instance: "Of considerable importance, significance, or distinction; important, weighty; distinguished, prominent; famous, renowned; impressive. Also in weakened sense: highly commendable, praiseworthy" (*OED*, "great, *adj.*, *n.*, *adv.*, and *int.*" A.III.13.a.), or the colloquial use as "excellent, admirable, very pleasing, first-rate" (A.III.22.).

For the purposes of the following discussion, we shall assume that the scale activated here is an underspecified scale of measurement (MEAS, see (4)). Context determines the relevant scale. We come back to MEAS below.

(4)   ⟦great⟧ = λd. [λx. MEAS(x) ≥ d]

In the poem, "Great" occurs in the Positive form (see e.g. in von Stechow 1984). This form makes reference to a degree by comparing the degree that the property talks about to a contextually given standard. It is this standard which lies at the heart of S's considerations, and it may differ from one context to another, which becomes evident in the following example:

(5) a. (about a four year old:) Pascal is tall.
         (true e.g. if Pascal is 1.20 m)
    b. (about an adult basketball player:) Pascal is tall.
         (not true if Pascal is 1.20 m; true e.g. if Pascal is 2.10 m)

Hence the analysis in (6):

(6) a. ⟦Pascal is tall⟧^{c} = 1 iff Height (P) ≥ s$_c$ (where s$_c$ is the contextually given size threshold)
    b. "Pascal's height reaches s$_c$."

This property of the Positive is relevant to the interpretation of "Great" as used by S: there is no fixed or independently given standard in our example. The meaning of the embedded clause in the first sentence is the following:

(7) a. MEAS(S) ≥ s$_c$
    b. "The speaker's measure reaches a contextually given measurement threshold."

The sentence meaning in (7) thus identifies two values that have to be determined contextually: the standard s$_c$ and the nature of the measurement. For both, we need to look within the text of the poem. In the following lines, S offers up different possibilities. In lines two and three, S relates the properties that apply to her to the addressee's estimation. The most plausible[6] way to semanti-

---

6 We say "most plausible" because there are several ways to resolve the scopal relationship between the disjunction ("or") and the conditional structure. However, this structural ambigui-

cally resolve the elliptical structure of the two lines can be seen in the paraphrase in (8):

(8)   "If that pleases A, the property true of S is 'great' (an interval high up on the size scale), or if that pleases A, the property true of S is 'small' (an interval would be situated low on the size scale), or if that pleases A, any size property (no matter which) is true of S."

Essentially, S assumes that MEAS is size and lets A choose whether or not S's size is equal to or more or less than the standard.[7]

(9) a. Size (S) ≥ s_c
    b. Size (S) = s_c
    c. Size (S) < s_c

She offers three possibilities to A: either he can choose that she is above the size standard ("Great"), or he can choose that she is below ("Small") or, rather, it is not important what he chooses: as long as it pleases him, all sizes are equally suitable values for where S is on the size scale. The text does not specify whether that means that A manipulates the standard only, or whether A is capable of manipulating S's size (see our discussion below on stanza two).

S finishes the discussion of the logical possibilities offered here by stating what the only relevant criterion is for choosing her size – the size that suits A:

(10)   I'm (of) the size that suit(s) thee –
    a. Size (S) = the unique d: d suits A & d ∈ SIZE
    b. "The speaker's size is the degree on the SIZE scale that suits A."

---

ty does not lead to a decisive change regarding the overall text meaning, which is why we assume for this sentence and all following examples that involve this scopal relationship that the disjunction always outscopes the conditional or modal.

7 Barker (2002) calls this a "sharpening use": a context-dependent utterance like "Chris is great" informs us about the present context within which the utterance is made, i.e. what counts as "great" in this particular situation. Barker contrasts this with a normal "descriptive use," which takes the context for granted and informs a hearer about the facts – we would simply conclude that Chris fulfils the criterion for greatness.

2.3 Stanza Two, Lines 5–8

In this stanza, S continues the reasoning introduced in the first stanza but varies the assertive mode into an interrogative one. She asks A which property he would choose for her. In parallel to the first stanza, all three possibilities depend on A's estimation. The scale here is specified and defined as referring to physical size or, more specifically, to height, where the "Stag" is situated rather high on the scale, while the height of the "Wren" is situated much lower than the stag. Either one of the examples S mentions can serve as the property that is applied to S, a fact which S uses to state that, whatever A wants to consider "Great" will be fine with S, no matter if it be a standard interval that is high on the height scale or low.

The most plausible way how to resolve the elliptical structure in a paraphrase is presented here:

(11) "Would it please you if I was tall like the stag or would it please you if I was lower like the wren or would it please you if I was of other heights of other ones I've seen?"

Concurrent with the logical structure in stanza one, S offers three possibilities to A; she also stresses that it does not matter which size A chooses. What is important is that the size pleases A.[8] The speaker's suggestion to being the size of either the stag or the wren corroborates the ambiguity mentioned above: either the standard changes, or it is possible within the text worlds that S can manipulate her size (or A can manipulate it for her).

2.4 Stanza Three, Lines 9–12

In the same vein as the previous stanzas, S continues to reflect on the contextual information necessary to fully interpret A's utterance "You are great." Unlike the first two stanzas, where we encountered the two sentence modes of assertion and question, now Dickinson includes a third option: the imperative. S tells A to identify which property it is that pleases him and that applies to S. The use of three different moods, i.e. indicative, interrogative and imperative, in the first

---

8 Smith (1996) reads the poem as "absolutely malleable to the desire of its addressee/reader" and suggests that one reading could be to see the poem itself as speaker (139f.). We discuss this idea in more detail in chapter III.2, "Formal Linguistics as a Tool in Literary Analysis."

three stanzas also suggests that S is trying out different ways of addressing A and thus exploring the quality of their relationship.

The consequence of not knowing what exactly pleases A is then formulated in the following sentence:

(12)   And I must be Rhinoceros
          Or Mouse –
          At once – for Thee –

"At once" is ambiguous. It may mean either "immediately, this instance" or "simultaneously." As we shall see, both meanings are present in the poem. Interpreting "at once" to mean "immediately" seems fairly straightforward: S does not want to wait any longer but asks for A's immediate decision. This reading is supported by the exclamation in line 9: "Tell which – it's dull to guess –," which can also be read as an expression of S's impatience. Reading "at once" to mean "simultaneously" leads to a seeming contradiction: the scalar item "or" in (12) normally triggers a "not both" implicature, strengthening the statement to an "either-or" statement (see (13)).

(13)   S must be rhinoceros or S must be mouse, and S doesn't have to be both.

The contradiction we perceive stresses the conflict the speaker is in, and the impossibility of fulfilling the addressee's wishes. At the same time, it is not impossible to reinterpret the sentence so that this conflict disappears. What we have seen in the previous chapter becomes evident once more at this point: because we read a lyrical text, readers do not abandon the poem because of a local semantic problem but tend to continue reading and try to resolve the conflict.[9] In order to resolve the conflict, the logical structure S introduced in the previous stanzas comes into play. The following logical possibilities were offered there:

(14) a. Stanza One: S's size is defined as either B (great) or C (small) or ALL (any size at all)
      b. Stanza Two: S's size is defined as either B (stag) or C (wren) or OTHERS (other heights of other ones)

---

[9] We will observe a parallel example in the discussion of "I'm Nobody" in chapter I.3.

The beginning of the third stanza seems to go along the same pattern: B (rhinoceros) or C (mouse). However, the third aspect that played a role before and that evoked a notion of plurality (see in (14a): "all" and in (14b): "others") seems to be missing at first sight. But this is exactly where "at once" comes in: "at once" evokes this plurality without its being overtly uttered. Thus, the rescue strategy that is put forward through the context of the poem is to abandon the implicature triggered by "or" and interpret the sentence in the following way:

(15)   S must be a rhinoceros for A, or S must be a mouse for A, or S must be both at once for A.

Even though the implicature of "or" is very strong and perceived to be present, "at once" makes the pragmatically weaker meaning accessible. What we as readers are left with is a parallel reasoning that is so salient that it may overrule the pressure to derive the implicature:

(16)   Stanza 3: B (rhinoceros) or C (mouse) or BOTH (at once)

This strong statement brings S's wish to please A even more into focus and hints at how S sees her relation to A. The interpretative possibilities and related conflicts as well as the possible resolutions stress the complication of pleasing A, the conflict S is in, and S's desire to be what seems impossible.

2.5 Stanza Four, Lines 13–18

The last stanza marks the finale of S's semantic game. In addition to the explicitly mentioned gradable adjective "Great" at the beginning, the text is full of expressions indicating size or dimension: S names "Great" (twice), "Small," "any size," "the size suit Thee," "Tall," "lower," and "other heights" as possible options for understanding A's utterance "you are great." In the last stanza, two things happen with regard to the understanding of "great": first, the meaning of "great" is shifted, and, second, the last stanza combines all previous options. In the first two lines of the last stanza, S again offers two possibilities for A to assign a property to her. This time, the measurement is one of social rank. In imperative sentence mode, S requests A to decide if S should be associated with being high on the scale, as the queen, or lower on the scale, as a page. These two options each depend on A's preference:

(17) "So say if my being great like a queen would please you or if my being small like a page would please you."

We notice that there is a shift with respect to the scale that "great" refers to and realise that the (mis)interpretation of "you are great" as a reference to S's size was deliberate. S shows that she has of course understood that "great" could mean "supreme; illustrious" (Webster 1828, "great, *a.*" 8.), "wonderful; admirable" (9.) or "Dignified in aspect, mien or manner" (13.). The ambiguity of "great" with regard to "page" underlines this: though the "page" may be lower on the scale that defines the "queen" as "great," he may be higher on another scale defined by "greatness."

In the last four lines of the poem, S concludes her logical game by including all possibilities that S offered to A and by stating once more that the only relevant criterion for the interpretation of the contextual information given in the predicate "great" is that S should suit A. The sentence structure is paraphrased as follows:

(18) "As long as S suits A, S is queen or page, or none of the properties hold for S or if there is some other property, this property holds for S."

The options given here include all options that were given in the previous stanzas and they also include additional options:

(19) (B (queen) or C (page)) or nothing or (any) OTHER THING

In the last two lines, S then presents an apparent resolution to the dilemma of choosing a meaning for "great": "With just this Stipulus – / I suit Thee –." However, the meaning of "Stipulus" is obscure. The word "stipulus" does not exist in English, and the closest equivalent would be the Latin adjective "stipulus" meaning "firm." The similarly sounding verb "to stipulate" is defined by Webster as to "make an agreement or covenant with any person or company to do or forbear any thing" ("stipulate, *v. i.*" 1.), suggesting an agreement or understanding between S and A that connects the two. The noun "stipulation" also has a meaning that makes sense in the context: "The action of specifying as one of the terms of a contract or agreement; a formulated term or condition of a contract or agreement" (*OED*, "stipulation, *n.*" 4.). "I suit thee" would then be the condition for S being "that – or nought – / Or other thing –." Yet the relation between S and A remains open, similar to word meaning in this poem, which is anything but "firm." Another conceivable alternative against which to read "stipulus" is the similarly sounding "stimulus," i.e. "[a]n agency or influence that stimulates to action or [...] that quickens an activity or process" (*OED*, "stimulus, *n.*" 2.a.), which fits well with S prompting A to address the meaning of "great." Yet the poem ultimately does not provide an answer by A, and, thus, just as the meaning of "great" is left open, the ending only apparently presents a solution.[10]

S does not simply either reject or acknowledge A's compliment but plays with the notion of greatness and wishes to be what suits A. By this strategy, however, S proves to be much "greater" than A in this exchange, as she takes up his rather unoriginal statement and transforms it into a complex expression of her wish to be determined by A. Through the choice of animals she uses, we see that S lovingly (and mockingly) deals with A's verbal helplessness by treating it as an expression of genuine admiration. The poem is thus revealed as an elaborate game that is played with the apparently banal compliment that A pays S. In conclusion, both the underspecified MEAS and the standard s_c can be assigned values arbitrarily, as long as it is to the liking of A. In other words, S requests that A choose MEAS and s_c.

(20) $MEAS(S) \geq s_c$

2.6 Overall Text Meaning

We arrive at an overall text meaning by combining all individual sentence meanings: that proposition in which everything the text says, and thus in which everything each individual sentence says, is simultaneously true. On the one hand, S presupposes that, at a previous time, A made the utterance "you are great."

(21) $\lambda w.$ there is a past time t in w where A uttered "you are great" to S

On the other hand, we can draw the following inference on the basis of the rest of the poem, where this utterance of A is analysed more closely:

---

[10] The manuscript of the poem shows "Reservation" as an alternative to "Stipulus," which would have provided a different and much clearer reading of the last two lines.

(22) a. ∀ MEAS: if it pleases A that MEAS(S) ≥ s_c then MEAS(S) ≥ s_c
b. "For all measures MEAS: if it pleases A that S reaches the standard for MEAS, then the speaker does indeed reach the standard for MEAS."

What does S mean by making such a statement? As hinted at in the introduction, this statement cannot be true in the actual world: for every individual, there is one physical size, one degree or rank, etc. It is impossible to have more than one height. What seems rather to be the case is that the speaker does not care which one value for MEAS and s_c will be chosen by A: whatever value chosen by A defines greatness.

Additionally, the choice of animals and occupations by S to illustrate possible meanings of "great" is telling with regard to the relationship between S and A. Throughout the poem, there is a progression: after the adjectives "Great" and "Small," S goes on with "Tall" and "lower," and illustrates her apparent conceptions of these adjectives with the help of comparisons in pairs (stag-wren, rhinoceros-mouse, queen-page) and sets up dichotomies between them (great-small, tall-lower).

This progression is another instance of S's playfulness. While a "Stag" can be seen as a majestic animal, and "Wren" is used by Dickinson several times without particularly negative connotations, it is difficult to see "Rhinoceros" as a compliment. It appears almost equally difficult to call someone a "Mouse" in a positive sense, though Dickinson does use "Mouse," similarly to "Wren" to describe neutral, if not positive characteristics;[11] she mainly seems to use "Rhinoceros" and "Mouse" in order to contrast a particularly large animal with a particularly small one, regardless of the connotations they may transfer to a person. S thus shows that her comparisons lead nowhere (just like the attempts to classify her "greatness"). With the subsequent reference to "Queen" and "Page," S retracts from the humour entailed in the possibility of calling her a "Rhinoceros." Moreover, "queen" and "page" refer to status and thus serve not only to lead the interpretation of "great" back to a consideration of rank or position, but they also point to human relationships: a queen is commanding and superior to most people, whereas a page is submissive and inferior to those at

---

11 "Mouse" appears in seven other poems besides J738/Fr736. In J636/Fr700A, for instance, the mouse assumes a similar function in that it refers to a small creature whose presence the speaker is wary of because she wants to be alone. J793/Fr753A, on the other hand, begins with the line, "Grief is a Mouse": here, the literal meaning of mouse yields to the metaphor more clearly than it does in J738/Fr736.

court. If S were a queen or page in A's perception, S would inevitably be placed above or below A (unless A were also a queen or page or their equivalent, which seems unlikely). However, as even this (more accessible) option is not chosen, the nature of the relationship between S and A is left open.

The poem's two central concerns – the meaning of "great" and the relation between S and A – are linked by the exploration of "great," which becomes symbolic of their relationship: the apparent necessity of defining "great" links S to A and provides an occasion for their communication. Thus, the poem is also about the communication taking place between S and A. S asks for a response ("You said," "Tell which," "So say"), and the central matter – the meaning of "great" – is dependent on something A must provide, namely to specify the values for MEAS and s_c.

The poem ostensibly presents a private conversation in which a specific addressee on a previous occasion, "one Day," said something to S, and S is all the while addressing this A with her response. S and A are partaking in a – rather one-sided – fictional conversation to which the reader is a witness who is invited to make sense of it. The poem thus also becomes a poem **about** communication and understanding. The context of this instance of fictional communication is not explicit; accordingly, we can read the poem as an explication by the speaker made in the context of an intimate or personal conversation.

There are thus two possibilities for how we can read the relationship between S and A: either S expresses that she is everything A requires her to be because A says so, thereby putting A in control of the situation. Alternatively, that quality of S which is declared as "Great" by A has always been so, but only now given the particular name "Great" by A. In this case the scales are tipping in S's favour (who has always been "great" anyway). Or in other words: greatness is defined by stating that S has this property and can thus do no wrong in the eyes of A. In both cases, S is "great" because the scale on which this is defined "suits" A.

To summarise, the following interpretations reflect on the meaning in (22):

(23) a. Interpretation 1: S will be everything A requires her to be
b. Interpretation 2: A defines greatness by way of S's properties

Let's go back to the literal text meaning, i.e. the combination of (21) and (22):

(24) λw. there is a past time t in w where A uttered "you are great" to S & $\forall$ MEAS: if it pleases A that MEAS(S) $\geq s_c$ then MEAS(S) $\geq s_c$

We can apply FictionalAssert to (24):

(25) $[\![\text{FictionalAssert}]\!](24) = 1$ iff $\forall w$ [there is a past time t in w where A uttered "you are great" to S & $\forall$ MEAS: if it pleases A in w that MEAS(S) $\geq s_c$ then MEAS(S) $\geq s_c \rightarrow R(@)(w)$]

A value for R can reflect upon the specific relation between A and S, given the overall text meaning. If we take the text meaning to be that either S submits to the judgment of A in that S attempts to fulfil A's requirements of what it means for A to be great (cf. (23a)), or that S can do no wrong in the eyes of A because anything S represents can count as being great (cf. (23b)), we may come up with a relation R that includes both options: the text itself does not give any indications which of these two versions of the relationship is the preferred reading.

(26)   "The relation R between the text worlds w and the actual world @ holds iff the text worlds w are maximally similar to @ except that S and A in w are the reader in @ and the reader's admirer in @, and A's utterance in w corresponds to an utterance of the reader's admirer in @ and as S plays with A's utterance in w, so does the reader with her admirer's utterance in @."

In (26), the speaker of the poem is mapped to the reader in the actual world. Alternatively, the speaker could be mapped to someone else, e.g. someone that the reader knows. The same is true for the addressee, who is mapped to the reader's admirer in (26). This mapping could also be different, i.e. the addressee could be mapped to someone that the reader knows.

Apart from relating the poem to themselves, readers can thus also arrive at a subjective interpretation of the poem by relating the ideas expressed in the poem to other people they know and thus to other relationships than their own.

Thus, two possible pragmatic interpretations could be either, that people want to please each other constantly (see (27a), or that they can do no wrong in the eyes of their partners (see (27b).

(27)   a.   "If everything the text says is true, then there are people who want to please each other constantly."
       b.   "If everything the text says is true, then there are people who can do no wrong in the eyes of their partners."

A more abstract alternative for R is to highlight the communicative play in the poem and to see it as a commentary on how much meaning can get lost in communication, either because the phrasing is not precise enough, or because it cannot be precise enough – and that language always expresses a multiplicity of connotations that can be dealt with in a playful, creative fashion. This version of R results in the following pragmatic interpretation of the poem:

(28) "If everything the text says is true, then people like A are at the mercy of people like S, who can both analyse a well-meant compliment as well as implement it."

2.7 Conclusion

Our interpretation reveals that a reading of the poem which is primarily informed by semantic criteria may be more plausible than previous explanations. According to Hagenbüchle (1988), for example, the poem shows that the wish to acquire an identity appropriate to the addressee cannot be realised; he sees this futility in S's agonising quizzing game, vacillating between extremes (240). The recognition of S's playful analysis of her interlocutor's compliment, however, makes us aware of the fact that S is not agonised at all but quite in control of the situation. S finds it "dull to guess" what she is to A not because it is impossible to fix the standard or scale but because guessing becomes superfluous when S is whatever A has given the adjective "great." It is noteworthy that in Webster's *Dictionary*, the lengthy entry on "great" ends with the elaboration that "[t]he sense of *great* is to be understood by the things it is intended to qualify." What defines the meaning of "great" hence is, ultimately, S herself – both consciously in her play with scales and degrees as well as unconsciously with regard to her being the way she is, which is what prompted A to call her "great" in the first place.

In this poem, we are dealing with one single utterance that is taken apart, and a deep reflection on the semantic ingredients of this utterance follows, such that the one utterance becomes a mirror image of what S wishes the relationship between S and A to be like. Here, the speaker's analysis of the sentence "you are great" can be read as a play on the linguistic properties of the sentence, and, thus, S acts as a linguist. This embedding of linguistic notions in the primary text has not been observed in the previous chapter. The deliberate underspecification of what it means to be "great" may serve as a complex mirror of relationships and the weaknesses of communication in general. Hence, the underspecified values for MEAS and s_c serve as a tool for the speaker to express her view on the relationship between her and the addressee.

Tab. 1: Chapter Summary

Core Phenomenon

Scales and Contextual Parameters
$[\![great]\!] = \lambda d. [\lambda x. \text{MEAS}(x) \geq d]$

Text Interpretation

Meaning of the Text: there is a past time t in w where A uttered "you are great" to S & ∀ MEAS: if it pleases A that MEAS(S) ≥s_c then MEAS(S) ≥ s_c
"There is a past time t in w where A uttered "you are great" to S and for all measures MEAS: if it pleases A that MEAS assigns the standard s_c to S, then MEAS assigns s_c to S."

Relation R: "The relation R between the text worlds w and the actual world @ holds iff the text worlds w are maximally similar to @ except that S and A in w are the reader in @ (or an acquaintance of R, g_1(R)) and an acquaintance of the reader, g_2(R) in @, and A's utterance in w corresponds to an utterance of g_2(R) in @ and as S plays with A's utterance in w, so does R (or g_1(R)) with g_2(R)'s utterance in @."

Pragmatic Interpretation:
"If everything the text says is true, then people like A are at the mercy of people like S, who can both analyse a well-meant compliment as well as implement it."

Scales in other Chapters

In chapter I.6: Though I than He – may **longer** live / He **longer** must – than I –
"It is possible that I live longer than he, and it is necessary that he live longer than I." **or**
"My maximum life expectancy exceeds his maximum life expectancy, and the minimum required lifetime of his exceeds the minimum lifetime required of me"

Other Phenomena in this Chapter

Pronouns:
$[\![I]\!]$ = the speaker in the context
$[\![you]\!]$ = the addressee in the context

Disjunction:
And I must be Rhinoceros / **Or** Mouse – / **At once** – for Thee –
"S must be a Rhinoceros for A, or S must be a Mouse for A, or S must be both at once for A."

Presupposition Accommodation:
Accommodate earlier conversation, triggered by citation (A uttered "you are great" to S)

I.3 "I'm Nobody!": Interpreting Quantifiers

> Attention: This chapter presupposes familiarity with quantifiers, possible world semantics and speech act operations. For an explanation of these concepts in the framework we adopt, see the appendix.

```
1   I'm Nobody! Who are you?
2   Are you – Nobody – Too?
3   Then there's a pair of us!
4   Don't tell! they'd advertise – you know!

5   How dreary – to be – Somebody!
6   How public – like a Frog –
7   To tell one's name – the livelong June –
8   To an admiring Bog!
                          (J288/Fr260)
```

3.1 Introduction

The poem "I'm Nobody," c. 1861, reflects on the topic of identity, and on recognition of the self in relation to others. The speaker is concerned with evaluating the merit of public recognition for one's work or person. The quantifiers "nobody" and "somebody" play a key role. Because of their properties and the possible combinations within the text, the reader is compelled to reinterpret them.

In this context, it makes sense to briefly recapitulate the characteristics and the regular use of quantifiers as introduced in the appendix. Quantifiers are interpreted as non-referential. Their semantic contribution is to relate two sets. For example, "no" relates two properties, saying that there are no individuals that share both properties:

(1) $[\![no]\!]^g = \lambda P_{<e,t>}. \lambda Q_{<e,t>}.$ there is no x such that P(x) & Q(x)

While quantifiers never make reference to specific individuals, in the present poem, Emily Dickinson uses quantifiers in order to make statements about specific individuals, namely the speaker S and the addressee A. This turn is, from a semantic perspective, rather risky. We as readers are forced to reinterpret the quantifiers, and the way we reinterpret them influences the overall interpretation of the text. Specifically, in J288/Fr260 it is impossible to find one consistent reading of the text. Instead, two options for the reinterpretation of "nobody" emerge, each of which can only partially be combined with the individual sentences of the text. What we arrive at as a consequence are two interpretations of parts of the text, neither of which covers the whole. The overall text meaning then lies in the combination of those two readings, and the question is how this overall text meaning comes about. This combination of the two readings is to be seen in contrast to other analyses (such as the ones in chapter I.4, "This was a Poet," and chapter I.6, "My Life had stood"), where also two readings of the overall text emerge. However, in those cases, the combination of the readings and the consequence of this combination for the text interpretation differ. In the following, we will discuss each stanza in turn and then proceed with the interpretation of the overall text.

3.2 Stanza One, Lines 1–4

The speaker's initial statement "I'm Nobody!" is, strictly speaking, uninterpretable, since the semantic type of "nobody" does not go together with the rest of the sentence: "I" refers to a specific individual (the speaker of the poem), while "nobody" denotes a set of properties.

(2) $[I_{<e>} [am [nobody_{<<e,t>,t>}]]]$

(3) $[\![I]\!] = S$ (the speaker in the context c)

(4) $[\![nobody]\!] = \lambda P.$ there is no person x such that $P(x)$

"Nobody" says that the set that it combines with has an empty intersection with the set of people. This, however, leads to a mismatch since "nobody" in this sentence would need to combine with "I," an individual. Semantically, "nobody" and "I" cannot be combined. In order to still make sense of the utterance, we have to reinterpret "nobody." There are two possibilities: treating it as being referential or as a being a property. Taking "nobody" to be referential amounts to understanding the structure in (2) in analogy to (5a), an identity statement. Taking "nobody" to denote a property leads to understanding (2) in analogy to (5b): attributing a property to the subject (while "is" remains vacuous).

(5)   a.   Referential analogy: I am the boss
              $S = [\![the\ boss]\!]$
       b.   Property analogy: I am important
              $[\![important]\!] (S)$

In analogy to (5), one way of reinterpreting the sentence is to reinterpret the meaning of "nobody" from being a quantifier to being a referential proper name, e.g., "I am the unique person called Nobody." Then "Nobody" refers to a specific individual. The use of "Nobody" as a proper name has a prominent predecessor in the story of Odysseus and the Cyclops.[1] When asked for his name, Odysseus calls himself "Οὖτις," ("No-one," "no man" or "nobody," *Odyssey* IX.366). Because of the ambiguity inherent in this expression – that it can be read as a proper name but also as a quantifier – Odysseus is not pursued upon his escape. When the Cyclops shouts that he has been attacked by "The man called 'Nobody,'" the other Cyclopes understand his exclamation as "There is nobody who has attacked me." Additionally, the name of the Cyclops, "Πολύφημος" (Polyphemus, "many-voiced" or "much spoken of," *Odyssey* IX.403) can be seen parallel to being "Somebody" in Dickinson's poem. Reading "I'm Nobody" as an allusion to the episode of Odysseus and the Cyclops supports the overall reading of the quantifiers "nobody" and "somebody": the secretive and reticent Odysseus is clearly seen in a positive light, while the well-known ("public") and loud Cyclops is a man-eating monster. In addition, Odysseus is able to grasp the detailed meaning of words and use it for his own purposes, while Polyphemus is unable to understand the possible meanings of "Οὖτις."[2] The interpretation proceeds as in (6) and (7).

(6)   ⟦nobody$_{<e>}$⟧ = Nobody

(7)   ⟦I am nobody⟧ = 1 iff S = Nobody

---

[1] Eberwein (1983), in discussing possible sources for Dickinson's poem, notes both Desdemona's last words ("Nobody, I myself; farewell") and Charles Mackay's poem "Little Nobody," which also plays with the notions of being Nobody or Somebody. She regards the Odysseus episode as an even more significant influence (9f.). We find another parallel in Lewis Carroll's *Through the Looking-Glass* (1872), in which the King reinterprets one of Alice's utterances ("I can see nobody on the road"; 7.199) to refer to an individual called "Nobody": "'I only wish I had such eyes,' the King remarked in a fretful tone. 'To be able to see Nobody! And at that distance too!'" (7.199). For a discussion of this passage with regard to the parallel to Dickinson, see Winter-Froemel & Zirker (2010).

[2] A predecessor for Dickinson's play with the meaning of "Somebody," though not as well-known as the episode from the *Odyssey*, can be found in Dickens's novel *Bleak House*: "They said there could be no East wind where Somebody was; they said that wherever Dame Durden went, there was sunshine and summer air" (Dickens 378). "Somebody" and "Dame Durden" both refer to the protagonist Esther Summerson, who perceives of herself as insignificant, while she is in fact highly significant within the novel. Additionally, "Somebody" here is used as a proper name that denotes a specific individual, namely the protagonist.

This reading is strengthened by the capitalisation of "Nobody," and by the question following it.

(8)   Who are you?

(9)   Are you – Nobody – Too?

(8) and (9) are both questions, not propositions. The answer to the question in (8) requires that the addressee identify herself, similarly to the statement by the speaker, who identifies herself as the specific individual "Nobody." Reading on to the next line, however, we are confronted with a problem: the reinterpretation of "Nobody" as designating a specific individual cannot be combined with the other elements of question (9) in line 2.

The additive particle "too" triggers the presupposition that another proposition is also true. In our case, this is the proposition that someone other than the addressee is "nobody":

(10) $[\![\text{You are nobody, too}]\!]^{c,g} = \lambda w: \exists x\ [x = \text{nobody}\ \&\ x \neq A].\ A = \text{nobody in } w$

And here we see that it is not possible for two individuals, speaker (S) and addressee (A), to be the same specific individual "Nobody."[3] The referential reinterpretation of "nobody" is not plausible, hence we are forced to find another possibility to reinterpret "nobody." This is by treating "nobody" as a property, in parallel to (5b). Plausibly, this is the property of being insignificant:[4]

(11) $[\![\text{nobody}_{\langle e,t\rangle}]\!] = \lambda x.\ x$ is insignificant

(12) $[\![\text{I am nobody}]\!] = 1$ iff S is insignificant

With this reinterpretation, the compositional interpretation of (9) "Are you – Nobody – Too?" is possible as both S and A may be insignificant. However, this

---

3 We disregard the possibility that "Nobody" is a proper name that can refer to more than one individual; compare, for instance, the substitution of "Emily" for "Nobody": "I'm Emily! Who are you? Are you – Emily – Too?" The reading of "Nobody" as a proper name is unlikely at this point, as one would rather ask, "Are you **called** Nobody too?" In simply asking "Are you Nobody too," S puts a focus on A's identity rather than on A's actual name.

4 The idiomatic use of "nobody" meaning "insignificant" is attested in the 19th century and earlier; see *OED* "nobody, *pron.* and *n.*" A.2.

second reinterpretation of "Nobody" does not go together with the question in (8), "Who are you?," which is a question asking about A's identity and not about A's properties ("What are you?"). Each of the two questions in (8) and (9) allows for only one of the two reinterpretation mechanisms. Semantically, we encounter a problem: we cannot find one way of consistently interpreting all sentences.

This impossibility of deciding in favour of one consistent interpretation is then continued in the next line: while "pair" says that S is talking about two specific individuals that make up a pair (since the lexical semantics of "pair" require there to be exactly two elements), it is not entirely clear what she means by "of us." Somehow, the pronoun "us" seems to mean more than just a reference to S and A together and to suggest that S means a pair of "us nobodies," so that both speaker and addressee are identified as being insignificant. Within the sentence itself we thus find that we need to sustain both options: the notion that "Nobody" refers to a specific individual, and the notion that "nobody" refers to the property of being insignificant. This combination through "pair" and "us" accordingly hints at the peculiarity of the overall text meaning: both readings have to be taken into account.

The last line of the first stanza then turns around the quality of the property "nobody": it is presented as a secret between S and A and should be kept as such, else "they" would advertise it; because we lack more explicit context it is left open who exactly "they" refers to.[5] It seems that being "nobody" is something special that only applies to S and A, and no one else.

We hence arrive at the following interim summary: the type mismatch triggered by the combination of "I" and "nobody" leads to two possible reinterpretations. Those are exploited in two possible readings that go along with either of the two reinterpretations: the reading where S is identified as a particular individual called "Nobody," from here on I_{Ind}, and the reading where S characterises herself as having the property of being insignificant, from here on I_{Prop}:

(13) I_{Ind}: S is Nobody. S asks A who she is. S and A are a pair.

---

5 In any case, "they" must be the others that oppose or are different from A and S. Freedman (2011) refers to Dickinson's variant of "advertise," which is "Banish us"; she points out the Edenic imagery of the frog/bog imagery in the poem and imagines the two voices as possibly those of Adam and Eve after eating the apple (59). See also Lindberg-Seyersted (1968), who points out that the "use of the phrase *you know* is a congenial device for underlining bonds of camaraderie between speaker and addressee" (218).

(14) I_{Prop}: S is insignificant. S asks A if A is insignificant, as well. There is a pair of two insignificant people. Being insignificant is something special.

3.3 Stanza Two, Lines 5–8

The second part of the poem begins with "How dreary – to be – Somebody!" which contains a quantifier parallel to line 1. The expression "to be – Somebody!" can be reinterpreted. Because of the infinitival structure of the sentence that assigns to a nonspecific, generic subject the property of being "somebody," one way of reinterpretation is to treat it, similar to "nobody" above, as the property in (15). This goes along with I_{Prop}:[6]

(15) $[\![somebody_{\langle e,t\rangle}]\!] = \lambda x.\ x$ is important

This property is then depicted as "dreary" and frog-like. But once more, this line of interpretation breaks down in line 7: "To tell one's name" again can be seen in parallel to the question "Who are you?" Here again, the person that is identified as "Somebody" is described as telling her name – we have to come back to the referential option of reinterpretation, reading "Somebody" as a reference to a specific individual, in accordance with I_{Ind}:

(16) $[\![somebody_{\langle e\rangle}]\!]$ = Somebody

Being "Somebody" is contrasted with being "Nobody" above and is "public" and "dreary"; imparting this fact is compared to the constant croaking of frogs. While both readings of "nobody," i.e. "nobody" as being insignificant as well as reading it as the identity of the individual called "Nobody," at first glance appear negative in the first stanza, S claims that being "Nobody" has to be preferred over being "Somebody" in the second stanza: being "Nobody" is special, a quality shared only between S and A, and it therefore needs to be kept secret from others.

---

[6] This interpretation, too, shows a common idiomatic use of "somebody" (cf. *OED*, "somebody, *n.*" 2.a.).

3.4 Overall Text Meaning

We have seen that neither I_{Ind} nor I_{Prop} can be consistently combined with all sentences of the text: Some sentences are so explicit in their semantic properties that they only allow for one of the options, while others are similarly explicit but allow only for the other line of reinterpretation. A possible solution, as already alluded to in the introduction to this chapter, is that the text proffers two partial interpretations I_{Ind} and I_{Prop}; combining them via conjunction will lead to an adequate interpretation of the text as a whole. I_{Ind} only includes those sentences that are compatible with it:

(17) I_{Ind}:
        S_1: S is "Nobody"
        S_2: S asks A who A is
        S_5: S tells A not to tell. They'd advertise – you know!
        S_6: How dreary – to be – Somebody!
        S_7: How public – like a frog –
        S_8: To tell one's name – the livelong June –
            To an admiring bog!

For this reading, all other sentences are ignored. Those sentences are part of I_{Prop}:

(18) I_{Prop}:
        S_1: S is insignificant
        S_3: S asks A if A is insignificant, too.
        S_4: Then there's a pair of us!
        S_5: S tells A not to tell. They'd advertise – you know!
        S_6: How dreary – to be – significant!
        S_7: How public – like a frog –

Only sentence 1, sentence 5, 6 and sentence 7 go together with both readings. As we can see, we arrive at a zigzag schema of interpretation, and both readings alternate in combining one of the two possible reinterpretations of "nobody" with the individual sentences:

(19)

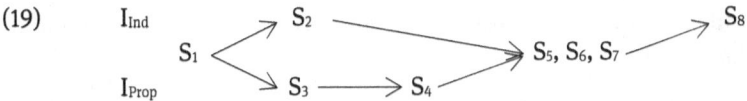

Intersecting the sentences of the two respective possible interpretations gives us two overall readings of the text that are (roughly) paraphrased below:

(20) Reading I_{Ind}: "I'm the individual 'Nobody.' Who are you? Don't give away your identity, as they will advertise it. It is dreary to be the individual 'Somebody' and to advertise this name over a long time-span, like the frog croaks about himself continuously."

(21) Reading I_{Prop}: "I'm insignificant. Are you insignificant, too? Then there's a pair of us insignificant people. It's dreary and public to be important."

It seems plausible that both readings can now be conjoined and thus form the overall text meaning, as paraphrased in (23).

(22) $T = I_{Ind}$ & I_{Prop} = (20) & (21)

(23) "In the worlds described by the text, the speaker is the individual 'Nobody' and the speaker asks the addressee which individual he is, telling him not to give his identity away. Being the individual 'Somebody' and advertising this is dreary. It is simultaneously the case that the speaker is insignificant, asking the addressee if she is insignificant as well, in which case there is a pair of insignificant people; this is contrasted with the property of being important, which is dreary and public."

By conjoining both partial text meanings, none of the information given in the text gets lost. FictionalAssert applies to this overall text interpretation in (24).

(24) $[\![FictionalAssert]\!]((23)) = 1$ iff $\forall w'\ [I_{Ind}(w') \ \&\ I_{Prop}(w') \rightarrow R(@)(w')]$

In this poem, one reading is only complete in combination with the other. We arrive at a very specific interpretation where both options of reinterpretation are combined. Therefore, both have to be considered as equally valid and are intended to be evoked; deciding in favour of one or the other is neither possible nor desired. We will see later that in other poems, it is more likely that two readings are available for the whole text. The interpretive effect is somewhat different – see the next chapter.

Next, we ask what R is. Remember that a value for R determines how the reader relates the text to her actual situation. Through the limited possibilities of reinterpreting the quantifiers "nobody" and "somebody," Dickinson points us to a reflection about identity, in particular about identity in relation to others.[7] In order to find one's place in the world as an individual, human beings are confronted with the characteristics other people assign to them and are also often forced to belong to a group. What plays a role when we discuss someone's identity is not only the individual as such but also the properties that apply to them, and the relation between these properties as well as to other people. It is striking that reinterpreting the semantics of a quantifier (i.e. a function that relates properties) into either an individual or a property can be an image of the difficulty of finding one's identity. Dickinson thus uses linguistic mechanisms as a means of describing one of the fundamental questions of human existence.[8]

The overall text meaning gives us the information that being "nobody" is associated with being secluded and quiet, while being "somebody" is linked to being public and talkative, "dreary" and frog-like (i.e. loud). Furthermore, the speaker places much emphasis on the fact that she is "Nobody" and makes the question of being "Nobody" or "Somebody" the central concern of this short poem. "I am" is a strong statement (especially right at the beginning of the poem) and shows that the speaker is aware of herself and has some notion of her identity. This fact contributes to the impression that being "nobody" is a special and valuable condition which merits reflection. The common notions of being "nobody" and being "somebody" have thus been reversed.

These qualities converge in the relation R. By establishing the value of R, the reader maps elements of the poem to elements of the actual world. As the text is written as an address by the speaker to the addressee, possible values for R map speaker and addressee to individuals in the evaluation world of the reader, taking into account the missing contextual information about who is referred to by "I" or "you." Through the lack of more explicit contextual information, the

---

[7] Some critics have read this poem as Dickinson's rejection for public recognition; see Porter (1966, 62) and Juhasz, Miller, Smith (1993, 15). Mudge (1975) represents a minority opinion in that she reads the poem as Dickinson's worries "about inconsequence," though she notes the "element of irony" as well (20). Richards (2013), in contrast, emphasises that ED "reverses the subject position; she valorises the idea of being a nobody, enlists the nobody as a comrade, and asserts their superiority over the somebodies" (144). See also Weisbuch (1975), who reads the poem as a rejection of conventional identity and quest for individual identity (172).

[8] See also Budick (1985) who reads the poem against the background of Puritanism (145). Kher (1974) interprets the poem as showing the paradoxical creation of personality through impersonality (75).

reference is unclear.[9] As readers we could simply be observers of a part of a one-sided conversation between two individuals, or we could be conversational partners ourselves, being directly addressed by the speaker. This indeterminacy will influence the choice of the reader when assigning the two conversational partners to individuals in her evaluation world and illustrates the space of R, for which some specific interpretations are possible but others are outside of it. The reader might just as well identify herself with the speaker of the poem or consider herself to be the addressee. Both speaker and addressee are assigned specific properties in the text, and these properties have to be transferred to the evaluation world of the reader, functioning as an interpretative frame given by the semantics of the text. Accordingly, whoever she assigns the speaker or addressee to be, both have to have the property of being special, because they do not reveal their identity to the public ("Don't advertise – ") and because being insignificant (the property that the speaker assigned to them) is contrasted with the dreariness of being important. A simple paraphrase of a possible value for R could then look like this:

(25)   "The relation R between the text worlds w and the actual world @ holds iff @ is exactly like w, except that the addressee in w corresponds to the reader in @ who is asked to reflect on her identity in relation to others."

Note that we simplify in the paraphrase in (25) in that we map the addressee of the poem to the reader. We think that in this particular case, it is quite plausible to assume that the reader feels that the questions are asked of her by the speaker of the poem. However, this need not always be the case. Individual readers might well think of persons they know for whom what the poem reflects might be more relevant. Still, these persons have to be familiar to the reader. We imagine that as a first step, the reader likely identifies herself with the speaker or

---

[9] Pollak (2004) reads the poem as being about "Dickinson's anxiety about the twin forces of democracy and technology that were transforming rural Amherst and moving America from the country to the city in the nineteenth century" (151). Others have read it in the context of feminist criticism, for instance Grabher (1998, 230); and Wardrop (1996, 40f.). Erfani (2013) places it in the context of Dickinson's existentialism, where she expresses that Dickinson is "suspicious of the knowledge crowds hold because it unburdens the self of its responsibility" (179). Freedman (2011) addresses the religious link to Jesus Christ and his making himself "of no reputation"; she points out that the poem's speaker ridicules this notion, and partakes in "disobedient acts which subvert the idea that, as a process of naming and bonding into Christ's obedient sacrifice, Baptism undoes original sin" (59).

addressee (the latter as above), and only in a second step might relate the text to other individuals.

On the basis of (25), a pragmatic interpretation of the poem could be the following:

(26)   "If everything the poem says is the case, then being unknown to the public is more precious than being a hotshot."

The reader has now related the poem to her own world and world-views. For example, the poem may be read as a general statement about the value of being reserved and silent (yet perceptive and understanding) in contrast to being public, loud, and insensitive. More specifically, it may be read as a reclusive poet's opinion about more "public" talkers and writers.

3.5 Conclusion

Once again, Emily Dickinson demonstrates her intuitive knowledge of the possibilities and rules of semantic composition in this poem. By deliberately violating standard interpretation mechanisms, she forces the reader to reinterpret certain words, here quantifiers, and by doing so is able to reflect on the main concern of the poem: identity. In the reader, this leads to a thought process about the interpretive differences and similarities between the original phenomena, in our case the quantifiers "nobody" and "somebody" and their alternative reinterpretations. On the level of the poem as a whole, the ambiguity created by the possible options of reinterpretation likewise contributes to a reflection on what it means to be "Nobody" or "Somebody."

An important effect of Dickinson's unconventional use of quantifiers is therefore that it draws the attention to the words themselves – both to their meaning and to their function. The reader is made to think not only about what it means to be nobody or somebody, but also about what the words "nobody" and "somebody" mean if considered in general and how they can (or cannot) be employed, or to what ends. The reader thus gains more insight into the possible applications of quantifiers, and into the way language works. "I'm Nobody" also shows a quality that is characteristic of Dickinson's poetry: an interpretation of a poem on the level of content and general notions alluded to or discussed therein is directly intertwined with the poem's structure and with the complex meanings that arise when linguistic phenomena are used by a poet deliberately. While we have observed in the two preceding chapters that Emily Dickinson exploits semantic mechanisms to arrive at a complex system of overall text meanings, this chapter presents an extreme case of pushing semantic composition to its limits. Here, similar to chapter I.2 ("You said that I 'was Great'"), linguistic analysis is part of the text itself. In "I'm Nobody," the text interpretation reveals that a deliberate violation of the semantic composition principles is a necessary part of the meaning of the text as it initiates a discussion about identity.

Tab. 1: Chapter Summary

Core Phenomenon

Quantifiers
⟦nobody⟧ = λP$_{<e,t>}$. there is no person x such that P(x)

Type Mismatch leads to **Reinterpretation**:
⟦nobody$_{<e>}$⟧ = Nobody (*Individual*)
⟦nobody$_{<e,t>}$⟧ = λ x. x is insignificant (*Property*)

Text Interpretation

Meaning of the Text:
Reading I$_{Ind}$ **(Individual-Interpretation):** "I'm the individual 'Nobody.' Who are you? Don't give away your identity, as they will advertise it. It is dreary to be the individual 'Somebody' and to advertise this name over a long time-span, like the frog croaks about himself continuously."
Reading I$_{Prop}$ **(Property-Interpretation):** "I'm insignificant. Are you insignificant, too? Then there's a pair of us insignificant people. It's dreary and public to be important."

→ **Text Interpretation:** I$_{Ind}$ & I$_{Prop}$

Relation R: "The relation R between the text worlds w and the actual world @ holds iff @ is exactly like w, except that the addressee in w corresponds to the reader in @ who is asked to reflect on her identity in relation to others."

Pragmatic Interpretation:
"If everything the poem says is the case, then being unknown to the public is more precious than being a hotshot."

Quantifiers in other Chapters

Modals as intensional quantifiers (in chapter I.6): Though I than He – may longer live / He longer must – than I –
⟦must⟧ = λR$_{<s,<s,t>>}$. [λp$_{<s,t>}$. [λw. ∀w' [(R)(w)(w') → p(w')]]]
⟦may⟧ = λR$_{<s,<s,t>>}$. [λp$_{<s,t>}$. [λw. ∃w' [(R)(w)(w') & p(w')]]]

Other Phenomena in this Chapter

Presupposition: Are you – Nobody – Too?
⟦too⟧^{c,g} = λp$_{<s,t>}$. [λw: there is a proposition q such that q ≠ p & q(w). p(w)]

Pronouns:
⟦I⟧^{c,g} = the speaker in c
⟦you⟧^{c,g} = the addressee in c

I.4 "This was a Poet": Identifying Referents – Definites and Demonstratives

> Attention: This chapter presupposes familiarity with variable assignments, possible world semantics and speech act operations. For an explanation of these concepts in the framework we adopt, see the appendix.

1 This was a Poet – It is That
2 Distills amazing sense
3 From ordinary Meanings –
4 And Attar so immense

5 From the familiar species
6 That perished by the Door –
7 We wonder it was not Ourselves
8 Arrested it – before –

9 Of Pictures, the Discloser –
10 The Poet – it is He –
11 Entitles Us – by Contrast –
12 To ceaseless Poverty –

13 Of Portion – so unconscious –
14 The Robbing – could not harm –
15 Himself – to Him – a Fortune –
16 Exterior – to Time –

(J448/Fr446A)

4.1 Introduction

J448/Fr446A, "This was a Poet" (c. 1862), describes a reciprocal relationship between the poet and "us," the readers of poetry as implied within the poem. Two readings of the poem emerge through the use of heavily fragmented syntactic structure, emphasising that both poet and readers are active agents in their interaction with each other. Moreover, the use of the demonstratives "this" and "that" in this poem poses a challenge as to their interpretation[1]; the poem sug-

---

[1] Heginbotham (2003) suggests that since "This was a Poet" is located opposite J613/Fr445A, "They shut me up in Prose," on fascicle 21, the two poems are discoursing with each other thematically (16). Some authors argue that J448 was written as a eulogy of Elizabeth Barrett

gests a self-referential reading, wherein it not only reflects about the poet-reader relationship but its own creative moment. Referential indeterminacy and structural underspecification thus lead the way to a complex (but never arbitrary) meaning of the poem in which local ambiguities interact to form two main readings.²

4.2 The Nature of Poetry – Lines 1–8

From the beginning of the poem, we are presented with an interpretational difficulty that is related to the interdependency of the syntactic structure in the first two stanzas. The syntactic complexity interacts with two context-dependent elements in the first line, the two demonstratives "this" and "that."³ Both come without contextual clues on how to interpret them. In the following, we will first explain how to interpret demonstratives generally. In a second step, we will relate this general analysis to the meanings of "this" and "that" in (1). We will see that both demonstratives introduce the basic theme of the text, poetry, which will lead to the two main readings.

(1)   This was a Poet – It is That

We analyse demonstratives in terms of Büring (2011). According to this analysis, demonstratives underlie rather heavy restrictions as to when they are felicitous-

---

Browning (e.g. Schöpp 1997, 96; Sherwood 1968, 211), who died in 1861. Although the poem was written around 1862 (Heginbotham 1998, 285), there seems to be no conclusive evidence for this claim; in fact, there is no evidence other than the temporal proximity of Barrett Browning's death and the composition of the poem as well as Dickinson's admiration for her. Textually, Heginbotham also points out the poem's closeness in word choice to Emerson's essay "The Poet" ("the verbs—'Distils,' 'Arrested,' 'Entitles'—are all in Emerson's 'The Poet'"; 1998, 286); see also Farr (1992, 323). Dickinson moreover recalls Higginson's "Letter to a Young Contributor": "Literature is attar of roses, one distilled drop from a million blossoms" (410). Her style shows a great deal of indebtedness to Higginson's after the publication of the "Letter," see Sherwood (1968, 205).

2 When we speak of "global" and "local" phenomena, we categorise them according to whether they apply on the level of the text as a whole (global), or on only a specific part of it, for instance a phrase or a line (local).

3 Of course, there is another reading: "that" may be read as a relative pronoun; in this case, the line can be read the following way: "This was a poet, it is [this] that / Distills amazing sense." The noun it refers to is elided; going along with a self-referential reading, it is conceivable to insert "poem": "This poem distills amazing sense." We simplify by not including this reading in the discussion.

ly employed since they share their basic semantics with pronouns. Let us assume for now that demonstratives, like pronouns, carry an index that points towards a specific individual in a given context (cf. Heim and Kratzer 1998; Büring 2011).[4] A variable assignment function is responsible for this mapping mechanism (see the appendix). This assignment function takes indices as arguments and returns contextually salient individuals as values:

(2)   ⟦this$_1$⟧^{g,c} is only defined if $g_c(1)$ is proximal. Then, ⟦this$_1$⟧^{g,c} = $g_c(1)$

(3)   ⟦that$_2$⟧^{g,c} is only defined if $g_c(2)$ is distal. Then, ⟦that$_2$⟧^{g,c} = $g_c(2)$

Let us assume a context where I, one of the authors of this chapter, sit at my desk. On my desk, there is a mug of tea right next to me, and a textbook that I need for my work is on the far right side of my desk. Suppose now that I ask my student assistant to take the mug away and to pass me the textbook:

(4)   Can you take this$_1$ and pass me that$_2$?

The variable assignment maps the first demonstrative to the mug and the second to the textbook. Interpretation of both happens smoothly as the relevant information is given by the context:

(5)   ⟦this$_1$⟧^{g,c} = $g_c(1)$ = the tea mug in c (well-defined since the mug is proximal)

(6)   ⟦that$_2$⟧^{g,c} = $g_c(2)$ = the textbook in c (well-defined since the mug is distal)

However, if a referent for "this" and "that" as given in (5) and (6) was not immediately available, this lack of a referent would generally be perceived as a semantic violation against the **Appropriateness Condition**.

(7)   **Appropriateness Condition:**
        A context c is appropriate for an LF [**a sentence structure**] ϕ only if c determines a variable assignment g_c, whose domain includes every index which has a free occurrence in ϕ (Heim and Kratzer 1998: 243).

---

[4] Assuming that pronouns and demonstratives are both variables is a simplification. See a more detailed analysis of demonstratives in Büring (2011).

As a result, compositional interpretation would fail and no meaning at all would be assigned to the structure. A reader's or listener's response in a conversation might be: "Hey, hang on – what do you mean by 'this' and 'that'?" (cf. Matthewson 2006; von Fintel 2004). Poems create a pragmatically different context. The reader cannot ask for clarification. Since we assume that the poet is a cooperative speaker and wants to convey meaning, readers assume that there must be a reason for the poet to use a sentence where a fixed referent is lacking. For the purpose of interpreting the poem, the **Appropriateness Condition** is temporarily suspended. The question is thus how the reader can deduce possible referents. In the following, we will address this question.

The only contextual information that we have access to is the poem itself. We may still find plausible referents for the demonstratives after we have read the poem as a whole, i.e. once we have gathered information about what the poem is about. This means, however, that it is impossible to interpret the demonstratives immediately. A dynamic system of interpretation can help us out (cf. Heim 1982; Kamp 1981; Poesio 1996; Stalnaker 1978; Groenendijk and Stokhof 1991): instead of interpreting every individual sentence relative to a particular contextually given variable assignment function, we will determine more abstract sentence meanings by abstracting over the possible assignments that make the sentence true. This is captured by analysing sentences as functions from assignments to propositions. Similarly, the parts of the sentence are functions from assignments into their usual denotations. In this way, the meaning of "this" is just the set of functions from variable assignment functions to the values to which they give the index:

(8) $[\![\text{this}_1]\!] = \lambda g.\ g(1)$

With the switch to a dynamic interpretation, readers can go on accumulating information about "this" (and likewise for "that") in order to eventually pick out a variable assignment function at the global level of the text. The **Appropriateness Condition** can thus also be fulfilled at the global level of the overall text. In chapter I.5, we will see a similar case of a global resolution of the pronoun "it."

To be able to combine the dynamic meaning of "this" in (8) with a dynamic meaning of the verb phrase in (9a), we need to make use of a dynamic version of Functional Application as well, defined in (9b). This extension of our system derives the meaning in (9c).

(9) a. ⟦was a poet⟧ = λg. [λx. [λw. x was a poet in w]]
   b. Dynamic Function Application (DFA), from Bade & Beck (2017):
      Let <g> be the type of variable assignment functions. Then:
      If α is a branching node with daughters β and γ and β is of type <g,<x,y>> and γ is of type <g,x> then ⟦α⟧ = λg. ⟦β⟧(g)(⟦γ⟧(g))

   c. ⟦This₁ was a poet⟧ = λg. [λw: g(1) is proximal in w. g(1) was a poet in w]

We now consider the meaning of the sentence "This was a Poet" as it is given in (9): it is a partial function from variable assignments to a proposition which says that the referent for "this" chosen for the index 1 by the assignment was a poet in w (if the referent is proximal). Similarly, the sentence embedding the second demonstrative can receive the sentence meaning in (10a) (assuming the most plausible sentence structure for the first and second stanza). Ignoring the cleft-structure of the sentence for now to somewhat reduce its complexity we analyse a simplified version of the sentence as given in (10b). Its meaning is (10c).

(10) a. It is that (which) distills amazing sense from ordinary meanings and (which distills) attar so immense from the familiar species that perished by the door.
   b. S₂ = That₂ distills amazing sense from ordinary meanings and (distills) attar so immense from the familiar species that perished by the door.
   c. ⟦S₂⟧ = λg. λw: g(2) is distal in w. g(2) distils sense [...] and attar [...] in w

One possibility that helps with accumulating information about the referent is to interpret the presuppositions of the demonstratives to delimit the possibilities for referents to come: the first demonstrative "this" refers to something immediately in the context, something proximal, whereas "that" stands in contrast to it by referring to something distal or abstract. There have to be two different referents for the demonstratives which are nonetheless connected to each other in S₂.

The following lines provide an explanation of what the referents of "that" and "this" do: the referent of "that" distills sense from meanings and attar from the familiar species. At the semantic level, we are presented with a mismatch of the selectional restrictions of the verb "distill" and the object "sense," as "distills" requires a physical substance as object, suggested by the juxtaposition of distilling attar from the familiar species that follows this line, but "sense" is an abstract notion:

(11)   ⟦distill⟧ = λy. [λz. [λx: z is a liquid. x distills y from z]]

Since the second argument of "distill," namely "ordinary meanings," is also an abstract concept, the most plausible way to arrive at a sentence meaning is to reinterpret "distill" and read it as metaphorical:

(12)   ⟦distill$_{Reint}$⟧ = λy. [λx. [λz. z transforms y into x]]

With that meaning, the first conjunct states that "that" transforms "ordinary meanings" into "amazing sense." In the second conjunct, we seem to need the literal meaning of "distill," as here, "that" distills attar, i.e. "[a] very fragrant, volatile, essential oil obtained from the petals of the rose; fragrant essence (of roses)" (*OED*, "attar, *n*.") from "the familiar species."[5]

But even though the verb and the object match in this literal interpretation, a metaphorical interpretation is still needed for the combination of "distill" and "ordinary meanings" as shown above. In the metaphorical interpretation, the whole VP, distilling attar from species, could be read as taking something beautiful that is temporal or ephemeral (e.g. the blooming of a flower) and transform it into something timeless and lasting. This transformation of something short-lived into something that endures over time is further strengthened by the subordinate clause that describes the familiar species as having perished by the door:

(13)   [$_{main}$ That distills attar so immense from [the familiar species [$_{subord}$ that perished by the door]]]

As the context of the poem is rather restricted and does not make reference to a specific door, there is, technically, a multitude of different doors that could be possible referents to the one where the familiar species perished by, e.g. on its threshold as part of the transformative process that is being described.[6] In order

---

5 Eberwein (2013) contextualises "This was a Poet" (and other poems, such as J501/Fr373A "This World is not Conclusion") as influenced by Darwin's *The Origin of Species*, particularly with reference to the word "species"; see especially pages 64f.
6 Deppman (2013) – who places the poem in the context of Heidegger's philosophy – reads the door as "a threshold between this world of everydayness [...] and the next or other world out-

to accommodate the uniqueness condition of the definite article, one possibility is a metaphorical reading of *the door*: in this case, the door stands for a transition, i.e. the transformation from flowers to attar. "The door" then is a representation of the act of transition that takes place when flowers perish at the precise moment they are turned into attar, i.e. when something ephemeral passes away as it is transformed into something everlasting.[7] In this way, we are also dealing with a paradox: something has to perish in order to be turned imperishable as a consequence.[8]

Taking both conjuncts together, the referent for "that" is described as fulfilling two main purposes: creating sense, and at the same time creating a very dense essence. Because of the conjunctive sentence structure it is clear that both the sense and essence have to be part of the product of the transformation process. On the basis of the information about the actions of "that," one plausible variable assignment function could map "that" to poetry, as it creates both sense and a lasting aesthetic experience. Similarly, due to the locality presuppositions of proximity and distance, the same variable assignment function could map "this" to the poem itself.

(14) $\quad g = \begin{bmatrix} 1 \rightarrow \text{poem} \\ 2 \rightarrow \text{poetry} \end{bmatrix}$

We will keep this possible mapping in mind and see whether at the overall level of text, it is borne out and remains the most plausible one.

Interpreting the last two lines of the second stanza presents a problem in terms of the syntactic structure which is mainly caused by "before." "Before" creates a syntactic ambiguity that will introduce the relationship between the

---

side, usually male, dangerous, exposed, mysterious, and radically transformative" (241) across Dickinson's poetry.

[7] According to Cameron (1979), the process in the poem indicates that "[t]o keep meaning from perishing is to lift it out of the context where it is sheer mediacy, to make of mediacy a totality and of totality a meaning" (198), explained as the poem's "ability to isolate meaning from time, to spatialize it" (197). How "spatializing" meaning should serve to achieve "totality" remains unclear.

[8] The Christian imagery is striking, as the process of distilling attar from roses can be likened to the passing from an earthly existence into life everlasting. Although we will not pursue this line of argument in this context any further, we note that it certainly is a possibility to make the connection between Poet and God (or Creator) in this poem. For the poet as creator, see e.g. Sir Philip Sidney's *Apology for Poetry* (1595): he ascribes the poet "divine force" (84) and argues that the poet "doth grow in effect into another nature, in making things either better than Nature bringeth forth, or, quite anew, forms such as never were in Nature" (85).

poet and the group of speakers "we." "Before" can take both an NP or a CP as arguments. In the poem, we cannot be sure whether we are faced with a case of ellipsis and the NP argument of "before" has been left out, or whether the third stanza is the CP continuation of the sentence.

(15)   We wonder it was not Ourselves –
        Arrested It – before –

Two possible readings arise:[9]

(16) a. NP: We wonder (that) it was not ourselves who arrested it before the poet (arrested it).
      b. CP: We wonder (that) it was not ourselves who arrested it before the poet (who is the discloser of pictures) entitles us, by contrast, to ceaseless poverty.

In each case, the group of speakers "we" is contrasted with the poet in that they did not arrest something that the poet, in turn, did arrest. In order to arrive at a complete interpretation, we have to find the referent of "it." Only then can we pin down the content of the action that the poet performed and the speakers did not. Because of the structure of the sentence, which includes the cleft-structure "it was not ourselves," the content that some arresting-event has happened is presupposed rather than asserted. This arresting-event should have been mentioned before in order for the sentence with the cleft to be felicitous. In the preceding lines, there are two possible referents for the arresting-event that "it" could refer to: the distillation of amazing sense and the distillation of attar. As both are connected via conjunction, they occupy parallel hierarchical positions in the LF and are equally plausible candidates for "it":

(17) a. We wonder (that) it was not ourselves (who) arrested the sense before.
      b. We wonder (that) it was not ourselves (who) arrested the attar before.

---

[9] There is also the possibility of "before" not taking any arguments. In that reading, the sentence could best be captured by the following meaning: "We wonder it was not ourselves who arrested it earlier." However, this reading is closely related to (17a), because we still have to find out to which earlier time "before" refers – the context gives us only the activities of the poet, which again leads to us, in contrast to the poet, having not arrested it before the poet did.

In more formal terms, we see that the text makes available two plausible variable assignment functions which each provide a different referent for "it". As in the dynamic analysis for "this" in (8), "it" in (18) is not assigned a referent right away, but it rather marks that different variable assignments could possibly assign different referents to the variable.

(18) $[\![it_3]\!] = \lambda g.\ g(3)$

In one case, let us call this variable assignment function g_1, "it" is mapped to the sense (see (19a)), while in the other variable assignment function g_2, "it" is mapped to the attar (see (19b)).

(19) a. $g_1 = \begin{bmatrix} 1 \to \text{poem} \\ 2 \to \text{poetry} \\ 3 \to \text{sense} \end{bmatrix}$

   b. $g_2 = \begin{bmatrix} 1 \to \text{poem} \\ 2 \to \text{poetry} \\ 3 \to \text{attar} \end{bmatrix}$

We will see later how and when this mapping actually occurs. For now, let it suffice to say that both variable assignments provide plausible referents for "it" and we keep both options in mind. Combining both options for the reference of "it" and both ways of how to resolve the syntactic ambiguity caused by "before" leaves us with four possible interpretations:

(20) a. Interpretation according to g_1: We wonder it was not ourselves (who) arrested the sense before the poet did.
   b. Interpretation according to g_2: We wonder it was not ourselves (who) arrested the attar before the poet did.

(21) a. Interpretation according to g_1: We wonder it was not ourselves (who) arrested the sense before the poet entitles us to poverty.
   b. Interpretation according to g_2: We wonder it was not ourselves (who) arrested the attar before the poet entitles us to poverty.

Since attar and sense both complement each other and are defined as being both part of the process that poetry is responsible for, it seems as if the conjunction of both readings in (20) and (21) best captures the overall meaning in each case. As we are confronted with poetic discourse, and the context of the poem is such that none of the two options is preferred over the other, only both options taken together seem to reflect on a complete interpretation of the pronoun. In more technical terms, it seems as if we do not decide for one of the two variable assignment functions g_1 and g_2, but rather, both contribute to the meaning of this line. We will see later how the simultaneous existence of two plausible variable assignments can yield an overall text interpretation.

In an interim summary of the first part of the poem, we come to the conclusion that a complex definition is given of what "that" does. As we have seen, a plausible variable assignment which is compatible with the information about "that" given in the poem maps "that" to poetry. With this mapping, poetry is described as transforming something ordinary into something extraordinary, while at the same time preserving something sensual and beautiful to last for a very long time. In the present case, it is natural language which is used poetically, i.e. transformed. This distillation or arresting of both the sense and the aesthetics of ordinary things is ascribed to the poet as an ability proper only to her, unlike the group that the speaker is part of.

4.3 The Relation between Poet and Readers – Lines 9–16

In the following discussion, we will assume the most plausible sentence structure of stanza three:

(22)   The poet, the discloser of pictures, it is he (who) entitles us, by contrast, to ceaseless poverty.

The lexical entries of "entitle" and "poverty" force us to reinterpret either the one or the other, since else we would arrive at an implausible statement. Our first option is to interpret "entitles" as ironical and actually meaning something like "condemn." The poet condemning us to ceaseless poverty can be seen as a consequence of our failure to distill or arrest the sense. Such a reading suggests a causal link in which arresting the sense could have prevented our impoverishment caused by the poet. Since this did not happen, and he has left us (entitled) with perpetual (ceaseless) poverty, we are poor, whereas the poet is rich. Alternatively, we reinterpret poverty to be seen as something positive, whereas the poet's richness is not necessarily so. This reading is based on taking "entitles" literally; it suggests that our poverty may have its advantages and may therefore not really be poverty. These two reinterpretation possibilities lead to different readings of the line, paraphrased as follows:

(23) a. The poet condemns us, in contrast to himself, to poverty (which is the inability to disclose pictures).
b. The poet entitles us, in contrast to himself, to keeping pictures undisclosed.

The first reading of (22), given in (23a), goes along with a reinterpretation of "entitle" where it receives the same meaning as "condemn." In this reading, the group of speakers was not able to arrest the sense/attar (i.e. unable to disclose pictures in the way the poet does)[10]. The second reading of (22), given in (23b), is the positive reinterpretation of "poverty" and incorporates the causal link between "entitle" and failing to arrest or distill sense: the group of speakers was not able to arrest the sense/attar before the poet arrested it, and thus, the poet relieves the group of speakers of the responsibility to disclose pictures. The group of speakers, in turn, is at liberty not to do the work the poet does for them. We suggest that the most illuminating interpretation of the text is to take both readings simultaneously. Accordingly, both poet and the group of speakers gain and lose something, or rather take something away from the other. This is further supported by the apposition "in contrast," which puts focus on the diametric relation of the two parties: the poet takes the ability to disclose pictures from the speakers, while, at the same time, the speakers take the possibility to leave pictures undisclosed from the poet.

We can summarise stanzas one to three by providing two readings reflecting the reinterpretations within them. In one reading, the inability of capturing something special with ordinary tools has the effect that the poet impoverishes the group of speakers; in the second reading, the poet only managed to do so earlier, while the group referred to by "us" could possibly have done the same. In parallel, the different reinterpretations of "entitle" and "poverty" contribute to these two readings:

---

[10] Deppman (2013) reads Dickinson's "Discloser" as an approach to the "Heideggerian vocabulary of aletheia, of truth as disclosedness [*Erschlossenheit*] rather than as adequation of language or concept of reality" (238). Wardrop (1996) points out that the "Discloser" is not only "one who reveals, but also the dis-closer, one who willingly opens the door. ... The speaker insists on dis-closing her house in the way that the poet who dwells in the House of Possibility throws all the doors and windows wide, letting in the familiar, the detritus from which poetry can be crafted, converting death into life, distilling from ordinary meaning amazing sense" (30). For a discussion of J657/Fr466A, "I dwell in Possibility," see chapter II.2 below, "The Linguist as Poet."

(24)   Lines 1-12 according to Reading 1:
"Poetry transforms something ordinary into something extraordinary and preserves something sensual and beautiful to last for a very long time. The speakers wonder why they did not use poetry in that way before the poet condemned them to ceaseless poverty."

(25)   Lines 1-12 according to Reading 2:
"Poetry transforms something ordinary into something extraordinary and preserves something sensual and beautiful to last for a very long time. The speakers wonder why they did not use poetry in that way before the poet entitled them to leaving pictures undisclosed."

We propose that both the impoverishment in Reading 1 and the hidden capability of the speakers in Reading 2 are true at the same time. Their combination elucidates this part of the poem and yields the most comprehensive interpretation. Furthermore, the simultaneity of the poet impoverishing us and our basic ability to do the same introduces one of the main topics of the poem: namely the reciprocal relation between the poet and the group referred to by "us."

This diametric relation of poet and the group of speakers is further dramatised in the fourth stanza, especially in lines 13 and 14:

(26)   Of portion – so unconscious –
         The Robbing – could not harm –

Because of the ellipsis, we cannot be entirely sure of the sentence structure. A plausible way to resolve the structural indeterminacy, given the information in the preceding lines of the poem, is as follows:[11]

(27)   The robbing of portion could not harm

The definite article of the NP "the robbing" triggers a uniqueness presupposition of the form in (28):

(28)   ⟦the robbing⟧ = ⟦the⟧(⟦robbing⟧) =
         λg: there is a unique e such that e is a robbing. the unique e such that e is a robbing

---

[11] For clarity's sake, we have left out "so unconscious" in this paraphrase, but we will come back to it later.

This uniqueness presupposition requires that there be one unique robbing event. The preceding sentences therefore have to have introduced this particular robbing event. A second point relevant for the NP is the semantic ellipsis involved: the lexical information of "robbing" requires an agent and a patient, so we need the semantic information as to who has done the robbing and who was robbed. Thus, "robbing" requires two additional covert arguments in order for us to arrive at a complete interpretation:

(29) 〚robbing〛 = λx. [λy. [λe. e is a robbing of y by x]]

(30) [$_{NP}$ the [$_{N'}$ [$_{N'}$ robbing PRO$_4$] PRO$_5$]]

(31) 〚the robbing〛 = λg: there is a unique e such that e is a robbing of g(4) by g(5). the unique e such that e is a robbing of g(4) by g(5)

The internal structure of the NP in the LF (given in (30)) thus has to include two covert pronouns, PRO$_4$ and PRO$_5$, which are the two arguments needed by "robbing." (31) is the fully specified meaning of the NP. Once more, as with the demonstratives and the pronoun "it," we assume a dynamic interpretation of PRO$_4$ and PRO$_5$ where once more two variable assignments offer up different plausible referents for the covert pronouns here.

The most likely candidates for the referents of the pronouns are the poet and the group of speakers, as those are the only referents mentioned in the poem. As a consequence, two variable assignments are plausible: one possibility is to choose the poet as the agent and the speakers as the patient. The other possibility is the reverse case: the speakers are the agents whereas the poet is the patient. In the first case, a possible variable assignment assigns the poet as referent to the index 4 and the speakers as referents to the index 5. The alternative is to assign the speakers to the index 4 and the poet to the index 5.

(32) $g_1 = \begin{bmatrix} 4 \rightarrow \text{poet} \\ 5 \rightarrow \text{speakers} \end{bmatrix}$

(33) $g_2 = \begin{bmatrix} 4 \rightarrow \text{speakers} \\ 5 \rightarrow \text{poet} \end{bmatrix}$

Depending on which variable assignment is chosen, two possible meanings arise for the NP:

(34) a. Reading according to g_1: the unique e such that e is a robbing of the poet by the speakers
b. Reading according to g_2: the unique e such that e is a robbing of the speakers by the poet

We see that each option contributes to one of the two readings established in the previous stanzas: (34a) fits Reading 2 in (25), while (34b) fits Reading 1 in (24). We will refer to Reading 1 as the "Poet Robber" reading and to Reading 2 as the "Reader Robber" reading to draw attention to this central passage of the poem, in which the lack of an overt agent and patient for "robbing" makes a local, ambiguous interpretation of the NP possible. Emily Dickinson's establishing the two meanings can thus be seen as a strategic move to maintain the global ambiguity of the poem.

The ambiguity between two equally plausible variable assignment functions which provide mirror image mappings of the agent and patient to either poet or speakers interacts with the assignments of "it" in line 8. Remember that at that point, we suggested that variable assignment functions which mapped "it" to either "attar" or "sense" seemed to be equally plausible options. As a consequence, four variable assignment functions provide plausible mappings that are compatible with the information provided in the text:

(35) $$g_1 = \begin{bmatrix} 1 \rightarrow \text{poem} \\ 2 \rightarrow \text{poetry} \\ 3 \rightarrow \text{sense} \\ 4 \rightarrow \text{poet} \\ 5 \rightarrow \text{speakers} \end{bmatrix}$$

(36) $$g_2 = \begin{bmatrix} 1 \rightarrow \text{poem} \\ 2 \rightarrow \text{poetry} \\ 3 \rightarrow \text{attar} \\ 4 \rightarrow \text{speakers} \\ 5 \rightarrow \text{poet} \end{bmatrix}$$

(37) $$g_3 = \begin{bmatrix} 1 \rightarrow \text{poem} \\ 2 \rightarrow \text{poetry} \\ 3 \rightarrow \text{sense} \\ 4 \rightarrow \text{speakers} \\ 5 \rightarrow \text{poet} \end{bmatrix}$$

(38) $g_4 = \begin{bmatrix} 1 \rightarrow \text{poem} \\ 2 \rightarrow \text{poetry} \\ 3 \rightarrow \text{attar} \\ 4 \rightarrow \text{poet} \\ 5 \rightarrow \text{speakers} \end{bmatrix}$

In all four variable assignment functions, the mapping of "this" to the poem itself and "that" to poetry stays the same. However, in variable assignments g_2 and g_4, "it" is mapped to attar, whereas in variable assignments g_1 and g_3, "it" is mapped to sense. As these two mappings are equally plausible, they should be compatible with both a reading where either the poet robs the readers (captured by the mappings in variable assignments g_2 and g_3) or the readers rob the poet (g_1 and g_4). Regarding the two overall lines of interpretation "Poet Robber" and "Reader Robber," we see that variable assignment functions g_2 and g_3 are compatible with the "Poet Robber" reading, while g_1 and g_4 are compatible with the "Reader Robber" reading. The possible assignments taken together can capture possible text interpretations.

Coming back to the presupposition that there has to be a salient robbing event available in the context of the sentence, a salient possibility is to read the distilling of sense/attar as the ability that the poet takes away from us, and thus the portion that he robs from us. This is in accordance with the "Poet Robber" reading. In the second reading, "Reader Robber," in which the speakers are the robbers, the end-product could equally be the distillation that we take away from the poet, because we do not have the ability to do the distillation ourselves.

Let us now combine the meaning of the NP with the meaning of the rest of the sentence. Two additional elements are relevant for its interpretation: the modal "could" and the VP "harm," in combination with the negation.[12] In the LF structure, we will assume the negation to have widest scope:

---

[12] We will exclude the possibility that "himself" is the argument for "harm." According to our two analyses of the sentence, neither of them provides a basis where it is grammatical to use "himself" as an argument for "harm." In the reading where the speakers rob the poet without harming him, the reflexivity would not make any sense as the poet is not the agent of the robbing event; the other reading would fully account for the reflexivity of the pronoun, and, given that if the poet robs somebody else, it is less plausible (but possible) that this action leads to him harming himself. Since the first reading suggests that it is not the poet who is responsible for the robbing but the speakers, using a reflexive is dispreferred.

(39)   [CP not [IP could [VP [NP the [N' [N' [N' robbing of portion] PRO₄] PRO₅]] harm]]]
"It is/was not possible that the robbing of portion from g(4) by g(5) caused harm."

One more local ambiguity needs to be addressed at this point: the interpretation of "could." In one case, the morphology of "could" points towards an event that happened in the past, when the robbing was not able to do harm. In the other case, the temporal reference is irrelevant and "could" is interpreted purely modally. This means that, in the first case, we have to anchor the reference to a past time, while, in the second case, the sentence is a general statement about possibility. The two options lead to the following two propositions:

(40)   a. λg. [λw. ¬ ∃w' [R$_{circ}$(w)(w') & ιe [e is a part of w and e is a robbing of portion of g(4) by g(5)] harms g(4) at t$_{past}$]]
       b. "The function that maps any assignment g and world w to true iff it is not the case that there is a world that adheres to the same circumstances as w in which the robbing of portion event of g(4) by g(5) harms g(4) at the relevant past time t$_{past}$."
           "It's not the case that there was the possibility that g(5) robbing g(4) would harm g(4)."

(41)   a. λg. [λw. ¬ ∃w' [R$_{circ}$(w)(w') & ∃t' [ιe [e is a part of w and e is a robbing of portion of g(4) by g(5)] harms g(4) at t']]]
       b. "The function that maps any assignment g and world w to true iff it is not the case that there is a world w' that adheres to the same circumstances as w in which the robbing of portion event of g(4) by g(5) ever harms g(4)."
           "There isn't any possibility that g(5) robbing g(4) could harm g(4)."

The two readings of "could" contribute to the ambiguity of the semantic ellipsis of "robbing" and thus also to the ambiguity between "Poet Robber" and "Reader Robber": we suggest that both options in conjunction contribute to the interpretation: neither in the past, nor ever, will any of the two robbings of either the poet robbing the speakers or the speakers robbing the poet harm the respectively robbed entity.

The final item that requires explanation in this sentence is the apposition "so unconscious." To which element of the sentence does it belong? Due to its position, it can either modify "portion" or the "robbing." Accordingly, in the first case, the portion that is taken away is held unconsciously, meaning that the person having this portion is not aware of it. This fits the reading where the poet robs the speakers without harming them, i.e. the "Poet Robber" reading, as they are not aware that they are missing something – and it also refers back to the presuppositional element of the NP, namely that the poet robs us of the ability to distill sense/attar, though we were not aware of this ability in the first place. The second option, where "unconscious" modifies "robbing," fits the "Reader Robber" reading quite well: the speakers rob the poet without him being aware of it, and, thus, he is not harmed. This latter reading also accommodates the presupposition of the poet's lack of awareness of the fact that we rob him of the end-product of his ability to distill sense/attar, because he can repeat this process as often as he wishes to.

(42)   Himself – to Him – a Fortune –
        Exterior – to Time –

We cannot be sure how to interpret the sentence due to its elliptical structure: the problem is that the main verb is missing. But the two readings "Poet Robber" and "Reader Robber" can help with a reconstruction of sense. In the "Poet Robber" reading, it is the poet who robs the speakers of a portion or ability that the speakers were not aware they had; hence, they are not harmed, because they do not know that and what they have lost. In consequence, the poet is the only one who has the ability to disclose pictures and distill sense/attar. Through this ability, a timeless fortune is available to him, because he can be sure that no one else will interfere with this unique ability. Thus, an informal paraphrase of the reading that follows "Poet Robber" can be seen below:

(43)   "He has gained a fortune for himself that is timeless."

His fortune is timeless because the work will survive the poet. The alternative reading is closely connected to the "Reader Robber" reading: here, the speakers rob the poet without him being aware of it and without him being harmed. He is not harmed by the robbing because he is sufficient unto himself. As he has the ability to distill sense/attar and can repeat this process whenever he wishes to, he is independent from the robbing by the speakers, who could only take away the end-product, i.e. the poem and its meaning. His creativity is his fortune. Accordingly, an informal paraphrase of this reading can be seen below:

(44)   "He is a timeless fortune for himself."

The poet is the creator who has the power to turn something ordinary into something extraordinary; the robbing by the speakers could never harm him. Seen in conjunction, both readings interact: it is simultaneously the case that, through robbing us, the poet gains a fortune and because our robbing of him could never possibly harm him, he is his own fortune.

In the third and fourth stanzas, the contrast between poet and the group of speakers ("we") is fleshed out in more detail. The two readings identified at the end of stanza two, "Poet Robber" and "Reader Robber," are sustained by considering structural and referential local ambiguities of the text:

(45)   Lines 9–16 according to "Poet Robber," with matching variable assignments g_2 and g_3: The poet as agent condemns us to poverty and thus robs us of an ability that we were not aware of, gaining a fortune only he has access to.

(46)   Lines 9–16 according to "Reader Robber," with matching variable assignments g_1 and g_4: The speakers are agents and entitled to poverty in that they do not have to disclose pictures; in turn, they rob the poet of his portion of ingenuity without him noticing it, and, since he can repeat the process of distilling sense and attar, he is not harmed by this action either.

Since both readings are simultaneously present, taken together do these readings of either poet as agent or "we" as agents constitute the text meaning. In either reading, the speakers are always poor, because they do not have the poet's ability, yet still can rob him in one scenario. Simultaneously, the poet is the one who produces or creates but simultaneously benefits from "us" because he can take away an ability that we were not aware of. In both readings, the poet gains a fortune and is himself his biggest fortune. These two readings are similar in that we are always poor and the poet always gains a fortune, yet the circumstances of this distribution are evaluated in drastically different ways each time.[13]

---

13 See also Bauer & Brockmann (2017).

4.4 Overall Readings of the Text

In order to arrive at an overall understanding of the text, let us come back to the interpretation of the five demonstratives and pronouns we have encountered in the poem. We have seen that the text provides information about plausible referents. For "this" and "that" in the first line, we can gather that both have to refer to something that a poet creates in contrast to a group of speakers. Accordingly, at the global level of the text, given that the only information available to us is the poem itself, it seems as if "this" is most plausibly to be interpreted self-reflexively in pointing towards the poem itself as something a poet creates. Through the contrast between "this" and "that" and their simultaneous connection, we can derive that, if "this" refers to the poem itself, "that" may refer to the broader concept of poetry in general – given that the poem is proximal, while poetry is a concept that is more abstract or distal.[14] Thus, our preliminary assumption that "this" refers to the poem itself, while "that" refers to poetry in general is confirmed. For "it," we have seen that attar and sense are equally plausible referents. Similarly, the two covert pronouns PRO$_4$ and PRO$_5$ can either be mapped so that the poet robs the speakers or the other way around. These possibilities are not resolved throughout the poem, so that also at the global level, the four variable assignments we identified before remain the assignments which provide the most plausible mappings given the information within the poem (see (35) through (38)).

Given these variable assignment functions, and that we have found two main lines of interpretation, the meanings of the four stanzas can be paraphrased as in (47) and (48) below.

(47)   "Poet Robber" according to variable assignments g$_2$ and g$_3$:
    a.   Stanza 1/2: This poem was created by a poet. It is poetry which transforms ordinary meanings into amazing sense and which derives an essence from short-lived species that do not survive the transformation process. We wonder that it was not ourselves (in contrast to the poet) who arrested the sense/essence before …

---

14 Miller (1987) reads "that" as referring to the poet, and thus "reduc[ing] the poet's humanity" (119). Farr (1992), however, perceives the peculiar mixture of "this," "that," and finally "He" as Dickinson's "definition of the poet as a nearly suprapersonal asexual force," since "[t]he artist [...] transcends sex in this poem" (324); her rather speculative argument is moreover based on the collocation of what she considers feminine-connoted fields, such as "wearing [...] perfume" and "the beautiful" (324) in combination with the male pronoun "He."

b. Stanza 3/4: ... the poet condemns (i.e. ironically entitles) us to ceaseless poverty (of the ability to disclose pictures). Thus, the poet robs us of an unnoticed share without (ever/in the past) harming us since we do not know what we lose. In this way, he gains a fortune for himself that is timeless.

(48) "Reader Robber" according to variable assignments g_1 and g_4:
a. Stanza 1/2: This poem was created by a poet. It is poetry which transforms ordinary meanings into amazing sense and which derives an essence from short-lived species that do not survive the transformation process. We wonder that it was not ourselves who arrested the sense/essence before the poet.
b. Stanza 3/4: The poet, who is the discloser of pictures, is the one who entitles us, in contrast to himself, to keeping pictures undisclosed. We can in turn rob the poet of his share of ingenuity without him being aware of it. This robbing was and will never be able to harm the poet, as he himself is his biggest and timeless fortune.

The poem is composed in a way that defies disambiguation and the decision in favour of one single interpretation. This, we would like to argue, is the point of the poem, and both (47) and (48) are both plausible readings. We assume that Emily Dickinson makes use of these ambiguities not accidentally or to be obscure, but rather to create a more complex meaning of the poem. The coexistence of two interpretations points us to the reciprocal relationship between poet and readers and is an important component of the overall interpretation.[15] Expressing the reciprocity through ambiguity is not the same as simply asserting it. The interaction of two interpretations throughout the poem mirrors the complex relation between the poet and the group of speakers, who could plausibly be the readers of both this poem in particular and poetry in general. We can actually see in the syntax of the poem that these three elements – poet, poem, and reader – are the core of what the poem is about. They are all foregrounded through cleft-constructions:

---

[15] Miller states that Dickinson uses non-recoverable deletions in her poetry to create density and syntactic or logical ambiguity (1987, 28ff.). She gives J448/Fr446A as an example of this technique, and discusses the non-recoverable deletion in line 1 that may be resolved in different ways.

(49) a. This was a Poet – It is That –
      b. We wonder it was not Ourselves
      c. The Poet – it is He –

The poem consciously exploits structural and referential ambiguity to reveal the triangular relationship between poem, poet, and reader, and this complex relationship is addressed in a very economic way, namely by consistently available double interpretation.

Having determined the different readings of the text, our final step is to connect them in order to arrive at a global interpretation of the poem, and consequently formally capture the triangular relationship delineated above and the poem's global ambiguity. We have shown that all possible readings of the sentences depend on which variable assignments can plausibly map the demonstratives and pronouns to their referents. For example, the "Poet Robber" reading comes about by employing the variable assignment functions g_2 and g_3. Similarly, the "Reader Robber" reading came about by employing the variable assignments g_1 and g_4. We have also argued that both readings are simultaneously true. Thus, in other words, the text must be true for all four variable assignment functions.

At this point, let us come back to our extension of the formal system. We have interpreted each sentence as a function from variable assignments to propositions. Thus, the semantics of the text is also a function from variable assignments to a proposition and leaves open which mappings do actually occur. In order to accommodate this semantics, we revise FictionalAssert so that it is able to operate on a text meaning of type <g,st>. We propose (50).

(50) $[\![\text{FictionalAssert}_@]\!] = \lambda T_{<g,<st>>}. \forall g,w\ [T(g)(w) \rightarrow R(@)(w)]$

The formula in (50) universally quantifies over all possible variable assignment functions and all worlds which make the text true. This says that in all worlds in which what the text says is true under any assignment, R holds.

However, this revision does not yet account for the fact that not any variable assignment function is appropriate, but that rather the four assignment functions we identified before are the plausible candidates. Those four variable assignments preserve the **Appropriateness Conditions** (i.e. the presuppositions) triggered by the linguistic material. As a consequence, we have to make sure that universal quantification is over those variable assignment functions:

(51) $[\![\text{FictionalAssert}_@]\!] = \lambda T_{<g,<st>>}. \forall g,w\ [g \in \{g_1, g_2, g_3, g_4\}\ \&\ T(g)(w) \rightarrow R(@)(w)]$

The version of FictionalAssert as given in (51) gives us the desired interpretation: it says that for all four variable assignments g1 to g4 and for all possible worlds in which what the text says under that assignment is true, the relation R between the text worlds and the actual world holds. In other words, all relevant mappings of variables to values lead to the relation R being inferred. Thus, as a consequence, we achieve that the two readings in (47) and (48) both go into the pragmatic interpretation of the poem J448/Fr446A and that the reciprocal relationship between poet and readers is captured.

The actual pragmatic interpretation of the text depends on what we infer as the relation R. A plausible value for R for the present poem can be roughly paraphrased as below:

(52)   "The relation R between the text worlds w and the actual world @ holds iff w is exactly like @ except that the group of speakers in w are readers of poetry in @ and the poet in w is the poet in @ and the relation between the readers in @ and the poet in @ reflects a reciprocal relation as given for the speakers in w and the poet in w."

The combination of (51) and (52) leads to the pragmatic interpretation in (53):

(53)   "If everything the poem says is the case, then poetry in general and this poem in particular create a creative and reciprocal relation between readers and poet."

In summary, we arrive at the conclusion that both poet and reader rob someone, and that both are getting robbed. The robbing is, on a basic level, the very fact that the poet has written the poem, which may also be put in relation to poetic originality, and that the speaker has been robbed of the originality to write the poem first. Nonetheless, the reader has the capability to also harness the creative potential that is seen in the poet and his writing, and she gets to share the poet's originality in reading and interpreting the poetry he produces. When the reader applies interpretive tools, whether consciously or not, in reading the text, they correspond to the tools the poet used in producing it, and hence a reciprocal relationship is created between the two. The actions of both the reader and the poet are original and utilise creative potential. If the reader thus plays an active role, she "robs" the poet.

With this in mind, lines 7-8, "We wonder it was not Ourselves / Arrested it," show another local ambiguity that arises from ellipsis. The text does not provide any clue whether we are to "wonder why" or "wonder that" or "wonder if ... it was not Ourselves." The last of these possibilities ("wonder if") serves to approximate the "Poet" and "Us," which up to this point had appeared as opposing parties, and ties them together.

4.5 Conclusion

Local ambiguities that Dickinson creates through ellipsis and fragmentation in interaction with presupposition and anaphora resolution serve to induce at least two strands of interpretation of the whole poem that are simultaneously present and that depend on the global resolution of the demonstratives and pronouns. Both of these are coherent in their own right, but the juxtaposition of the two that arises due to the formal structure and linguistic tools Emily Dickinson employs suggests that an overall meaning of the poem is intended to convey the simultaneous truth of the poet robbing his environment and his environment robbing the poet. This interpretation highlights the reciprocal relationship between poet and speakers in the poem, and, similarly, between author and reader on another level of communication. The poem itself serves as an example of the interaction between the poet and reader and becomes the very thing it describes in the creative potential of the poet: it is "amazing sense," an aesthetic product, and filled with verbal richness ("Fortune").[16] Only if all parts of the poem are taken together and parallel interpretations are combined in conjunction does J448/Fr446A reveal itself as a brilliantly devised composition.

---

[16] Critics differ on their evaluation of the poet's depiction: whereas reading "This was a Poet" as a celebration of the poet has a long tradition (a particularly strong interpretation is Sherwood's, who writes that "the creation of a poem is not an intellection so much as it is the saving of a life"; 1968, 211), it has also been pointed out that the poem can be read as a criticism of poetic skills: "The poet, in other words, may, in the very attempt to preserve nature, also become a destroyer of the natural order, a burglar who (unintentionally perhaps) succeeds in impoverishing his or her intended beneficiaries" (Budick 1985, 123). Budick supports this reading by pointing towards the vocabulary used in the poem, which circles around poverty, theft, unconsciousness, and harm. As is often the case, this interpretation neglects the very active role that the readers play as well, and instead places all influential power on the poet alone.

Tab. 1: Chapter Summary

Core Phenomenon

Demonstratives/Definites
$[\![this_1]\!]^{g,c}$ is only defined if $g_c(1)$ is proximal. Then, $[\![this_1]\!]^{g,c} = g_c(1)$ = this poem
$[\![that_2]\!]^{g,c}$ is only defined if $g_c(2)$ is distal. Then, $[\![that_2]\!]^{g,c} = g_c(2)$ = poetry
$[\![\text{the robbing}]\!] = \lambda g$: there is a unique e such that e is a robbing of $g(4)$ by $g(5)$. the unique e such that e is a robbing of $g(4)$ by $g(5)$
$[\![this_1]\!] = \lambda g.\ g(1)$

Text Interpretation

Meaning of the Text:
Reading "Poet Robber": This poem represents a poet. It is that (either poetry in general, produced by the poet, or the poet himself) which transforms ordinary meanings into amazing sense and which derives an essence from short-lived species that do not survive the transformation process. We wonder that it was not ourselves (in contrast to the poet) who arrested the sense/attar before the poet condemns (i.e. ironically entitles) us to ceaseless poverty (of the ability to disclose pictures). Thus, the poet robs us of an unnoticed share without (ever/in the past) harming us since we do not know what we lose, nor the linguistic expressions themselves – which are unconscious, i.e. have no consciousness. Thus, he gains a fortune for himself that is timeless.

Reading "Reader Robber": This poem represents a poet. It is that (either poetry in general, produced by the poet, or the poet himself) which transforms ordinary meanings into amazing sense and which derives an essence from short-lived species that do not survive the transformation process. We wonder that it was not ourselves who arrested the sense/attar before the poet. The Poet, who is the discloser of pictures, is the one who entitles us, in contrast to himself, to keeping pictures undisclosed. We can in turn rob the poet of his share of ingenuity without him being aware of it. This robbing was and will never be able to harm the poet, as he himself is his biggest and timeless fortune.

→ **Text Interpretation:** Poet Robber & Reader Robber (conjunction)

Relation R: "The relation R between the text worlds w and the actual world @ holds iff w is exactly like @ except that the group of speakers in w are readers of poetry in @ and the poet in w is the poet in @ and the relation between the readers in @ and the poet in @ reflects a reciprocal relation as given for the speakers in w and the poet in w."

Pragmatic Interpretation:
"If everything the poem says is the case, then poetry, and this poem in particular, creates a creative and reciprocal relation between readers and poet."

Demonstratives / Definites in other Chapters

Definites (in chapter I.6): **The Owner** passed – identified – / And carried Me away –
⟦the owner⟧ = λg: there is a unique x such that x owns g(3). the unique x such that x owns g(3).
Demonstratives (in chapter I.1): **This** would be Poetry – // Or Love – the two coeval come –
⟦this$_1$⟧^{g} = g(1) = the property of piling like thunder piles to its close, while everything created hid, then crumbling grandly away

Other Phenomena in this Chapter

Structural Ambiguity: We wonder it was not Ourselves – / Arrested it – before
⟦before⟧(NP) or ⟦before⟧(CP)

Reinterpretation:
⟦distill⟧ = λy. [λz. [λx: z is a liquid. x distills y from z]]
⟦distill$_{Reint}$⟧ = λy. [λx. [λz. z transforms y into x]]

I.5 "If it had no pencil": Identifying Referents – Pronouns

> Attention: This chapter presupposes familiarity with variable assignments, presuppositions, counterfactual conditionals, possible world semantics and speech act operations. For an explanation of these concepts in the framework we adopt, see the appendix.

```
1   If it had no pencil
2   Would it try mine –
3   Worn – now – and dull – sweet,
4   Writing much to thee.
5   If it had no word,
6   Would it make the Daisy,
7   Most as big as I was,
8   When it plucked me?
                    (J921/Fr184A)
```

5.1 Introduction

"If it had no pencil" (J921/Fr184A) was probably written sometime between 1861 (Sewall 1975, 526) and 1864 (Dickinson 1961, 433) but not published until 1945. An interpretation of this poem presents the reader with a peculiar problem: unlike other poems discussed in this book (and the majority of Dickinson's poetry in general), J921/Fr184A is written as a question rather than a statement. This challenges a number of assumptions about what information is given and how the context can be reconstructed. The question form of the poem allows for a philosophical reflection about the means given to someone and what to do with them – it invites the reader to wonder with the speaker, as it were, and imitate the performance of the question. Our approach to interpreting the poem is focused on its use of presuppositions in counterfactuals, and the puzzling use of pronouns, especially "it," which seems to lack a referent intratextually.

A further complication is the material form in which the poem has survived: it is not written in one of Dickinson's notebooks but rather on a slip of paper pinned around the stub of a pencil and signed "Emily" (Sewall 1975, 526).[1] This

---

[1] As it is, the circumstances of the poem's creation and its addressee have been the subject of most of its criticism. Jackson (2005) reads it as "an invitation to written exchange," addressed at the time to "Samuel (or perhaps Mary) Bowles," who "was meant to write back, or if he could

specific mode of preservation provides us with an extra-linguistic context for the poem which we will take note of later in our interpretation. Though it suggests the context of a non-fictional communication, we contend that this is a possible but not necessary assumption,[2] and therefore consider the poem a fictional text.

Although the first sentence of the poem lacks a question mark, it contains subject auxiliary inversion, which structurally marks questions in English: "If it had no pencil would it try mine." Semantically, the denotation of a question is the set of propositions that are possible answers (Hamblin 1973; Karttunen 1977):

(1)   ⟦If it had no pencil would it try mine⟧ = {If it had no pencil it would try mine, If it had no pencil it would not try mine}

In this case, the two possible answers are counterfactual conditionals. They receive a similar analysis as "would" in chapter I.1. A counterfactual presupposes that its antecedent is false, remember (2).

(2)   If it were Tuesday, Peter would come.

In (2), the counterfactual presupposition holds in the actual world, i.e. it is not actually Tuesday. In the case of the counterfactual conditionals in the poem, however, the counterfactual presupposition holds in the text worlds. In other words, whatever "it" refers to, "it" does have a pencil in the text worlds and "it" does have a word. The conditional talks about worlds in which everything is just as described by the text, but in these worlds "it" has no pencil. As regards the question structure in (1), the difference between the two propositions that are possible answers to the question is the consequent of the conditional. The first possible answer says that "it" would try the speaker's pencil in the counterfactual worlds; the second possible answer says that "it" would not.

Unlike statements, questions are not asserted. Therefore, we need to proceed slightly differently than before: we will begin by analysing the presuppositions given within the text which contain information about "it" as well as those presuppositions we can derive from the speaker's references to herself. Accord-

---

not write (Bowles was ill at the time), at least draw in response" (135f.). Sewall (1975) likewise believes it to have been addressed to Samuel Bowles, but reads it as "another, though muted, complaint that he has ignored or rejected her" (526).

2 See, for a thorough explanation, chapter III.2.

ingly, this chapter is structured unlike other analyses in Part I of this book in that we will not proceed chronologically through the sentences of the poem, but rather begin by figuring out what we know about "it" and the speaker in section 5.2. In section 5.3 we consider how the poem as a whole can be interpreted, given its question form.

5.2 "It" and the Speaker: What We Know

5.2.1 "it"

A striking problem is the lack of a referent for the pronoun "it." There is nothing in the immediate local context "it" could refer to.

Parallel to the interpretation of demonstratives in the previous chapter, we can make use of a dynamic system to interpret the pronoun, where we take all sentences to be functions from variable assignments to propositions. In that way, the meaning of "it" is the function from variable assignment functions to the values to which they give the index:

(3) $[\![it_1]\!] = \lambda g.\ g(1)$

With the switch to a dynamic interpretation,[3] readers can accumulate information about "it" in order to eventually pick out a variable assignment function at a global level of the text. One possibility that helps with accumulating information about the referent is to interpret the features of the pronoun to delimit the possibilities for referents to come. The features of "it" are that it is third person; it is rarely used to describe human beings. The presuppositions of the features of the pronoun "it" are therefore the following (cf. Kratzer 2009):

(4) $[\![it_1]\!] = \lambda g:\ g(1)$ is a non-human, single individual, and is not the speaker, nor the addressee. $g(1)$

Due to its presuppositions, it is very unlikely that "it" denotes a human individual or more than one individual, with the exception that it may refer to a child. This is one possible interpretation which we will pursue later.

---

[3] For simplicity's sake, we will present the dynamic extension only for the pronoun and at the level of sentences in this chapter. In chapter I.4, the technically complete way to implement the dynamic system is defined with Dynamic Function Application.

Even when the reader makes these assumptions and proceeds with interpretation, the meaning of the question "If it had no pencil would it try mine" remains unclear. As mentioned before, the counterfactual presupposes that the antecedent is false. Hence, we know that the referent "it" has a pencil at its disposal,[4] and also has the possibility to use the speaker's. However, in order to be able to have a pencil at one's disposal, the referent is required to be human, because only human beings can write. Thus, combining the VP with "it" would lead to uninterpretability. Yet again, we assume that the utterance is not uninterpretable, but that the poet intentionally made use of this conflict in order to convey something meaningful. Thus, we have to reinterpret either the VP or "it" as referring to a human referent.

A possible linguistic argument for reinterpreting the VP is the presupposition of the pronoun. A strategy for reinterpreting the VP could involve some kind of generalisation. This superset could be something like (5), which has a wider domain including individuals that fit the features of the pronouns more easily.

(5) $\lambda x.$ x has the means to express x's ideas

"It" under this line of interpretation might refer to the personification of an abstract concept like "love" or "creativity," since it is possible to assign a property like the one in (5) to them. This is due to the fact that metaphors of this sort are fairly common language use, for example "language of love" or "love rules the world."

So far, we have been able to derive the presupposition that "it" has a pencil from the counterfactual conditional in the first line. A parallel construction can be found in line five which begins with the counterfactual "If it had no word," and then segues into another question: "Would it make the Daisy / Most as big as I was / When it plucked me?" Analogous to the first line, the counterfactual conditional presupposes that its antecedent is false: "it" has a word. Again, we can encounter a mismatch between "having a word" (a property of human beings exclusively) and the features of the pronoun (referring to a non-human entity), so that reinterpretation becomes necessary.

---

4 An alternative is to interpret "have" as "to own," such that the speaker asks about what if "it" did not possess a pencil of its own. This reading is not necessarily the most plausible one, since it invites implications about ownership and suggests a different relationship between hypothetical pencil and "it," whereas the reading illustrated above ("it" has a pencil ready to use) is more neutral in its terms.

Because of the presupposition of the pronoun, the reader could reinterpret the predicate in a way that makes it fit a non-human agent. Parallel to generalising from "having a pencil" to "having the means to express oneself," one could say that "having a word" means "having the ability to express oneself." This incorporates a notion of authority but also a mental capacity. For instance, people can have no word in the sense that words fail them in an overwhelming situation. Alternatively, the option that "it" refers to a child is also available as well as the option that "it" might have a human adult as a referent.[5] One could easily imagine what it means for a child to "have no word," namely that it cannot speak yet or not express itself properly. Reading "it" as a child in relation to "have a word" moreover opens up the Christian context of *logos*, i.e. a name or title of Jesus Christ, which can be translated as "Word" as well.[6] This would lead to a topical wordplay of the Word having no word, that is by becoming an *infans* in the birth of Jesus Christ.[7]

---

5 A case in point of Emily Dickinson's using "it" for a human adult is the second of her so-called Master Letters, which begins: "Oh – did I offend it –" (Franklin 1986, 22). The Master Letters are three drafts of letters, composed in spring 1858, early 1861, and summer 1861 (Franklin 1986, 7), i.e. around the time when J921/Fr184A was written, though it is not known for certain whether these letters were ever sent off, or even meant for a real addressee. In the draft of the second letter, "it" apparently refers to a human addressee, a "you." Although "it" is no form of direct address, "it" seems capable of answering the speaker's question (and also of "wanting" something), thus functioning like an implicit addressee intended to "overhear" what the speaker is saying. This shows that an interpretation of "it" as a human being, not necessarily a child, can be substantiated within the context of Dickinson's writings.

6 *Logos* appears in "three passages of the Johannine writings of the N.T. (where the English versions render it as 'Word') as a designation of Jesus Christ; hence employed by Christian theologians, esp. those who were versed in Greek philosophy, as a title of the Second Person of the Trinity" (*OED* "Logos, *n.*"). See, for instance, John 1:1: "In the beginning was the Word, and the Word was with God, and the Word was God" and 1:14: "And the Word was made flesh, and dwelt among us, (and we beheld his glory, the glory as of the only begotten of the Father,) full of grace and truth." For more discussion about the Word made flesh in Dickinson's poetry, see Bauer 2006.

7 Cf. John Donne's "La Corona" ("4. Temple"):
　　The Word but lately could not speak, and lo,
　　It suddenly speaks wonders. (Donne 2010, 481, ll. 5-6)
On the topic of wordplay (or "word" play), see, for instance, Dickinson's poem J8/Fr42B (c. 1858), which begins as follows:
　　There is a word
　　Which bears a sword
　　Can pierce an armed man – [...]

To summarise for now, there are three possible kinds of referent for "it" that interact with how the mismatches in the two counterfactual questions are interpreted. The choices of referents can be captured by choosing a specific variable assignment function that assigns "it" a specific referent:

(6) a. variable assignment g_1, where $g(1)$ is a child
Presupposition: it has a pencil at its disposal and it has a word
b. variable assignment g_2, where $g(1)$ is an adult
Presupposition: it has a pencil at its disposal and it has a word
c. variable assignment g_3, where $g(1)$ is a nonhuman concept (e.g. creativity; or supernatural power)
Presupposition: it has the means to express itself

Let's examine the consequent.

The definite description "the daisy" in "Would it make the Daisy, / Most as big as I was, / When it plucked me?" presupposes that there is some unique x in the discourse which is a daisy.

(7) $[\![$the daisy$]\!]^g$ is only defined if there is a unique x s.t. daisy(w)(x).
Then, $[\![$the daisy$]\!]^g$ = the unique x s.t. daisy(w)(x)

Since no other referent for "the daisy" is mentioned in the poem, the reader has to accommodate that there is some unique entity in the discourse that is a daisy. Another complication is added to the interpretation of the conditional by "most." It is plausible to assume that "most" in American English is used like "almost" in this context, which gives rise to the implication that the height of the daisy did not reach the height of the speaker when it was plucked.

The question immediately arises what it means "to make a unique daisy almost as big as the speaker when she was plucked."[8] A standard semantic analy-

---

For one thing, this is obviously a pun, in that the letters of "word" make up 4/5ths of the word "sword" and can thus be seen as "bear[ing]" it; moreover, the "word" is mighty enough to affect a human being in a powerful way, not unlike the "it" in J921/Fr184A.

8 Sewall (1975) suggests: "For all the pronominal difficulties, [the last four lines] seem to say, 'If I don't hear from you, does that make me the little girl I was when I fell in love with you?'" (526). This paraphrase assumes a number of reinterpretations, hardly any of which he explains (only that "it" must be read as "you" since it appears as such in the Master letters), in order to accommodate the biographical context he believes to be the case (i.e. that Dickinson is in love with Bowles, but not satisfied with his correspondence). Farr (1992), by contrast, reads these lines as Dickinson "telling Bowles—since he was not writing to her—to draw her a picture of a

sis of "making the daisy big" assumes that it is a resultative construction (cf. von Stechow 1996) which says that there is a making event of which "it" is the agent that causes "the daisy" to reach a degree of "bigness" that is no bigger than the degree to which the speaker is big at a certain time. Since the verb "make" is underspecified here and it is unclear at what point of the daisy's existence the influence of "it" is located, we have two possibilities of reading "make big":

(8) $[\![\text{make\_big}_1]\!] = \lambda y. [\lambda x.\ x \text{ creates } y \text{ and } y \text{ is big}]$

(9) $[\![\text{make\_big}_2]\!] = \lambda y. [\lambda x.\ x \text{ causes } y \text{ to grow}]$

Consequently, the reader has to assume that the referent of "it" has enough power to cause the daisy to grow (see (9)), and also to "pluck" the speaker. Hence, there is a clear imbalance of power between "it" and the speaker. This is consistent with "it" referring to a supernatural being, which might exert power on a human being. Another option would be to see "make big" as a process in which the daisy is created, and in which the daisy is already big from the beginning of its creation (see (8)). This reading, too, would assume a mighty "it" with creative power. The use of the verb "to make" is conspicuous in this passage, because – in combination with the extraordinary power which "it" has over the speaker – it may hint at a religious reading of the poem in which "it" is God, the maker *par excellence*,[9] thus linking back to the wordplay on "Word"/"word" and "it" as referent for an infant Jesus Christ mentioned above. In a reading where "it" is a child, "making a daisy" could mean "drawing a daisy." In addition, the (seemingly ungrammatical) phrase "most as big as I was" sounds like something a child would say, rather than an adult, and a speaker's use of the third person (in this case, "the Daisy") is also something we would associate with children's speech.

The "it" mentioned in the poem not only has the power to "make" the daisy but also to "pluck" the speaker. "Pluck" is defined as "to pluck (up) a plant" (Webster 1828, "pluck, *v. t.*"), a rather violent action, ripping out by the roots, or is applied to plucking fruit from a tree (*OED*, "pluck, *v.*" 1.a.). But pluck could also be seen in a more positive light. The motion of plucking is an upwards

---

daisy" (283), and avoids dealing with the question what precisely "pluck" must mean in this context.

9 The pronoun "thee" is prominently used in the Authorized Version, and may thus be in (minor) support of such a religious reading.

movement, lifting, elevating the speaker, chosen perhaps for grander purposes (see *OED*, "pluck, *v.*" 5.a.: "To bring (a person or thing) forcibly into or out of a specified state or condition; †to bring (disaster, etc.) *upon* a person (*obs.*). Now *esp.*: to snatch or rescue *from* danger, to take *from* obscurity, etc.").[10] Regardless of whether "pluck" is seen as good or bad, it reveals a power relation where an overwhelming "it" can "make" daisies and "pluck" the speaker.

If we regard having "word" and "pencil" as essential properties of "it," "it" has the tools of an artist, and most likely of a poet. "It" could use word and pencil to write and to "make" the daisy.[11] In addition, the link between words and creation has biblical connotations: in Genesis, Creation is the result of speech acts.[12] Two creative processes are thus alluded to by the counterfactuals that let us draw inferences about the nature of "it": firstly, that of writing or drawing, since "it" has a pencil, and, secondly, that of speaking (and possibly creating through speech acts), since "it" has a word.

As we have seen, the "it" mentioned in the poem is very powerful and dominating. "It" can "make" the daisy "big," that is, either create the daisy or make it grow. Considering that daisies are not made by human beings, "it" seems godlike (also, considering that "it" has a "word"), creative but also potentially

---

10 For the ambiguous connotations of the word, see also J499/Fr369A (c. 1862), in which Dickinson describes people from the past only visible to the speaker through their portraits:

Those fair – fictitious People –
The Women – plucked away
From our familiar Lifetime –
The Men of Ivory –
[...]

These people are separated from the speaker, "plucked away" to "places perfecter" – ostensibly a metaphor for death as a passage into life everlasting. The verb "to pluck" thus works both in the semantic field of literally plucking a flower as well as in relation to human beings, both by a supernatural force such as God as well as figuratively by other people. See also a quotation from Charles Dickens's *Our Mutual Friend* ([1864-5] 1997): "The grim life out of which she had plucked her brother" (518).

11 See also our discussion of the poet as maker in chapter I.4.

12 See, for instance, Gen. 1:3: "And God said, Let there be light: and there was light"; the notion of "making" that we find in this poem can similarly be connected with Creation in Genesis, e.g.: "And God said, Let us make man in our image, after our likeness [...]. So God created man in his *own* image, in the image of God created he him" (Gen. 1:26f.). The expression "make the daisy [...] big" is moreover reminiscent of "The Word was made flesh" (John 1:14), an expression Dickinson used in J1651/Fr1715A, "A Word made Flesh is seldom," in which she also links this topic to the power of language (cf. Bauer 2006, 382-86). Taken in connection with the biblical passage, something inanimate (the Word and the Daisy respectively) is turned animate by an act of creation, or "made" animate.

destructive.[13] Having now collected all the information given in the text for "it," we can summarise the state of our knowledge and delimit the number of possible interpretations. Through the features of the pronoun and the presuppositions resulting from the counterfactual conditionals, the following information is provided by the text about "it":

(10)   g(1) is singular & g(1) is not speaker, nor addressee

(11)   Presuppositions resulting from the Counterfactual Conditionals:
    a.   λw. g(1) has a pencil in w
    b.   λw. g(1) has a word in w

These presuppositional properties restrict the possibilities for referents but do not resolve all interpretation problems posed by the text. Though we cannot exclude that "it" refers to an adult human being, this reading turns out to be much less plausible than interpreting "it" as either a child or as a creative agency or a divine person, i.e. God. If the agent is God (rather than a human child), the imbalance in power between the agent who plucks and the patient who is being plucked is more appropriate; this also does justice to "plucking" as an act of selecting (and possibly elevating) someone or something. The consequent thus confirms and specifies (6), resulting in the following plausible types of referent:

(12)   a.   variable assignment g_1, where g(1) is a child.
    b.   variable assignment g_2, where g(1) is God
    c.   variable assignment g_3, where g(1) is an abstract concept like creativity

---

13 There is evidence for Emily Dickinson's use of "it" referring to a human being in a number of her poems (Sewall 527). J462/Fr697A (c. 1862), for instance, begins with "Why make it doubt – it hurts it so," where "hurt" is a transitive verb that requires the argument "it" (in the sense of "it_1 has caused physical or mental damage to it_2" and "it_2" thus must refer to a sentient being capable of feeling pain). This does not exclude animals, for which, however (judging from many of her other poems), Dickinson would sometimes use a male or female pronoun; as she does for example in J328/Fr359, J500/Fr370 (birds); J1185/Fr1236 (cats and mice); J186/Fr237, J500/Fr370, J1185/Fr1236 (dogs). In J500/Fr370, the dog is even endowed with a mental capacity and associated with logic and philology, i.e. with exclusively human characteristics (cf. Bauer 1995, 214-16).

5.2.2 The Speaker

We have discussed the first line with regard to "it"; it is part of a structure in which the pronoun combines with the VP "try mine." This triggers further presuppositions. The first person use of the possessive ("mine") presupposes that the referent is the speaker (cf. Kratzer 2009). The possessive presupposes that the possessed element is unique in the discourse. It is plausible to assume the possessed element to be "a pencil" in this context (i.e. "mine" is "my pencil"). The content of the presupposition is thus that there is a unique pencil in the context which the speaker possesses. The corresponding semantics is given in (13a) below, a paraphrase of which is given in (13b).

(13) a. $[\![\text{mine}]\!]^g = [\![\text{my pencil}]\!]^g$ is only defined if there is a unique x such that pencil(w)(x) & the speaker has x in w. Then $[\![\text{my pencil}]\!]^g$ = the unique x such that pencil(w)(x) & the speaker has x in w.
b. (13a) is only defined if there is a unique x such that x is a pencil and the speaker has x. If defined, it denotes the unique x such that x is a pencil the speaker has.

Since this information is not explicitly provided by the context, the reader has to accommodate that the speaker of the poem possesses a unique pencil. The pronoun "it" combines with "try mine" and once more a mismatch occurs. "Trying a pencil" seems to prefer to combine with human subjects; however, as we have seen above, the overall text makes it more plausible that "it" refers to creativity, God or a child. If "it" refers to a child, "try mine" can be understood literally, such that this child uses the pencil. In the other two cases, "try mine" can be read as "use."

The following lines seem to be defining properties of the speaker's pencil: "Worn – now – and *dull* – sweet." The third line is structurally ambiguous in three respects. It is either a relative clause with an elided relative pronoun: "mine, which is worn now and dull – sweet," or it is an apposition. Moreover, the adjective "sweet" could either structurally belong to the relative clause or to the following line and thus be a form of address, an option that we return to below. Finally, the temporal adverb "now" can have scope over one, two, or all three adjectives. Depending on the structural position of "now," it delivers the time argument for all three adjectives "dull," "worn," and "sweet," or only for some of them. This is under the assumption that adjectives have an open argument slot for times:[14]

(14)   ⟦worn/dull/sweet⟧ = λt. [λx. x is worn/dull/sweet at time t]

"Now" deictically refers to a specific time and presupposes that this time includes the utterance time.

Consequently, the temporal adverb "now" can deliver the time argument for the adjectives "worn," "dull," and "sweet," and triggers a conversational implicature, which changes with the structural position of the adverb:

a. Temporal adverb "now" has scope over all three predicates
    conversational implicature: the speaker's pencil was not "worn," "dull," and "sweet" at some time before now
b. Temporal adverb "now" has only scope over "worn"
    conversational implicature: the speaker's pencil was new and not worn in the past, yet is worn now, and is – independently – dull and sweet
c. "now" has scope over "worn" and "dull" but not "sweet"
    conversational implicature: the speaker's pencil is now worn and dull, used to be shiny, sharp and new; it is also sweet, though temporally unspecified in that respect

"Dull" as an adjective most often refers to characteristics of a person or their wits,[15] which is less plausible in the context of the predicate modifying "pencil." It is more plausible to read "dull pencil" as "pencil that has often been used" (in that its tip is blunt and dulled), which in turn makes possibility (c) more prominent since "worn" and "dull" are related more closely to each other than either is to "sweet": "worn," just like "dull," can describe a result state such that they describe the result of extensive usage. However, in the reading where "it" refers

---

14 Generally, predicates and adjectives are both world- and time-relative. In order to simplify the presentation, we only allude to times when they are relevant for the interpretation, as is the case here.

15 See, for instance, Webster, in whose dictionary the first seven listed meanings for "dull" are all in relation to human beings in some way; only from meaning 8 onwards – "Gross; cloggy; insensible; as the *dull* earth" – does it refer to inanimate objects. "Dull" as a decidedly human quality is used by Dickinson in, for instance, J704/Fr734 (c. 1863): "Won't you wish you'd spoken / To that dull Girl?" Similarly, in J1130/Fr1156 (c. 1868); "Oh Life, begun in fluent Blood / And consummated dull!"

to creativity, "dull" could also be read as "Dim; obscure; not vivid" (Webster 1828 "dull, *a.*" 12.), such that creativity using the dull pencil can metaphorically mean that it uses average, obscure means to express itself. The syntactic ambiguity interacts here with lexical underspecification in this sequence of the poem (a more detailed analysis of lexical underspecification can be found in chapters I.1 and I.2). What seems uncontroversial is that the pencil of the speaker had all of these properties at some point in time and that the information is relevant to answering the question in the first two lines. Another fact is added in the fourth line: "Writing much to thee." It could plausibly be completed as "[from] Writing much to thee" meaning that the properties of being worn, dull and sweet come about because the pencil has been used.

The introduction of the addressee is noteworthy from a linguistic perspective. We analyse the pronoun "thee" in parallel to "it" and the demonstratives "this" and "that" in chapter I.4 as a variable that is further restricted by its features:

(15) $[\![\text{thee}_3]\!]^g = \lambda g: g(3)$ is the hearer in the context. $g(3)$

Assigning the pronoun "it" and the indexical "thee" to the same individual is semantically impossible. It is implicated that the addressed person could provide an answer to the question posed in the poem at this point. However, it is critical to notice that the "it" which most likely should be able to give an answer is not addressed. It is completely unclear why the addressee should be an expert on the decisions of "it."[16]

We have already discussed the second part of the poem (ll. 5-8) with regard to "it" and alluded to its possible actions towards speaker and "Daisy." It is important for our understanding of the speaker to acknowledge the inherent comparability between speaker and "Daisy": firstly, there is comparability in size; secondly, there is comparability in their susceptibility to being "plucked."

---

[16] As has been mentioned in the introduction to this chapter, the mode of preservation of J921/Fr184A (wrapped around a pencil) stands out. It is believed that the poem was meant as a present, and there are many speculations about the potential addressee based on various pieces of evidence, though the evidence is inconclusive. Still, the context of the poem's origin is relevant for our analysis of the poem, since it opens up additional possibilities of interpretation and introduces a degree of self-referentiality only available if the pencil is a real object. Considering this, the "pencil" implied in the second line ("mine," i.e. the speaker's pencil) could have a very real referent in the pencil around which the poem was wrapped. The "writing" in line four could then refer to the writing presented with the pencil, that is, to the poem itself.

As for a comparison in size between speaker and daisy, we return briefly to our analysis above, where we stipulated that "most" in line 7 is a short version of "almost." The speaker's question can thus be paraphrased as

(16)   Would it make the daisy almost as big as I was when it plucked me?

We discussed the possibilities of what it means to "make a daisy" above and concluded that the most plausible interpretations are either to draw a daisy or create it forthright, supporting our three main readings of "it" as child/creative agency/God, respectively. Without evidence to the contrary, we assume that the speaker is a human being and thus within the reasonable size range of human beings. If we take the unique daisy of the poem to be a common lawn daisy, the comparison in size between the two reveals a potential conflict. The common lawn daisy cannot grow to almost the size of a human. The presupposition of the speaker's question, i.e. whether "it" **would** make the daisy most as big as the speaker, is that it **could** do so. We also know that the speaker was "plucked" by "it" in the past. "Pluck" needs to be figurative in order to be applied to the speaker; we here paraphrase "pluck" as "select."

The daisy could also be read as referring to a human individual,[17] yet the unusual word choice of "pluck" in this context derives from a literal reading of

---

[17] There is some evidence that Dickinson regularly used "daisy" to refer to a being with human traits, for instance in J85/Fr87A; in addition, "daisy" in Dickinson's poems is often linked to humility and humble adoration (see, e.g. Seaton (1995), who lists as other meanings for the daisy the messages "I will think of it" and "I share your sentiments" (176f.); and also mentions one 18th-century text where the daisy is seen as a symbol of "timidity and humility" (65)), and contrasted with a mightier, adored being, which is sometimes addressed, as in J921/Fr184A. Other poems in which a "daisy" is given human traits are, for instance, J106/Fr161, J339/Fr367, J481/Fr460, and J124/Fr108. Moreover, in the Master Letters, there is plenty of evidence for an equation of "daisy" and a human being, in this case the speaker. In the third letter, the speaker is a daisy, while the addressee is grand and powerful: "Daisy's arm is small – and you have felt the Horizon – hav'nt you –" (Franklin 1986, 39). The speaker also describes herself as "No Rose, yet felt myself a'bloom" (Franklin 1986, 44). This letter also contains a long passage with hypothetical questions ("could ..." and "would ...") about their possible life together, similar in their syntactic form to the "would" questions in J921/Fr184A. In the second letter, the speaker is also a lowly daisy: "This Daisy – grieve her Lord – and yet it ↑she↓ often blundered –" but the addressee "teach[es] her majesty – Slow ↑Dull↓ at patrician things – Even the wren opon her nest learns ↑knows↓ more than Daisy dares –" (Franklin 1986, 25). Interestingly, Dickinson had originally written "dull" as an alternative to "slow" (Franklin 1986, 25). Their unequal relation is emphasised: "Low at the knee that bore her once unto <royal> ↑wordless↓ rest, <now – she> Daisy <stoops a> kneels, a culprit –" (Franklin 1986, 25).

the verb, which is only licensed if the daisy refers to a garden flower and not a human individual.

As an interim summary, we now combine the information about "it" and that about the speaker, in order to provide three readings of the poem:

(17)   Reading 1: "An individual, most likely a child, has a pencil and has a word. If that was not the case, would it use the speaker's pencil and would it draw the daisy and make it as big as it chose (to draw) the speaker?"

(18)   Reading 2: "Creativity has an outlet. If that was not the case, would it use average means to create meaning?"

(19)   Reading 3: "God has the means to express herself. If that was not the case, would she use the speaker's means and would she still make the daisy and make it almost the same size as the speaker when she plucked or chose her/him?"

Reading 1 in (17) above requires the afore-mentioned reinterpretation of "pluck": while the word choice makes sense if we talk of an actual daisy, this reading demands the effort of reading "pluck" as a metaphor for "draw," or "choose (to draw)." This reinterpretation can only take place because the daisy is mentioned in line 6, without which these lines of the poem would be nonsensical – Dickinson here suggests the semantic field from which to draw the meaning of the reinterpretation. Meaning is thus derived from intratextual context.

Reading 2 represents the most metaphorical reading, where "dull" is reinterpreted to mean "average," and where, on a metalevel, the comparison between the speaker and the Daisy is a means to create a specific meaning. In reading 3, the use of the pencil is reinterpreted as God expressing herself through the speaker's means.

5.3 An Analysis of the Text

Now that we have collected information about the speaker and "it" in the poem, we will proceed in this section with the interpretation of the poem as a whole. We do so in three steps. First, we propose a performative analysis of the question form of the poem. Secondly, we collect and accommodate the presuppositions about "it" and the speaker identified in the previous section. As a final step, we will parameterize the interpretation.

5.3.1 Step 1

The mode of the poem is important since it poses a question. As FictionalAssert only operates on assertions, we cannot employ this operator directly. We will pragmatically interpret the speaker's wondering about the counterfactual statements.

The poem contains two polar questions; see (20) and (21). These abstractly stand for the three readings identified in (17) to (19) above.

(20)   Question 1 (Q1): If it had no pencil, would it use the speaker's?

(21)   Question 2 (Q2): If it had no word, would it make the Daisy almost as big as the speaker was when it plucked the speaker?

Our solution to the problem of the mode of the poem is to interpret Q1 and Q2 performatively, that is, as if the speaker of the poem asks these questions within the fictional worlds of the text. The result is the proposition in (22).

(22) $\lambda w.$ the speaker asks in w Q1 and Q2

With this enrichment of the text meaning, it is possible to apply FictionalAssert.

5.3.2 Step 2

We consider the information which can be collected about both "it" and the speaker by means of analysing the presuppositions that derive from the counterfactual conditionals.

A summary of all available presuppositions are in (23) and (24) below:[18]

(23)   **Presuppositions about "it" (PSP_{it}):**
Presuppositions arising from Features:
   $g(1)$ is singular.
   $g(1)$ is not speaker, nor addressee.
Presuppositions arising from Counterfactual Conditionals:
   $\lambda w.\ g(1)$ has a pencil in w
   $\lambda w.\ g(1)$ has a word in w

---

[18] Some structural ambiguities have been neglected here for simplicity's sake.

(24)   **Presuppositions about the speaker (PSP$_{sp}$):**
         Presuppositions arising from Features:
           the speaker is singular.
           the speaker is not "it," nor addressee.
         Presupposition arising from the Possessive:
           λw. the speaker has a pencil in w, which is worn, dull, and sweet, and which has been used to write to the addressee.

Since the reader did not have the information conveyed by the presuppositions before, they are accommodated. Accommodation has the effect that even though the information is given as presupposition in the text, we treat it as if it was asserted. We add the content of the presupposition to what we hold as true for the text worlds. With accommodation, we have established yet another part of the text meaning: we combine all presuppositions about "it" and the speaker conjunctively, see (25).

(25)   (23) & (24) = λw. g(1), who is singular, neither speaker nor addressee, has a pencil and a word in w, and the speaker, who is singular and neither g(1), nor addressee, has a pencil in world w.

We thus arrive at the propositional text meaning that will be part of the argument of FictionalAssert. We apply FictionalAssert to the conjunction of the accommodated presuppositions in (25) and the performative interpretation of the two polar questions in (22), see (26):

(26)   ⟦FictionalAssert$_@$⟧(T) = 1 iff ∀ w [(25)(w) & (22)(w) → R(@)(w)]

5.3.3 Step 3

Though we have interpreted the question posed by the poem and the presuppositions that occur, we still cannot assign one definite interpretation to the poem: much depends on how we identify the referents for "it" and speaker (and, to a lesser degree, "the Daisy"). Leaving these choices open allows us to come up with a parametrised text interpretation, parallel to chapter I.4 "This was a Poet," and a set of plausible readings which differ in terms of which referents are picked. The rules of grammar help narrowing down the set of plausible interpretations. The main lines of interpretation derive from our referent for "it," as has been shown in (17), (18) and (19): does "it" refer to a creative force in general, or to God in particular, or to a child? If "it" is a child, then we get a poem asking questions about a "real" relationship. If "it" refers to an abstract concept, like love or creativity, or to God, we get a more philosophical poem asking questions about the nature of this creative entity and its impact on the speaker. Connected to this are of course further choices the reader can make, for instance how to interpret "make."

Assigning a referent to "it" now can be captured by choosing a specific variable assignment function. Previously, we identified three possibilities:

(27)   variable assignment g_1, where $g(1)$ is a child

(28)   variable assignment g_2, where $g(1)$ is God

(29)   variable assignment g_3, where $g(1)$ is an abstract concept like creativity

The central point of the poem does not seem to be so much identifying which of these three possibilities is meant by the text, but rather which relationship holds between the speaker and whoever "it" refers to. Intuitively, no matter which assignment function we pick to interpret "it," the same relationship will hold between these referents and the speaker. In order to capture this, we propose to use the revised version of FictionalAssert introduced in chapter I.4. The revised version allows us to consider that the text meaning is sensitive to interpreting "it" with respect to different variable assignment functions, g_1, g_2 and g_3, in our case. The dynamic text meaning is (30).

(30) $\lambda g. \lambda w.$ the speaker asks in w whether, if $g(1)$ had no pencil, would $g(1)$ use the speaker's and whether, if $g(1)$ had no word, would $g(1)$ make the daisy almost as big as the speaker was when it plucked the speaker

The pragmatic interpretation of the poem is derived with the version of FictionalAssert from chapter I.4:

(31) $[\![FictionalAssert_@]\!](T) = 1$ iff $\forall g\ [g \in \{g_1, g_2, g_3\} \rightarrow \forall w\ [(25)(g)(w)\ \&$ the speaker asks whether, if $g(1)$ had no pencil, would $g(1)$ use the speaker's and whether, if $g(1)$ had no word, would $g(1)$ make the daisy almost as big as the speaker was when it plucked the speaker $\rightarrow R(@)(w)]]$

> "For all plausible variable assignments g_1, g_2 and g_3, and all worlds in which g(1), who is singular, neither speaker nor addressee, has a pencil and a word in w, and the speaker, who is singular and neither g(1) nor addressee, has a pencil in w and in which the speaker asks whether, if g(1) had no pencil, would g(1) use the speaker's and whether, if g(1) had no word, would g(1) make the daisy almost as big as the speaker was when it plucked the speaker, stand in relation R to the actual world."

The important insight of this version of FictionalAssert is that for all three plausible variable assignments g_1, g_2 and g_3, the same relation R holds. In other words, no matter if "it" refers to a child, God or an abstract concept like creativity, this referent will have the same impact on the speaker, and the same relevance will moreover be established for the reader. (32) is a possible value for the relation R:

(32) "The relation R between the text worlds w and the actual world @ holds iff w is exactly like @ except that the speaker in w is the counterpart of the reader in @ and 'it' in w is a formative force working on the reader in @ and, as the speaker in w, the reader asks (or should ask) in @ Q1 and Q2."

With this relation R, a very intimate self-reflection of the speaker becomes evident. Through its question form, the poem can be seen as an invitation to wonder about which driving force and its instrument has a similar impact on oneself, and what would happen if this instrument were not there. An example: Monet (speaker) might wonder about Picasso (it) and his use of cubism (the pencil of it), and whether if Picasso did not paint this particular way he would employ the impressionist style like Monet (the pencil of the speaker). (33) is an approximation of a pragmatic interpretation of the poem resulting from applying FictionalAssert as in (31) and defining R as in (32):

(33) "If everything the poem says is the case, then I wonder about my relationship to the force that drives me and I ask myself how the driving force has impact on me and how it could have impacted my life, and how our instruments of choice are related."

Very broadly speaking, the poem ignites a deep reflection on identity – and here not only a personal identity, but also a shared one, as "it" in the poem not only plucks the speaker, but also the daisy: accordingly, a similar fundamental relationship seems to hold between daisy and "it."

5.4 Conclusion

In this poem, we see how underspecified reference is exploited to open up several but not arbitrary possible readings that interact in a meaningful way. Especially in combination with the status of the poem being posed as a question, we see a new way of employing FictionalAssert by looking at presupposition accommodation on the one hand and a performative interpretation of the question on the other. The result is quite surprising and contributes to in-depth philosophical questions about identity and its formative forces. It seems that the intent of the poem is to trigger a reflection on what drives us in life, and by what means. By employing the question mode and the semantics of pronouns and indexicals, Emily Dickinson creates the impression of a personal situation which may not be fully reconstructed and, at the same time, offers complex thoughts each reader may apply to herself.

Tab. 1: Chapter Summary

Core Phenomenon

Pronouns and Presuppositions
$[\![it_1]\!] = \lambda g$: $g(1)$ is a non-human, single individual, and is not the speaker, nor the addressee. $g(1)$

Presuppositions arising through Counterfactual Conditionals:
$\lambda w.\ g(1)$ has a pencil in w
$\lambda w.\ g(1)$ has a word in w

Text Interpretation

FictionalAssert, combining presupposition accommodation, dynamic text interpretation and a performative analysis of questions:
$[\![FictionalAssert@]\!] (T) = 1$ iff $\forall g\ [\ g \in \{g_1, g_2, g_3\} \to \forall w\ [\ (25)\ (g)(w)$ & the speaker asks whether, if $g(1)$ had no pencil, would $g(1)$ use the speaker's and whether, if $g(1)$ had no word, would $g(1)$ make the daisy almost as big as the speaker was when it plucked the speaker $\to R(@)(w)]]$

"For all plausible variable assignments g_1, g_2 and g_3, and all worlds, in which $g(1)$, who is singular, not speaker nor addressee, has a pencil and a word in w, and the speaker, who is singular and neither $g(1)$, nor addressee, has a pencil in w and in which the speaker asks whether, if $g(1)$ had no pencil, would $g(1)$ use the speaker's and whether, if $g(1)$ had no word, would $g(1)$ make the Daisy almost as big as the speaker was when it plucked the speaker, stand in relation R to the actual world."

Relation R: "The relation R between the text worlds w and the actual world @ holds iff w is exactly like @ except that the speaker in w is the counterpart of the reader in @ and 'it' in w is a formative force working on the reader in @ and, as the speaker in w, the reader asks (or should ask) in @ Q1 and Q2."

Pragmatic Interpretation:
"If everything the poem says is the case, then I wonder about my relationship to the force that drives me and I ask myself how the driving force has impact on me and how it could have impacted my life, and how our instruments of choice are related."

Pronouns in other Chapters

(In I.4):
$[\![this_1]\!]^{g,c}$ is only defined if $g_c(1)$ is proximal. Then, $[\![this_1]\!]^{g,c} = g_c(1) =$ this poem
$[\![that_2]\!]^{g,c}$ is only defined if $g_c(2)$ is distal. Then, $[\![that_2]\!]^{gc} = g_c(2) =$ poetry

---

Other Phenomena in this Chapter

Structural Ambiguity: Worn – **now** – and *dull* – sweet
Now [worn & dull &sweet] or [Now [worn & dull]] &[sweet] *or* [Now [worn]] & [dull & sweet]

Definites: Would it make **the Daisy**,
$[\![the\ daisy]\!]^g$ is only defined if there is a unique x s.t. daisy(w)(x). Then, $[\![the\ daisy]\!]^g =$ the unique x s.t. daisy(w)(x)

I.6 "My Life had stood – a Loaded Gun": Semantic Mismatches and Coercion

1   My Life had stood – a Loaded Gun –
2   In Corners – till a Day
3   The Owner passed – identified –
4   And carried Me away –

5   And now We roam in Sovereign Woods –
6   And now We hunt the Doe –
7   And every time I speak for Him –
8   The Mountains straight reply –

9   And do I smile, such cordial light
10 Upon the Valley glow –
11 It is as a Vesuvian face
12 Had let its pleasure through –

13 And when at Night – Our good Day done –
14 I guard My Master's Head –
15 'Tis better than the Eider-Duck's
16 Deep Pillow – to have shared –

17 To foe of His – I'm deadly foe –
18 None stir the second time –
19 On whom I lay a Yellow Eye –
20 Or an emphatic Thumb –

21 Though I than He – may longer live
22 He longer must – than I –
23 For I have but the power to kill,
24 Without – the power to die –
                    (J754/Fr764)

6.1 Introduction

"My Life had stood" (J754/Fr764) was written around 1863 and published in 1929 (Dickinson 1955, 574).[1] It is one of Dickinson's most controversial poems, as it has triggered a multitude of different interpretations, ranging from the de-

---

[1] An earlier version of this text was published in the *Journal of Literary Semantics* (Bauer et al. 2015).

scription of a male-female relationship over the battle and subversion by a suppressed woman to regarding it as a poem about language and what it means to be a poet (Leiter 2007, 145-47).² Robert Weisbuch (1975, 25) even calls it "the single most difficult poem Dickinson wrote." We have chosen this poem for the final analysis precisely because it seems to be difficult enough to prevent one straightforward interpretation. In fact, it suggests two distinct readings, both of which are upheld by the interaction of several coercion mechanisms and semantic mismatches that require reinterpretation. The complexity of the coercion mechanisms present in this poem provide the opportunity to fine-tune the linguistic toolkit. The possibilities that arise from this reveal the poem as stubbornly ambiguous: on the one hand, the literal reading describes a relationship between a gun and its owner, whereas on the other hand, the figurative reading describes a relationship between two human beings. While both readings can be substantiated, we will show that they cannot be combined conjunctively, and that a third reading of the poem emerges, regarding it as a reflection about language itself.

6.2 Stanza One, Lines 1–4

We begin with a syntactic analysis that will help us assign an interpretation to the first stanza and help us arrive at more global considerations. Since meaning is based on structure, it makes sense to break down the sentence that is the first stanza into smaller parts. It consists of the matrix sentence "My life had stood in corners," the apposition "a loaded gun" and the subordinate clause "till a day the owner passed – identified – and carried me away." The following bracketed representation illustrates the structure we assume:

(1)   [Matrix My life had stood – [Apposition a loaded gun] – in corners]
        [Subordinate till a day the owner passed – identified – and carried me away]

---

2 S. Leiter (2007) expounds different interpretations; E. K. Sparks (2011) lists 20 different (though some similar) interpretations between 1934 and 1992; and M. Freeman (1972, 271n18) notes seven main lines of interpretation of gun and owner.

6.2.1 Matrix Sentence: "My life had stood in corners"

The two features of the matrix clause to be examined are the occurrence of a past perfect and the plural of "corners." In order to illustrate how these forms are usually analysed in formal semantics, we shall consider the simpler example in (2a). An intuitive description of its meaning is suggested in (2c), and the corresponding formal semantic representation is given in (2b). Following a standard analysis of tense (cf. von Stechow 2009), the past perfect is analyzed as situating the time of the described event before the topic time which is in the past. Following a standard analysis for plurals (Link 1991; Beck and Sauerland 2000; Beck and von Stechow 2006), the sentence describes a plurality of standing events that take place in various corners. We take this to mean that John was habitually standing around before the past topic time.

(2) a. John had stood in corners.
 b. $\exists t \ [t < t_{Topic} \ \& \ t_{Topic} < t_{now} \ \& \ \exists E \ [\tau(E) \subseteq t$
 $\& \ \exists C \ [*corner(C) \ \& \ <E,C> \in **[\lambda e. \ [\lambda x. \ John \ stands \ in \ x \ in \ e]]]]]$[3]
 c. There is a time t before the time the discourse is about, which is before the speech time, and into t falls a plural event E such that there is a set of corners C such that in the relevant subevents of E, John stands in one of the corners.

Relating this interpretation to the poem yields the reading that "my life" was habitually standing around in corners at some point in the past. This leads to the most problematic feature of the matrix sentence, which is the mismatch between "my life" and "stand in corners."

The combination of "my life" and "stand" is in itself not problematic. Although it requires reinterpretation, it is a conventional combination found, e.g. in the phrase "My life stood still." However, the prepositional phrase "in corners" adds a physical dimension to the verb which is inconsistent with "my life." A basic lexical entry for "stand" as it appears with the prepositional phrase "in corners" is provided in (3a). "Stand" denotes a relation between an individual, a location, and an event. Moreover, there is a presuppositional component to "stand," namely that the individual argument for "stand" is a physical object that has a vertical dimension (represented in (3b)). The mismatch between "my life" and "stand in corners" is therefore a presupposition failure: since "my life" is not a physical object, the verb cannot apply to the subject.

---

[3] For a definition of the star operators * and **, see the appendix.

Thus, the meaning of the matrix sentence will be undefined. The linguistic notion of undefinedness captures that a sentence lacks a truth value – it is neither true nor false (cf. Frege 1892). This disrupts the interpretation process.

(3) a. ⟦stand⟧ = λe. [λx. [λy. y stand at x in e]]
    b. ⟦stand⟧ = λe. [λx. [λy: y is a physical object that has a vertical dimension. y is in location x in e and y is vertically oriented in e]]
    c. ⟦stand⟧(⟦my life⟧) is undefined.

In order to assign a meaning to the matrix clause, we either have to reinterpret the VP, or the subject, or both at the same time. A possible reinterpretation of "stand in corners" would be "to remain unnoticed, neglected." "My life" could be read metonymically as "I," or as "what is important about me" (especially considering the speaker's (S) consistent later use of "I" and "we" to talk about herself). Taking these possibilities into consideration, we arrive at the following readings:

(4) a. I stood around in corners.
       (NP reinterpretation)
    b. My life remained unnoticed.
       (VP reinterpretation)
    c. I (what is important about me) was neglected.
       (NP/VP reinterpretation)

6.2.2 Apposition

There are two possibilities for the interpretation of the apposition "a loaded gun": first, it can be taken to be an apposition in the sense "I am a loaded gun" (e.g. "My brother, a physicist, ..."); second, the apposition is an implicit comparison with "a loaded gun" (e.g. "This gardening catalogue, an invitation to buy plants, ..."). Taking the possible reinterpretations of "my life" from above, either the speaker herself or the speaker's life are such individuals. In combination with the matrix clause, this gives us the following plausible interpretations:

(5) a. The speaker (S), who was a loaded gun, had stood habitually in corners. In the following: S_{gun}
    b. The speaker (S), who was like a loaded gun, had remained neglected (or S's life/essence was like a loaded gun and had remained neglected). In the following: S_{ind}

At this point, we thus have two basic interpretive possibilities: the poem's speaker could be a gun, or the poem's speaker could be a person who is compared to a gun. Both readings require reinterpretation. In the first case, "my life" cannot be taken literally, and, in the second case, the predicate "stand in corners" cannot be taken literally.

6.2.3 Subordinate Clause

The next step is to identify those parts of the subordinate clause "till a day the owner passed – identified – and carried me away" which require clarification. The first issue is the meaning of "till" ("until") and what it tells us about the temporal order of events described in the poem. The second one is the definite description "the owner," and the third the structural ambiguity in the VP.

To get a clearer understanding of the meaning of "until," a slightly simplified version of matrix and subordinate clause combined is given in (6a), a paraphrase of which can be found in (6c). (6b) is the corresponding formal representation of this reading.

(6) a. My life had stood in corners until the owner passed.
  b. $\exists t \, [t < t_{Topic} \, \& \, t_{Topic} < t_{now} \, \& \, \exists e \, [\tau(e) \subseteq t \, \& \, my\_life\_stand\_in\_corners \, (e)]$
     $\& \, \exists e' \, [\tau(e') \subseteq t_{Topic} \, \& \, owner \, passed \, in \, e']$
  c. There is a time t before the topic time of the discourse, which is before the speech time, and into t falls an event of S standing in location l, and into the topic time falls the passing of the owner.

"Until" has a meaning which sets the right boundary for the described standing event. The whole subordinate clause thus has an implicature that S's standing ceases with the owner's arrival. In addition, the use of "pass" is underspecified as its meaning is not entirely clear. The most likely reading would be "to go by or move past" (*OED*, "pass, v." III.10.). The subordinate clause indicates, at any rate, the strong impact the owner has on S.

The subject of the sentence is "the owner." As can be seen in the lexical entry in (7a), "owner" denotes a relation between two individuals that holds at a time. The definite article "the" furthermore triggers a uniqueness presupposition.

(7) a. ⟦owner⟧ = λt. [λy. [λx. x owns y at t]]
  b. ⟦the⟧ = λf$_{<e,t>}$: there is exactly one x such that f(x)=1.
     the unique x such that f(x)=1

In order to check if this use of the definite article is felicitous, we ought to determine what the owned entity is as well as when the ownership holds, and then verify the presupposition triggered. As neither the time of ownership nor the owned entity are explicitly introduced in the poem, we accommodate certain facts. First, we assume that something is owned. Plausible candidates are S or S's life, since they are the two entities that occur in the context prior to the point where we encounter "The Owner." Second, we assume that there is a unique individual that is the owner of S/S's life.

The last issue arising in the subordinate clause is the coordination we find in the VP. The structure in (8a) invites two analyses: either as a coordination of two VPs with an apposition in between the two conjuncts (see (8b)), or as a coordination of three verbal categories (see (8c)).

(8) a. The owner passed – identified – and carried me away
 b. [VP [VP passed] [APP – identified –] and [VP carried me away]]
 c. [VP [VP passed] [VP [VP identified _] and [VP carried _] me away]]

The first version in (8b) would mean that the owner (O) was identified, presumably by S. The second version in (8c) would entail that O identified S. From a syntactic point of view, (8c) is the most plausible structure, and we shall focus on (8c) in the following.

Supposing that the individual arguments are O and S, we can ask as what S is identified. Most plausibly, in this case: O realises who S is. If we put things together for the subordinate clause, we arrive at the following reading:

(9) There is a unique individual O such that O owns S, and there is an event of O encountering and identifying S and taking S away.

Given the various possibilities discussed above for the matrix clause, this could describe different scenarios:

(10) a. Acquiring a gun. (S_{gun})
 b. Identifying a gun (as one that one owns?) and taking it. (S_{gun})
 c. Acquiring or recognising and taking a subordinate associate. (S_{Ind})

In terms of S_{gun}, it is not obvious how to read "identify." We know the gun would have to be very special in some way for us to make sense of the encounter described, but we do not know what it is that makes the gun special. The lack of a third argument, "as", for "identify" is more problematic in this case, since it would specify the property that makes the gun special (e.g., "O identified S as a Smith and Wesson").

In addition, the use of "me" instead of "it" rather strengthens the S_{Ind} reading ("gun" and "life" are inanimate, and would be referred to as "it"): S_{Ind} suggests that O recognises S as a desired inferior of some kind. The verb "carry away" confirms the implicature that the standing around in corners is ended. In addition, the use of the ambiguous expression "carry away" supports both the S_{gun} and the S_{Ind} reading. The literal meaning goes with S_{gun}, whereas the figurative meaning shows the strong impact O may have on S_{Ind}'s emotions (cf. also *OED*, "carry, *v.*" I.20.: "To impel or lead away as passion does, or by influencing the mind or feelings," and "carry, *v.*" I.21.: "to be carried: to be rapt, to be moved from sober-mindedness, to have the head turned").

6.2.4 Results

Two basic interpretations can be distinguished for the first stanza: one in which S is a gun, set in a fictional context in which inanimate entities can think, talk and feel as they are personified (see(11a)), and one in which S is an individual, creating some sort of fictional autobiography (see (11b)).

(11) a. S_{gun}: A rather special gun stood around loaded, disregarded, until it was recognised, possibly bought, and taken by its owner.
b. S_{Ind}: A person lived a neglected life, unrecognised in her or his dangerous nature, until someone came, recognised and took her or him as a suitable subordinate associate of some kind.

6.3 The Second and Third Stanzas, Lines 4–11

The reader's decision about the interpretation of stanza one determines how she will interpret the following verses, since they are compatible with both readings. However, there are linguistic factors that cause a slight tendency towards S_{Ind}. We will look at these factors next by comparing the interpretation of the second and third stanzas in accordance with an S_{gun} and an S_{Ind} reading, respectively.

6.3.1 The Second Stanza According to S_{ind}

Stanza two begins with a complex sentence consisting of three conjuncts (C1–C3):

(12)   [And [now we roam in sovereign woods]$_{C1}$ and [now we hunt the doe⁴]$_{C2}$ and [every time I speak for him the mountains straight reply]$_{C3}$]

The first two conjuncts describe collaborative activities of S and O. The personal pronoun shifts from the singular ("**my** life"; "me") to the plural "we," thereby stressing the cooperation between the two and their close relation. This fact points in the direction that we are dealing with two individuals.

Moreover, there is a shift from passive to active voice in the predicates describing S. In the first stanza, S was "passed," "identified" (as pointed out above, the analysis follows (8c) and regards S as the object of identification) and "carried [...] away." The only verb form attributed to S is a state ("stood [...] in corners"). By contrast, in stanza two, the verb forms associated with S refer to activities ("roam", "hunt" and "speak"). The personal pronoun "we" therefore entails that the activities are conducted both by S and O. Taken literally, this strongly suggests that S is at least animate, most likely human, which is why an S_{ind} interpretation seems to be slightly favoured.⁵

---

4 We might expect the more common "deer" instead of "doe" that is to be hunted, since does are usually not hunted for trophies, lacking antlers. The word "doe" only appears in one other poem of Dickinson's, J565/Fr527, which describes the hunting of a single, terrified doe. This evokes the use of hunting imagery and female deer in Renaissance love poems like Wyatt's "Whoso list to hunt, I know where is an hind" (Wyatt 1981, 77) and Spenser's *Amoretti* #67: "Lyke as a huntsman after weary chace" (Spenser 1958, 223). An alternative explanation is a phonetic one, in that "doe" allows the end rhyme with "foe" and "glow." Since Dickinson does not use rhyme regularly, this could hold significance but would need to be scrutinised more closely with regard to rhyme in Dickinson's poetry in general.

5 Another possibility to read S at this point is as an animate individual; rather than a human being, S could be a hound. The second stanza then works with a literal reading, as hounds can be said to "roam," "hunt," and even "speak" (*OED*, "speak, *v*." I.7.d.: "Of a hound: To give tongue; to bay"). The reading would also fit the Master-servant relationship proposed later in the poem, and that S must guard O. However, this reading is less likely if we draw evidence from the overall poem, which is why we will not consider it in more detail.

6.3.2 The Second Stanza According to S$_{gun}$

Following the S$_{gun}$ interpretation, one would have to reinterpret the predicates since inanimate objects do not "roam," "hunt," or "speak." This is manifested linguistically via the presuppositions of these verbs: essentially, the act of speaking is associated with human beings. Hence, the verb "speak" usually only allows for animate subjects to be its external argument. If S is not human, then the indexical "I" will refer to an inanimate entity, see (13b). Combining verb and subject would yield a presupposition failure in this case, as (13c) shows.

(13) a. ⟦speak⟧ = λx: x is human. x speaks
      b. ⟦I$_1$⟧^{g} = λg: g(1) is the speaker in the context. g(1)
      c. ⟦speak⟧(⟦I$_1$⟧^{g}) is only defined if g(1) is human

If the S$_{gun}$ interpretation is upheld, a reinterpretation of "speak" is required. We can suppose that it is used metaphorically and that human properties are transferred to the properties of a gun. A plausible way to do this is to find a generalisation for "speak" that can function as parallel between properties of both guns and humans. One possibility is to read "speaking" as a special way of making sounds. When human beings speak, they emit sounds. Guns emit sounds when they are fired. And, indeed, "speak" is conventionally used with reference to firearms (cf. *OED*, "speak, v." I.7.c.). Still, a very important distinction needs to be made between the interpretation of "speak" for S$_{ind}$ and S$_{gun}$. A human being can speak of his or her own accord; thus it becomes ambiguous what "I speak for Him" means under the S$_{ind}$ interpretation. Possible paraphrases are given in (14a) and (14b) below.

(14) a. When I speak, it is for his good/on his behalf.
      b. He is the reason for my speaking, he makes me speak.

A gun, by contrast, cannot fire itself. The intent is coming from O. Thus it would be transparent how "speak for Him" is most likely interpreted under S$_{gun}$, namely parallel to (14b): the reason for my firing is he, since he pulls the trigger ((14a) may still be implied, but (14b) is a sine qua non for S$_{gun}$).

The second part of the third conjunct describes reactions evoked by S. They have to be reinterpreted in both readings. One of them is described in lines 7-8, "And every time I speak for Him – / The Mountains straight reply –," the formal representation and paraphrase of which are given in (15a) and (15b) below.

(15) a. $\forall t\ [\text{speak}(S)(t) \to \exists t'\ [t' \subseteq t\ \&\ \text{reply}(\text{the\_mountains})(t')]]$
b. For every time t at which the speaker speaks there is a time t' which is included in t and at which the mountains reply.

Mountains, since they are not human, cannot reply in the same sense that humans can, hence there is a presupposition failure and a need for reinterpretation, which works analogously to the reinterpretation of "speak" in (13).

Again, decoding the metaphor is possible when taking properties of human beings to be transferred to properties of mountains. The reply of the mountains can be reinterpreted as the echo of S_{ind}'s speech or S_{gun}'s reverberation. The resounding noise a gun creates when fired is also called "report" (*OED*, "report, *n*." III.7.a.), which, in a less technical sense, usually refers to human speech, so that the mountains' "reply" can also be compared to a (spoken) "report." In both readings it is implied that S is powerful (being able to roam, hunt, speak and smile) and uses the potential of "a loaded gun" that was described at the beginning of stanza one.

6.3.3 The Third Stanza According to S_{gun} and S_{ind}, Lines 9-12

The third stanza begins with a sentence consisting of a matrix clause and a subordinate clause. The matrix clause verb is very plausibly "glow," although it has the wrong inflection.[6] The inversion in the subordinate clause is assumed to have a temporal clause meaning. These assumptions together yield the following paraphrase for the first sentence:

(16) And when I smile, such cordial light glows upon the valley.

Thus, S's smile evokes the existence of a cordial light. The semantic interpretation is found in (17a), a paraphrase of which is given in (17b).

(17) a. $\forall t\ [\text{smile}(\text{speaker})(t) \to \exists t'\ [t' \subseteq t\ \&\ \text{glow}(\text{light})(t')]]$
b. For every time t at which the speaker smiles there is a time t' which is included in t and at which the light glows.

Again, we need to reinterpret "smile" under the S_{gun} interpretation. Analogous to "speak" and "reply," "smile" is also a concept associated with human beings. If

---
[6] Miller (1987, 64-66) points out Dickinson's frequent use of verbs without inflection.

we follow the S_{gun} interpretation, a similar mismatch between the verb "smile" and its subject argument occurs as in the cases above. "Smile" can be reinterpreted as the muzzle flash of the gun (both smiling and a muzzle flash being temporary phenomena that manifest themselves nonverbally). Moreover, it is also consistent with the appearance of light (you can flash a smile). However, this reinterpretation is not as clear-cut as the reinterpretation of "speak": a smile, for example, can occur without speaking, but, following the reinterpretation of "speak" for S_{gun}, a muzzle flash can only occur in combination with shooting. Even though smiling and speaking follow each other in the poem, only the muzzle flash/shooting reinterpretation requires them to have a causal relationship.

The two interpretative possibilities are supported in different ways by the fact that the reaction is a "cordial light": although "cordial" is here applied to the (inanimate) light, the adjective "cordial" is derived from Latin "cor," or "heart" (*OED*, "cordial, *adj*. and *n*."), and the use of the word thus emphasises feeling and emotion. In Webster's 1828 *Dictionary*, "cordial" is defined in two ways. First, as "Proceeding from the heart; hearty; sincere; not hypocritical; warm; affectionate" ("cordial, *a*." 1.), a meaning which is suitably applied only to people or animals and which increases the need for reinterpretation when applied to inanimate entities. Secondly, as "Reviving the spirits; cheering; invigorating; giving strength or spirits" ("cordial, *a*." 2.).[7] If we relate this definition to the effect of firing a gun, we have to assume that Emily Dickinson's use – and especially the combination – of "smile" and "cordial" is ironic in this interpretation, since (although a volley or salvo in some cases may have an encouraging or invigorating effect) the firing of a gun is unlikely to be perceived as affectionate or reviving.

In any case, the combination of S's smile and the valley's glow and their possible interpretations links the two global interpretations S_{ind} and S_{gun} to each other. If S is an individual, S's smile can be taken literally, while the valley's glow must be seen metaphorically. If S is a gun, however, S's smile can only be interpreted metaphorically, while the valley's glow would be read literally as a valley glowing with a gun's fire.

It makes sense to compare the "cordial light" evoked by a gun to a "Vesuvian face" that lets "its pleasure through," since in both cases something danger-

---

[7] There seems to be no precedent for the phrase "cordial light"; however, in Ouida's novel *Under Two Flags* (1871) the expression is also used: "[...] his eyes rested with a kindly, cordial light on the new-comer [...]" (13). It is striking that the novel partly deals with the intimate relationship between a master and his servant.

ous is described as pleasant (and volcanoes, too, are in principle inanimate and are here endowed with the emotions of an animate being). The "Vesuvian face" in this line shares its properties with a gun, since both the "Vesuvian face" – which is "like or resembling Vesuvius" (*OED*, "Vesuvian, *adj.* and *n.*" A.a.) – as well as the gun possess "volcanic violence or power" (*OED*, "Vesuvian, *adj.* and *n.*" A.a.) released in eruption and firing respectively. This comparison takes place in the second half of the stanza, where we suppose an "if" is deleted.[8]

(18)   It is as if a Vesuvian face had let its pleasure through.

The reinterpretation necessary for the S_{gun} interpretation in the third stanza is thus more complex than the literal understanding if we take S to be human. It becomes clear though that S is dangerous and amiable at the same time, the second quality being more difficult to attribute to a gun.

Overall, the words used in stanza three indicate a positive atmosphere: "smile," "cordial light," and "pleasure." S seems to be able to evaluate the situation and show emotions. Since inanimate objects cannot do that according to our world knowledge, these expressions favour the S_{Ind} interpretation. In the interpretation S_{gun}, a gun must be able to have human properties within the poem.

6.3.4 Results

From a local perspective, the action and the evaluative description used in stanzas two and three allow for both interpretations of S.

Since the reading in which S or S's life is compared to a gun is slightly more prominent at this point in the poem, the nature of the relationship between S and O is a pressing question. Below are two rough paraphrases of how stanzas two and three contribute to S_{gun} and S_{Ind}:

(19) S_{gun}: S is being used, but is itself active by provoking reactions.

(20) S_{Ind}: S is an (unequal) partner that still acts herself.

---

[8] For a reference to Vesuvius, see also the Master Letters. In the third letter, the speaker compares herself to Vesuvius, talks about speaking and being silent, and about the "face" of a volcano: "Vesuvius dont talk – Etna – dont – <They> ↑2↓ said a syllable – ↑1↓ one of them – a thousand years ago, and Pompeii heard it, and hid forever – She could'nt look the world in the face, afterward" (Franklin 1986, 39).

The second and third stanzas, with their strong emphasis on "sovereignty," freedom ("roaming"), untamed wilderness ("doe"), mountains and the uncontrollable force of nature ("Vesuvian" power) remind us very much of the sublime.[9] S, by interacting with this sublime scene, acquires some of its power, and, in return, nature seems to "call back": the gun "speaks," and the mountains will reply; the gun "smiles" and this is linked to a "Vesuvian face."

6.4 The Fourth and Fifth Stanzas, Lines 13–20

6.4.1 The Fourth Stanza According to S_{ind}

Stanza four is a continuation of the events described by S in stanzas two and three. It consists of a temporal subordinate clause with an apposition and a matrix clause. One plausible structure for the temporal clause is the following:

(21)   [And when I guard my master's head at night [after our good day is done]$_{Apposition}$]$_{TempClause}$

According to the S_{Ind} interpretation, the VP "guard my master's head" can straightforwardly be interpreted as an actual guarding activity. Since guarding a person is usually not restricted to the head, this makes it plausible to take "my master's head" to be a metonymy that really stands for "my master." In linguistic terms this rhetorical figure has been described as an instance of predicate transfer (cf. Nunberg 1995) which requires a functional relation between the predicate described ("guarding the head") and the predicate derived ("guarding the person"). In this case the relation is defined via heads and their owners. The predicate transfer leads the reader to believe that the relationship between S and O is close. This closeness is stressed by the following matrix clause, which contains a comparative construction.

(22)   [$_{Matrix}$It is better than the eider-duck's pillow to have shared]

---

9 Cf., for example, Burke's (1990) statements that "Greatness of dimension, is a powerful cause of the sublime. [...] Of these the length strikes least; a hundred yards of even ground will never work such an effect as a tower an hundred yards high, or a rock or mountain of that altitude. [... A]nd the effects of a rugged and broken surface seem stronger than where it is smooth and polished" (66); and "Amongst [domestic animals] we never look for the sublime: it comes upon us in the gloomy forest, and in the howling wilderness, in the form of [wild animals]" (60f.).

This kind of judgement evokes the impression that S takes pleasure in protecting O, even in an uncomfortable position, and that all of S's actions are voluntary and conscious. Again, S seems to be capable of feeling and evaluating, which is more straightforwardly compatible with a S_{ind} interpretation.

At the same time, the relation is once again described as being unequal. On the one hand, guarding someone implies that there is a difference in strength and power; on the other hand, the description "my master" implies that the guarding person is inferior to O. This would suggest a very deep emotional or factual dependency, which is also supported by a more global perspective. Similarly, Dickinson's use of the word "Master" reminds us of her "Master Letters" and of other poems making reference to a "master."[10]

6.4.2 The Fourth Stanza According to S_{gun}

The fact that S is described as a possession and is protecting O is more compatible with a S_{gun} interpretation. The closeness implied by the use of "Head" could refer to the position of the gun: it is put close to O. If a S_{gun} interpretation is assumed, "guard my master's head" has to be reinterpreted. When we take the interpretation where the speaker is a gun with human properties seriously, however, the active mood is not surprising, since then the poem talks about worlds where guns are actually capable of "guarding." No reinterpretation would be necessary in this case.

However, the implicit agent of the guarding event is plausibly human, and thus it is reasonable to think that not the gun itself is doing the protecting but that it is O that uses the gun for his own protection. Yet, in the poem, the gun is not described as a passive instrument. This fact underlines the presence of a reading in which a human speaker is comparing herself to a gun (a human being is, after all, an active being, while an inanimate weapon is not), especially since the question in a S_{gun} interpretation arises **why** the feelings of a gun should be so important. It allows for an interpretation where S sees herself as a dangerous instrument as well as a human being capable of reflected decisions.

---

10 There are, of course, also many poems by Dickinson which present a similar relationship without explicitly using the word "master," for example, many of the poems in which the speaker is identified with a daisy also show an unequal relationship of the "daisy" to a higher being on whom the daisy is dependent (see e.g., J85/Fr87A, J106/Fr161, J339/Fr367, and J481/Fr460).

These reflections are not the ones of a defenceless individual but the ones of a dedicated, unconditionally loyal person.

6.4.3 The Fifth Stanza According to S_{Ind} and S_{gun}

The interpretive difficulties that arise in the fifth stanza seem to be largely independent of the question whether S is a gun or a human being. In both cases, stanza five stresses how protective S is of O and how dangerous to others, which becomes especially obvious in the first sentence of the stanza where the indirect argument "foe" is fronted so that it receives emphasis:

(23)   To foe of his I'm deadly foe.

This impression of a protective relationship is underlined by the use of the adverbial modifier "deadly," which fits a S_{gun} interpretation, since guns are known to be deadly instruments. Still, "being foe" to someone suggests human feelings and high emotional involvement, which strengthens the S_{Ind} interpretation.

The second sentence of the stanza consists of a main clause and a subordinate relative clause. The main (or matrix) clause is a quantificational statement, the relative clause functions as a restriction of the quantifier "none":

(24)   [None [on whom I lay a yellow eye or an emphatic thumb$_{Relative}$] stir the second time$_{Matrix}$]

It is unclear what "yellow eye" and "emphatic thumb" mean in this context. There is no clear semantic conflict or mismatch between the adjectives and the nouns; all four words are properties. The meaning of the NP should therefore be determined by intersecting the two sets the adjective and noun denote, respectively. Intersecting the predicates yields a set of individuals that have both properties. This is shown in (25).

(25)   a.   ⟦yellow eye⟧ = λx. x is yellow and x is an eye
        b.   ⟦emphatic thumb⟧ = λx. x is emphatic and x is a thumb

While in S_{Ind}, S has eyes and thumbs, human eyes are not usually yellow and thumbs are not usually called emphatic. If we consider S literally as a gun, the "Yellow Eye" could be the muzzle flash seen by the opponent immediately before being shot — the visual, "looking" activity accompanying the "speaking" in line 7. Dickinson uses the expression in a similar way in J590/Fr619: "Did you ever look in a Cannon's face – / Between whose Yellow eye – / And yours – the Judgment intervened – / The Question of 'to die.'"[11] On another note, the colour yellow is traditionally that of jealousy, and till 1858 the use of "yellow" to mean "jealous" is indeed documented (*OED*, "yellow, *adj.* and *n.*" A.2.a.). The expression "emphatic Thumb" could be associated with the holding and handling of a gun (the cocking piece of a gun, which can be manipulated with the thumb). Still, one must wonder why exactly this action should be described as "emphatic."[12] The adjective "emphatic" is used to describe utterances or verbal statements (see *OED*, "emphatic, *adj.* and *n.*," and "emphatic, emphatical, *a.*" in Webster). Therefore, the use of "emphatic" leads into the direction of a third possible interpretation of the poem outlined below in section 6.7, relating S's actions to language and poetry.

6.4.4 Results

At the end of stanza five the reader of the poem knows that the individual described as O is male (due to the pronouns "him" and "his" and "My Master") but knows very little about the identity of S. When assuming that S is an individual, one is drawn to see an intimate relationship based on the emotional component that is implied. This component primarily is expressed through the adjectives and nouns S uses to describe the surroundings and the activities ("Sovereign Woods," "cordial," "pleasure," "good Day").

---

11 The metaphor "yellow eye" for a flash of light can, for example, also be found in Stephen Crane's tale "Flanagan and His Short Filibustering Adventure" (1897): "One night the *Foundling* was off the southern coast of Florida and running at half speed toward the shore. The captain was on the bridge. 'Four flashes at intervals of one minute,' he said to himself, gazing steadfastly toward the beach. Suddenly a yellow eye opened in the black face of the night and looked at the *Foundling* and closed again" (1047).

12 Webster lists "Oversight; inspection" as a definition for "eye" and gives as an example the proverb "The eye of the master will do more work than both his hands" ("Eye, *n.*" 16.), while one of his definitions for "emphatic" includes "striking to the eye; as, emphatic colors" ("Emphatic, emphatical, *a.*" 4.). Although these definitions do not clarify the use of "Yellow Eye" and "emphatic Thumb," they suggest a link between the expressions. Looking at the "emphatic thumb" as a human gesture, we can find the idiom "to bite the thumb at" someone (*OED*, "thumb, *n.*" 5.e., and *OED*, "bite, *v.*" 16.), which describes a depreciatory and insulting gesture. Although this expression was no longer used in Dickinson's time, she is likely to have known it from Shakespeare's *Romeo and Juliet*, where an entire dialogue is dedicated to it (I.1.37-47). Lastly, there is also the idiom "to be under someone's thumb" – which with respect to the poem would add an ironic touch, since S (whether human or gun) is certainly under the Master's thumb, regardless of whether S threatens others with an "emphatic Thumb."

The two individuals are described as working together, more specifically, they hunt. S is powerful and takes pleasure in the activity. S does not share the pillow of O; S perceives him as S's master and is at the same time the one that protects him. S is becoming more active as the poem continues, which is represented by the mood of these four stanzas. At the same time, S is apparently only becoming active as an instrument of O and not of S's own accord. This is evidence that, even though slightly less plausible in the preceding stanzas, the interpretation where S is an actual gun is kept a possibility throughout. In this case, we have to assume that a personified gun which has human properties is described in the poem. Otherwise mismatches between the agent and the predicates that are used for the description ("speak," "smile," "Eye," "Thumb") would occur. As human feelings are also assigned to the gun, this interpretation would result in supposing that O has a deeply emotional, almost intimate, relationship with his gun.

6.5 The Final Stanza, Lines 21–24

The last stanza again displays high linguistic complexity. In order to get at its plausible interpretations, it is useful to analyse the two sentences it consists of very carefully and in detail, first separately and then in conjunction. These two sentences are given in (26) and (27) and will be referred to as S1 and S2 in the subsequent discussion.

(26)   [S1 Though I than he may longer live, he longer must than I]

(27)   [S2 For I have but the power to kill, without the power to die]

6.5.1 Interpretation of S1

Both sentences are structurally complex. To simplify things, the structure considered for the first sentence will be the one in (28), where the word order is adjusted and the ellipsis filled.

(28)   [S1 [subord though I may live longer than he][matrix he must live longer than I]]

The subordinate clause is given in (29). The comparison can be in the scope of the modal (30a), i.e. structurally lower than the modal in the logical form, or vice versa (30b), i.e. structurally higher than the modal in the logical form (see the appendix for a basic introduction to modals and scope). The modal force of a possibility modal like "may" is existential. This means it claims the existence of a possible world; in this case, a possible world where S lives longer than O (see, for a discussion of modals, the appendix and also Hacquard 2011; Kratzer 1991). The interpretation of the comparative "longer" comes about by separating the "-er"-morpheme from the adjective "long." The adjective introduces a scale of degrees, here the scale of temporal length, and the comparative morpheme introduces a relation between two degrees on that scale (see e.g. Beck 2011 for an overview).

(29) I may live longer than he.

(30) a. [may [[-er than he live _ long] [I live _ long]]]
      b. [[-er than he may live _ long] [I may live long]]

Moreover, the accessibility relation between possible worlds (see also chapters I.1 and I.5) tells us which worlds are relevant for us to consider. Accordingly, we can define this relation as considering only worlds compatible with the law (deontic reading), worlds compatible with what we know (epistemic reading), worlds compatible with the facts presented (circumstantial reading), and worlds compatible with what we desire (bouletic reading). We assume that the same laws, facts and desires hold in the text worlds as in the actual world, as the poem does not specify that these should be different. We formalise (30a) and (30b) as in (31a) and (31b) (with R standing for the accessibility relation):

(31) a. $\exists w\ [R(@)(w)\ \&\ \text{lifespan}(w)(S) > \text{lifespan}(w)(O)]$
      = It is possible that I live longer than he.
   b. $\max(\lambda d.\ \exists w\ [R(@)(w)\ \&\ \text{lifespan}(w)(S) \geq d]) > \max(\lambda d.\ \exists w\ [R(@)(w)\ \&\ \text{lifespan}(w)(O) \geq d])$
      = My maximum life expectancy exceeds his maximum life expectancy.

The matrix clause is given in (32). Like (29), it is ambiguous. A necessity modal like "must" has universal force. It states that a proposition — in this case that O lives longer than S — holds for all accessible worlds (accessibility modelled with R). The two structural possibilities in (32) correspond to the interpretations in (33).

(32) He must live longer than I.
    a. [must [[-er than I live _ long] [he live _ long]]]
    b. [[-er than I must live _ long] [he must live long]]

(33) a. $\forall w \ [R(@)(w) \to \text{lifespan}(w)(O) > \text{lifespan}(w)(S)]$
       = It is necessary that he live longer than I.
   b. $\max(\lambda d. \ \forall w \ [R(@)(w) \to \text{lifespan}(w)(O) \geq d]) > \max(\lambda d. \ \forall w \ [R(@)(w) \to \text{lifespan}(w)(S) \geq d])$
       = The minimum required lifetime of his exceeds the minimum lifetime required of me.

Putting together both the ambiguous subordinate clause and the ambiguous matrix clause, we theoretically have a total of four possibilities:

(34) a. Although (31a), (33a).
   b. Although (31b), (33a).
   c. Although (31a), (33b).
   d. Although (31b), (33b).

Since the two scopally parallel analyses (34a), (34d) are the most plausible, they will be pursued further (see (35), (36)). As it will make the analysis simpler, and since the difference is not relevant to make our point, we will here treat "although" as "and." The two interpretations and paraphrases for S1 are given in (35) and (36). Let us first consider (35):

(35) a. $\exists w \ [R(@)(w) \ \& \ \text{lifespan}(w)(S) > \text{lifespan}(w)(O)] \ \&$
       $\forall w \ [R(@)(w) \to \text{lifespan}(w)(O) > \text{lifespan}(w)(S)]$
   b. It is possible that I live longer than he, and it is necessary that he live longer than I.

If the relation R is the same for the two modals "may" and "must," (35) is a contradiction: it is not possible that all relevant worlds are such that O's life extends beyond that of S and that there is a world in which the life of S extends beyond O's. However, we know that there are various possibilities for R. (35) becomes non-contradictory if we suppose, for example, that the natural facts are such that S might live longer than O, but S's desires are such that O must live longer than S, and S will thus do her best to keep him alive beyond her own lifespan. In this case we assume a circumstantial reading of "may" and a bouletic reading for "must."

Next, the second interpretation will be considered, which is given in (36):

(36) a. $\max(\lambda d. \exists w\ [R(@)(w)\ \&\ \text{lifespan}(w)(S) \geq d]) >$
$\max(\lambda d. \exists w\ [R(@)(w)\ \&\ \text{lifespan}(w)(O) \geq d])\ \&$
$\max(\lambda d. \forall w\ [R(@)(w) \rightarrow \text{lifespan}(w)(O) \geq d]) >$
$\max(\lambda d. \forall w\ [R(@)(w) \rightarrow \text{lifespan}(w)(S) \geq d])$

b. My maximum life expectancy exceeds his maximum life expectancy, and the minimum required lifetime of his exceeds the minimum lifetime required of me.

c. t_1 t_2 t_3 t_4
|---------|--------|--------------|--------------|----------------------------->

The conjunction in (36) is not contradictory. It would be true for instance if, given all the relevant facts, S might die anytime between t_1 and t_4, while O might die anytime between t_2 and t_3. This means that the day of O's death can be narrowed down more closely than the day of S's death. Given what we already know about S and O, the interpretation in (35) might be the more plausible, since it is the more relevant one. But to be able to disambiguate between the different interpretations, the second sentence might be of importance.

6.5.2 Interpretation of S2

For the second sentence we will consider the structure in (37) below, assuming that "but" means "only" in this case.

(37)   [S2 I have only the power to kill, without the power to die]

If we consider the S_{gun} interpretation, this sentence is trivially true, since inanimate objects cannot die. The apparent banality of the statement invites the interpretation that more is meant than what is literally said; for example, that this specific weapon will always exist. Another small interpretive difficulty arises with "power to kill." It is not a gun itself that wields this power; being a mere instrument, it needs an agent. If we consider next the interpretation where S is an individual, the sentence is false, and once more rather trivially so, since all people die. Again, the apparent banality as well as the factual falsity invites reinterpretation. One possibility for the sentence to be read is: I cannot choose my death.[13]

6.5.3 Putting Things Together

The overall structure is "S1 for S2." This will be read as "S1 because S2," and we will paraphrase S2 for now as "S can kill, but S cannot die." Taking the two readings for S1 and putting them into this context yields the paraphrases in (38) and (39):

(38)   It is possible that I live longer than he,
        and it is necessary that he live longer than I,
        BECAUSE I can kill but I cannot die.

(39)   My maximum life expectancy exceeds his maximum life expectancy,
        and the minimum required lifetime of his exceeds
        the minimum lifetime required of me,
        BECAUSE I can kill but I cannot die.

These are the most plausible interpretations of the last stanza that a grammatical analysis can offer and on which more global interpretations can be based. If we assume everyday meanings for both "live" and "die" in (38), S is wishing for something impossible. If S cannot die, then S's lifespan necessarily exceeds the lifespan of any animate owner.

---

13 The phrase "the power to die" might be an intertextual allusion to a poem by Alfred Lord Tennyson: "Tithonus," which was published in *The Cornhill Magazine* in 1860, also includes this peculiar phrase ("[...] when the steam / Floats up from those dim fields about the homes / Of happy men that have **the power to die**"; 176). In this poem, Tithonus addresses Aurora about his unwanted immortality and compares himself to the "happy men that have the power to die." Dickinson's "My Life had stood" is dated by both Johnson (1955) and Miller (2016) at c. late 1863, which makes it at least plausible that Dickinson had the opportunity to have read the poem. While Dickinson alludes to Tennyson or references his poetry several times in her letters (e.g. L243, L320, L353, L486, L506), she never explicitly mentions "Tithonus," nor *Cornhill Magazine*, though the similarity of ideas (unwanted immortality) suggests that she may have become familiar with the poem at some point between its initial publication in 1860 and the composition of her own poem in 1863.

Under the S_{gun} interpretation, however, (38) is plausible. It may then be the case that O lives longer, since he is capable of living at all, whereas a gun can only exist. But this is contradicting the first line of the stanza where the possibility that S – a gun – lives longer is admitted.

It seems that, according to this reading, a reinterpretation of "live" and "die" is necessary. For S_{gun} to "live" might mean that it exists. This interpretation fits with the beginning of the poem. The gun's "life" was standing in corners; hence it existed although it was not used. The gun only functions and operates in the way described in the poem because O took it, but it existed even before O passed. The necessity that O exists longer is therefore only possible in a bouletic reading. Given the facts of the world, the length of existence of the gun can easily exceed the length of existence of the human owner.

Therefore, "die" cannot be the opposite of "live," since "to stop living" is impossible for inanimate objects. "To die" has to mean "to stop existing" in this case. What remains problematic is the interpretation of "power to kill" then. Strictly speaking, it is not the gun that is killing but O. If "power to kill" rather means "can be used for killing," then "without the power to die" has to be interpreted as "lacking the ability to be used for its own destruction." This means that the gun cannot end its own existence. It is damned to uselessness without O, since it cannot take action itself. It will always be able to function and never be able to stop existing. This reinterpretation could thus explain the causal relation between the existence of O and the existence of S when it is assumed to be a gun.

In terms of S_{gun}, a similar reinterpretation process has to be triggered in (39). If S cannot die, then the minimum lifespan reached in all worlds tends towards infinity and cannot be shorter than that of any animate owner O. Hence, the sentence in (39) also describes something that cannot literally be true, given natural laws of our world.

Next, we will consider the interpretations (38) and (39) under S_{ind}. Both interpretations completely change when S is assumed to be an individual. It is unproblematic to interpret "I have the power to kill" under this assumption. It is, however, unclear what it means for a human being to lack the "power to die." If we argue the same way as for the gun-case above, then "without the power to die" means that S is not capable of killing herself. This reading seems to imply that all her choices, even the ones that concern her own death, are really the choices of O, which is consistent with the analysis of the preceding stanzas, since a very deep dependency is suggested. The overall tone of the poem does not speak for an interpretation according to which this dependency is seen as unfair or negative.[14] We work with (38) in the following though (39) remains possible.

6.6 Overall Interpretation

The two lines of interpretation, S_{gun} and S_{ind}, which have guided our analysis, reveal a complex interplay. This is due to the fact that neither of the two can be applied without arriving at some interpretative difficulty at some point in the text. We paraphrase the two text meanings in (40) and (41):

(40) S_{gun}: I am a loaded gun and my existence was neglected until a day my owner came, identified me and carried me away. And now he takes me to roam in woods and hunt the doe and every time he shoots with me there is an echo in the mountains. When the muzzle flash of the shot appears, light appears upon the valley, it glows and is like the face of Vesuvius when it erupts. And when he is done hunting at night and places me next to his bed, this creates a comfortable atmosphere. He takes me to kill his foes, and I am very efficient. Although I may longer exist than he does, in order for me to function it is necessary that he lives, since I am an instrument for killing, but I have no life of my own.

(41) S_{ind}: I am a human being who is like a loaded gun; my life has been neglected until its owner came, identified me and took me with him. And now we roam in sovereign woods together and hunt the doe, and every time I speak for him, the mountains straight reply.

---

14 The use of the expression "power to die" does not seem appropriate for the negative associations of death and especially the passivity of dying. From a religious point of view, the "power to die" could be understood as the reassurance to die and be saved after death by Christ; see, e.g. Eberhard Jüngel's (1993, ch. 6) statement that mankind has achieved the power to die only through the death of Christ, that is, the power to die without fear in the knowledge that man's sins are forgiven through Christ's sacrifice. Dickinson herself also uses the expression "power to die" in J1651/Fr1715, "A Word made Flesh," in an explicitly religious context. In this poem, the "Word made Flesh" comes to life, and only through this coming to life can it then be subjected to life and death (Bauer 2006, 374), similarly to the gun in "My life had stood." A single word "that breathes distinctly," however, is only an instrument, and like S in "My life had stood" it has – standing on its own – only the "power to kill, / Without – the power to die" (Bauer 2006, 383f.). It can however, be made cohesive and "expire" through the power and condescension of Christ ("Made Flesh and dwelt among us").

> My smile is as pleasant as when the valley glows. The glow is like Vesuvius when it erupts. And when at night I guard him it is better than to have shared pillows with him. I will kill all his foes, and even though it is possible that I live longer than he, it is my wish that he will live longer than I do, since I have power with him but no life without him.

Now we come to the pragmatic interpretation of the text. We propose that a plausible analysis, rather unusually, applies the operator FictionalAssert to the disjunction of both readings. In the present poem, we see that both readings cannot be combined conjunctively as they contradict each other: the speaker cannot be human and be a gun at the same time.

Accordingly, the pragmatic interpretation of the poem is (42).

(42) $[\![\text{FictionalAssert}]\!]((40) \text{ or } (41)) = 1$ iff $\forall w'\ [(40)(w') \text{ or } (41)(w') \rightarrow R(@)(w')]$

Here, FictionalAssert results in the conditional statement that as long as (40) or (41) is the case, R holds. R, in turn, specifies the pragmatic meaning of the text, i.e. how the reader relates the text to her own context, by forming a relation between the text worlds and the actual world @. If the counterpart of the reader can be either a human being or a gun, what specific characteristics make guns and human beings comparable to each other? Accordingly, values for R reflect on the similarities between the two readings, and more specifically between human beings and guns. One possible way to specify it is paraphrased in (43). A resulting pragmatic interpretation is given in (44).

(43) "The relation R between the text worlds w and the actual world @ holds iff w is exactly like @ except that the speaker S in w, who is either human or a gun, is the reader in @ and the characteristics shared by human and gun apply to the reader in @ and there is an unequal relationship between the reader and someone in @ that shares the characteristics of the relationship between speaker and owner in w."

(44) "If everything the poem says is the case, then I am like S and if I do what S does, then I am either a lethal instrument in the hands of a superior power, or I am a superior power on whom the life of the other depends."

6.7 The Poem as a Reflection About Language

It seems unsatisfactory to assume the speaker simply to be a gun in one reading and make reference to fairytale settings. Instead, the speaker being a gun should probably not be taken literally, but metaphorically. This leaves the question open what the gun is a metaphor for. The context of the poem suggests that the gun stands for language or the word. References to language reverberate through the text: for example, "speak" and "reply" are verbal actions, the "Sovereign Woods" may evoke the literary tradition that likens writings to forests,[15] the use of "emphatic" is linked to speech, and the idea of immortality is also linked to poetry (see below).

Considering the vagueness of the last line in particular, we should keep in mind that weapons are not the only things without a "power to die." In J1651/Fr1715, the expression "power to die" is linked to religion but also to literature and speech. The "consent of Language" and "loved Philology" are compared to Christ's power over life and death, transforming a single "Word that breathes distinctly" into a "Word made Flesh." It is possible to read not having the "power to die" in two different ways, either as the possession of eternal life or as the incapability of dying (thus, a kind of powerlessness). One possibility therefore is to assume that the speaker of the poem is a poem or poetry in general, since words cannot die. But words are also powerless without someone who uses them. A second possibility hence is that the speaker of the poem is a poet who becomes immortal through the texts she writes. The idea that poetry has the power to immortalise its subject is a common notion familiar since antiquity (found, for example, in the ending of Ovid's *Metamorphoses*, in Horace's Ode IV.9, and in some of Shakespeare's sonnets, for example sonnet 18).[16] A

---

15 The figure that connects the woods (Lat. "silva" is "a wood, forest"; *OED*, "sylva/silva, n.") with writings goes back to a work by Statius, *Silvae*, a collection of poetry. This juxtaposition of woods and writings is then continued in, e.g. Simon Pelegromius's 16th-century dictionary *Silva Synonymorum* or Ben Jonson's *Timber*; see also the passage from Horace's *Ars Poetica* preceding the lines quoted below: "As the forests shed their leaves [...], so perish those former generations of words [...]" (Horace 2005, *Ars Poetica* 60-62).

16 The *Metamorphoses* end with "[...] a work which neither Jove's anger, nor fire nor sword shall destroy, nor yet the gnawing tooth if time. [...] If there be any truth in poets' prophecies, I shall live to all eternity, immortalized by fame" (Ovid 1980, 357). In Horace's Ode IV.9, the speaker states, "I shall not pass you over in silence, unhonoured by my pages; nor shall I allow jealous oblivion to erode your countless exploits" (Horace 2004, *Odes* 247). Shakespeare's sonnet 18 ends with "But thy eternal summer shall not fade, / Nor lose possession of that fair thou ow'st, / Nor shall death brag thou wand'rest in his shade, / When in eternal lines to time

dichotomy parallel to the two interpretations discussed above arises: we have an interpretation S_{poet} according to which the speaker is an individual, and we have an interpretation $S_{poem/poetry}$ in which the speaker is not human.

In "My Life had stood," we additionally get an ironic twist: S cannot die (which is seen as a lack of power) but can kill instead. Again, on the one hand, one may regard the poem itself as the "killer," since it can have destructive power by, for example, destroying clichés, relations or reputations with its content. On the other hand, one could also see the words as powerless without their creator, the poet, who thus has the power to destroy. A similar idea can be traced back to Horace's *Ars Poetica*, where the power(lessness) of words over the course of time is described. Here, what gives power to words (or takes it from them) is that words are being used (or not used) by human beings:

(45) Many words that are now unused will be rekindled,
Many fade now well-regarded, if Usage wills it so,
To whom the laws, rules, and control of language belong.
(Horace, *Ars Poetica* 60-72)

In J1212/Fr278, Dickinson describes the same notion:

(50) A word is dead
When it is said,
Some say.

I say it just
Begins to live
That day.

In Dickinson's poems, words can either live or die, or they are able to bring life or death. In J118/Fr103, Dickinson links the power of guns to the power of words, in this way giving words the power and status of weapons:

(51) My friend attacks my friend!
Oh Battle picturesque!
Then I turn Soldier too,
And he turns Satirist!

---

thou grow'st. / So long as men can breathe and eyes can see, / So long lives this and this gives life to thee" (Shakespeare 2000, 19).

> How martial is this place!
> Had I a mighty gun
> I think I'd shoot the human race
> And then to glory run!

The poem presents "Soldier" and "Satirist" as two alternatives complementing each other and involving the same kind of action ("attacking").[17] Of course, it is not possible to shoot all of mankind literally, but it is possible to shoot them in a literary way (as a satirist) and attain glory just as a soldier might attain glory through fighting. And, in fact, Dickinson does possess a "mighty gun" in the form of language. In the manuscript of J754/Fr764, line 23 originally read "For I have but the art to kill" (Dickinson 1955, 574) – "art" is a poet's strongest and only power. The "Owner" could then also refer to the power that inspired S to write poetry (and to write this particular poem), a muse or divine inspiration. This variation could also explain O's depiction as very powerful and S's depiction as more submissive (though S is of course the one who must necessarily speak throughout the poem). Porter (1966, 209-18) sees "My Life had stood" as a poem about an instrument (S) and a purpose (dependent on O), and, more specifically, as a poem about a poet and what she should do. He cites several other poems where language is used as a weapon or has the power and impact of a weapon (e.g., J479/Fr458A, "She dealt her pretty words like Blades").

Accepting this interpretation, we can see the use of the gun image as a twofold metaphor. If we assume a human speaker, she uses the gun metaphor to express his/her feelings. But the gun itself is then endowed with human sentiments and thoughts, and thus acquires characteristics of a human being. In this way, the gun is a metaphor to express the state and feelings of a human speaker; in addition, the gun leads the way to a second metaphoric level, where it is personified. The structure of this twofold metaphor is one of exchange, where a human being becomes a gun and speaks through the gun, and at the same time a gun becomes animate and "human," and speaks with a human voice. To summarise, we see that a two additional text meanings become available which are metaphoric:

(46) S_{poet}: I am a poet with the potential of a loaded gun, a potential which was not used till language, the owner of my art, came and inspired me. And now I roam through the jungle of words, and

---

17 By using the adjective "martial" (and thereby alluding to the Roman satirist Martial), Dickinson creates another link between war and satire.

every time I write it has an impact on the things around me, and my writing is powerful like Vesuvius when it erupts. And at night I prefer my service to language over soft pillows and intimacy. When someone does not appreciate my art I harm them through my writing. Though I may live longer than the language inspiring me, it should live longer than me, since I can only do harm through my writing, but (my poetry being immortal) I cannot die as a poet.

(47) $S_{poem/poetry}$: I am (in the beginning yet unwritten) poetry with the potential of a loaded gun, a potential which was not used till one day a poet came and wrote me. And now I am free through the poet, and we roam through the jungle of words, and every time the poet writes poetry I create a powerful impact on the things around me, as powerful as Vesuvius when it erupts. Being poetry is better than soft pillows and human intimacy. When someone does not appreciate my poet's art I help the poet to harm them through me. I, as written poetry, am immortal and will live longer than the poet, but he should live longer than me, since I am able to do harm, but I am nothing without the poet writing me and cannot even die.

Importantly, both metaphorical readings give rise to the same relation R as proposed above: even though the speaker can be interpreted as the poet, her relationship to the owner and the nature of this relationship stay the same, as the text itself stays the same, i.e. as the owner utilises the speaker, so does the poet his poetry. Coming back to (44), the reader in this case applies this text to actual poets or artists. The properties and relations are the same in the actual world as in the text worlds. Here, the poem is about actual art or poetry.

6.8 Conclusion

In this poem, Emily Dickinson primarily plays with the two interpretive possibilities that a gun or a human being are reflecting on their respective lives. It becomes obvious that neither of these two possibilities allows for an interpretive process to run coherently throughout the whole poem without having to reinterpret different parts for S_{gun} and S_{ind}, respectively. The image of the gun furthermore triggers two additional metaphorical readings in which the gun is an image of poetry.

"My Life had stood" is an example of Emily Dickinson's use of deviant structures. She prevents the reader from deriving a literal interpretation by exploiting mechanisms of grammar in such a way that the reader is forced to look for non-literal meanings. These reinterpretation processes allow for more freedom of interpretation, and, thus, the reader is left with more interpretative choices. This freedom is created at select points within a fixed structure, which is not arbitrary but created deliberately by Emily Dickinson to enable the coexistence of several threads of interpretation.

It follows that there cannot be one unique interpretation of the poem. It has been shown, however, that there is a set of plausible interpretations which can be identified, and that considering the relation between these different interpretations adds an additional level of meaning to the poem. Our claim is that plausible interpretations share the structural properties of the four interpretations we discuss (S_{Ind}, S_{gun}, S_{poet}, S_{poetry}).

Tab. 1: Chapter Summary

Core Phenomenon

Coercion
Reinterpretation Possibilities:
⟦stand in corners_Reint⟧ = λx. x is unnoticed/neglected.
⟦my life⟧ = the speaker in the context
see also *speak, reply*

Text Interpretation

Reading S_{gun}: I am a loaded gun and my existence was neglected until a day my owner came, identified me and carried me away. And now he takes me to roam in woods and hunt the doe and every time he shoots with me there is an echo in the mountains. When the muzzle flash of the shot appears, light appears upon the valley, it glows and is like the face of Vesuvius when it erupts. And when he is done hunting at night and poses me next to his bed, this creates a comfortable atmosphere. He takes me to kill his foes, and I am very efficient. Although I may longer exist than he does, in order for me to function it is necessary that he lives, since I am an instrument for killing, but I have no life of my own.

Reading S_{ind}: I am a human being who is like a loaded gun; my life has been neglected until its owner came, identified me and took me with him. And now we roam in sovereign woods together and hunt the doe, and every time I speak for him, the mountains straight reply. My smile is as pleasant as when the valley glows. The glow is like Vesuvius when it erupts. And when at night I guard him it is better than to have shared pillows with him. I will kill all his foes, and even though it is possible that I live longer than he, it is my wish that he will live longer than I do, since I have power with him but no life without him.
→ **Text Interpretation:** S_{gun} or S_{ind}

Relation R: "The relation R between the text worlds w and the actual world @ holds iff w is exactly like @ except that the speaker S in w, who is either human or a gun, is the reader in @ and the characteristics shared by human and gun apply to the reader in @ and there is an unequal relationship between the reader and someone in @ that shares the characteristics of the relationship between speaker and owner in w."

Pragmatic Interpretation:
If everything the poem says is the case, then I am like S and if I do what S does, then I am either a lethal instrument in the hands of a superior power, or I am a superior power on whom the life of the other depends.

Coercion in other Chapters

(In I.1): **distills** amazing sense – from ordinary meanings
⟦distill⟧ = λy. [λz. [λx: z is a liquid. x distills y from z]]
⟦distill_Reint⟧ = λy. [λx. [λz. z transforms y into x]]

Other Phenomena in this Chapter

Scales and Modals: Though I than He – may **longer** live // He **longer** must – than I –
⟦must⟧ = λR$_{<s,<s,t>>}$. [λp$_{<s,t>}$. [λw. ∀w' [(R)(w)(w') → p(w')]]]
⟦may⟧ = λR$_{<s,<s,t>>}$. [λp$_{<s,t>}$. [λw. ∃w' [(R)(w)(w') & p(w')]]]
'It is possible that I live longer than he, and it is necessary that he live longer than I.' or 'My maximum life expectancy exceeds his maximum life expectancy, and the minimum required lifetime of his exceeds the minimum lifetime required of me'

Definites and Structural Ambiguity: The Owner passed – **identified** – / And carried Me away –
⟦the owner⟧ = the unique individual O such that O owns S

Part II: Emily Dickinson: The Poet as Linguist, and the Linguist as Poet

Part II takes the analyses of individual poems from Part I as a point of departure to now consider the general behind the particular. In the following two chapters, we will show that Emily Dickinson's being a linguist has a profound influence throughout her poetry, and that linguistic peculiarities are not singular occurrences but essential to her meaning-making process. Moreover, we will also look at the significance of her linguistic dexterity from the point of view of her poetics, and integrate our findings into a consideration of what poetry as a text form means to Emily Dickinson.

II.1 The Poet as Linguist

1.1 Introduction

In this chapter, we will present Dickinson as an intuitive linguist who systematically exploits grammar to produce interpretative flexibility in her poems. As has been observed in the first part of this book, her particular use of linguistic techniques reveals that, though not a trained linguist, she was able to grasp and creatively use principles of how language and grammar work. Moreover, her deliberate exploitation of and non-compliance with certain grammatical rules and features leads to a specific structuring of her texts, which are characterised by a well-calculated number of readings. Her systematic use of language speaks against Dickinson arbitrarily violating grammatical rules to create vague and uninterpretable utterances that allow for an infinite number of textual meanings. Rather, it suggests a systematic approach that lends itself to the interpretation of her texts from a linguistic point of view. While our aim in the preceding analyses of individual poems was to offer in-depth and linguistically informed interpretations, the objective of this chapter is to systematise Emily Dickinson's use of the linguistic phenomena outlined below. These uses are not individual occurrences but phenomena found across her poetry. Even though the focus here will lie on these phenomena and not on an overall interpretation of the poems in which they occur, we conjecture that their use has a similar effect as the cases observed in the preceding chapters, namely that it contributes in a significant way to the overall interpretation of the text, of which several readings can be identified.

In the following sections, we will outline those linguistic phenomena that frequently appear in Dickinson's poetry,[1] starting with syntactic and structural phenomena, especially structural ambiguity and ellipsis.[2] We will then extend the discussion to semantic features Dickinson exploits, like lexical ambiguity and reinterpretation and, lastly, consider her specific use of phenomena that lie at the semantics-pragmatics interface, concentrating on context-dependent expressions like presuppositions and referential expressions, as well as possible resolutions of contradictions. In each section, we will first briefly come back to

---

[1] In many cases we have chosen the most plausible readings, disregarding that there may be additional interpretations available.
[2] This is an addition to what has already been observed and analysed in great detail by Cristanne Miller (1987).

one of the examples we have already encountered in the first part of the book and then discuss examples from other poems by Emily Dickinson.

1.2 Syntactic Ambiguity

1.2.1 Structural Ambiguity

Syntactic ambiguity may arise when a word or phrase exhibits more than one attachment option in the phrase structure:

(1)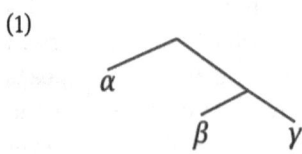

(2)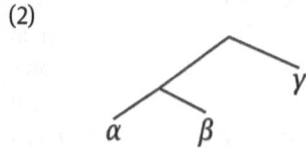

The same constituents α, β and γ can be structurally combined in two ways: in one case, β and γ form a subconstituent (see (1)), and, in the other, α and β form a subconstituent (see (2)).

This will make a difference in the poem's interpretation, as we have seen in the context of "If it had no pencil" (J921/Fr184A).

(3)   Worn – now – and *dull* – sweet,
       Writing much to thee.

Ambiguity arises as it is unclear which item the adverb "now" structurally belongs to (see chapter I.5). It could either be a modifier of the adjectives "worn," "dull," and "sweet," (see (4a)) or of "worn" and "dull" (see (4b)) only, or of "worn" (see (4c)):

(4) a.

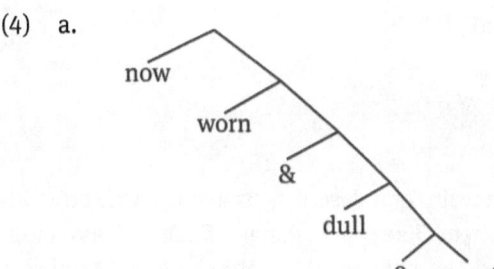

b.

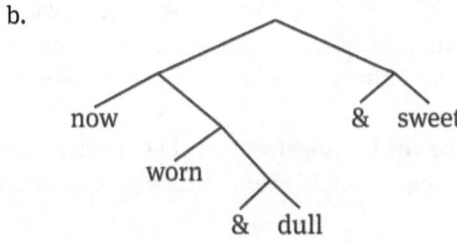

c.

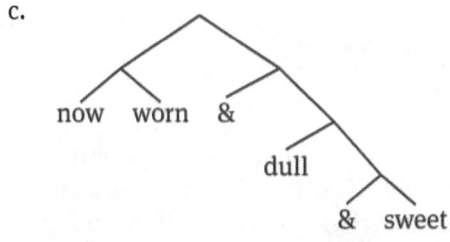

Another case of a structural ambiguity which, we assume, can be crucial for the overall interpretation of the poem is the one in (5) below, taken from Dickinson's "A Bird came down the Walk –" (J328/Fr359).[3]

---

3 Here, we refer to Miller (1987), who calls this phenomenon "syntactic doubling" (37). Ferlazzo (1976) discusses the ambiguity and concludes that "[i]t would be in keeping with Dickinson's sense of economy and use of highly compressed language to have the line working in both ways at the same time" (Ferlazzo 1976, 106). For a further analysis of the poem see also Weisbuch (1975, 137f.). For an analysis of versions with different punctuation see Vendler (2010, 158f.). See also Budick (1985), who reads the poem in a Christian context; she frames the syntactic ambiguity as "purposefully vague" (64) and as a recreation of a communion experience.

(5)   He stirred his Velvet Head

        Like one in danger, Cautious,
        I offered him a Crumb

In this poem, the speaker observes a bird and describes its actions. One possibility to read the passage above is to treat "like one in danger, Cautious" as a modifier within the sentence "He stirred his velvet head." In this reading, "cautious" modifies "He" (the bird) in the preceding line. However, a structurally equally plausible interpretation, encouraged by the stanza break, is one where the phrases modify the subject "I," where "Like one in danger" is a modifier within the sentence "I offered him a Crumb." The two readings are paraphrased in (6):

(6) a. He was cautious and like one in danger when I offered him a crumb.
    b. I was cautious and like one in danger when I offered him a crumb.

As a last example of structural ambiguity, consider the first two lines of "Who never wanted – Maddest Joy" (J1430/Fr1447):

(7)   Who never wanted – maddest Joy
        Remains to him unknown –

The structural interpretation of the relative clause "who never wanted" is dependent on the arguments that "wanted" selects; it can either be the object, such that "maddest joy" is the subject of the sentence, or it is the subject:

(8) a. Maddest joy remains unknown to (the person) who never wanted.
    b. (The person) who never wanted maddest joy remains unknown to him.

In (8a), "want" is interpreted as intransitive, i.e. "to be lacking or missing" (*OED* "want, *v.*" I.2.a.). With this structure, the sentence can be paraphrased such that the person who does not lack anything will not experience an extreme form of joy. (8b), in turn, interprets "want" as transitive, i.e. it selects a noun phrase as argument, such that the person who never had the desire to experience an extreme form of joy remains unknown to a third person "him."

The examples show that structural ambiguity systematically creates complex sentence meaning. Grammar, however, restricts which structures are possible, and consequently which interpretations are (linguistically) plausible. The options left open by local structural ambiguity are telling, since they often correlate with the global interpretative possibilities a text offers, as we have seen in Part I.[4]

1.2.2 Ellipsis

Dickinson frequently uses elliptical and fragmentary structures to create ambiguity. In these cases, ambiguity arises because there are multiple ways to resolve the ellipsis.[5] Ellipsis is subject to an identity condition (e.g. Johnson 2001), which says that the elided parts must be identical to an antecedent in the structure (see the appendix for details of the notation):

(9)

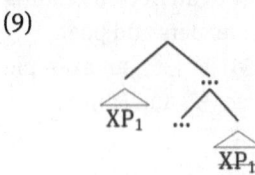

Here, the elided structure in (9), "XP₁" has to be identical with its antecedent. In Dickinson's poetry, the antecedent is often missing, which allows for more interpretative freedom. Moreover, we find cases where more than one antecedent qualifies to "fill the gap."

As we have seen in chapter I.4, line 14 of "This was a Poet" (J448/Fr446A) is elliptical (see a simplified structure in (11)):

(10)   The Robbing – could not harm –
       Himself – to Him – a Fortune

---

[4] An overview of additional examples of structural ambiguities can be found in the table at the end of the chapter.
[5] On ambiguity and ellipsis see, e.g., Winkler (2005); Bauer et. al. (2009); Konietzko and Winkler (2010); and Winter-Froemel and Zirker (2015).

(11)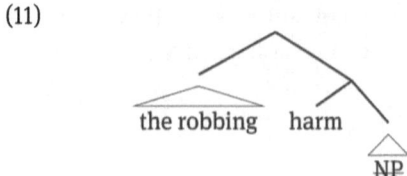

It is not clear who the object of "harm" could be. The preceding text makes two antecedents available: either the poet, or the referents for "we," which we refer to as "the readers." As discussed in detail in chapter I.4, the elided object of "harm" interacts with the question of who has done the robbing and who is being robbed. Thus, most plausibly, either the robbing harms the poet, or it harms the readers of the poem; this ambiguity contributes to an overall reading of the text that suggests a reciprocal relationship between readers and poet.

In the poem "I found the words to every thought" (J581/Fr436), an example of noun ellipsis after "your own" in line 6 can be found (see (12) and (13)):[6]

(12)   I found the words to every thought
         I ever had – but One –
         And that – defies me –
         As a Hand did try to chalk the Sun

         To Races – nurtured in the Dark –
         How would your own – begin?
         Can Blaze be shown in Cochineal –
         Or Noon – in Mazarin?

(13)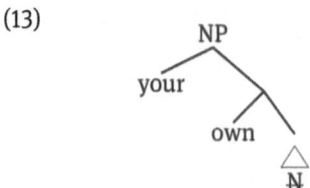

---

6 For further analyses see Wardrop (1996, 160f.; also stressing the ambiguity of "own"); Freedman (2011, 4-6); and Cameron (1981, 193f.).

The most prominent noun in the preceding discourse is "Hand"; accordingly, one plausible way of resolving the ellipsis would be "How would your own hand begin?" As the topic of the poem is finding words to every thought, another possibility is "How would your own thought begin?" As another ellipsis follows after "begin" – with an underspecification as to which event is to "begin" – the lines become enigmatic. The poem becomes even more complicated as it initially addresses the problem of finding words, but from line 4 onwards the process of writing is compared to painting. It would hence be possible to fill the ellipsis after "own" with "how would your own hand begin to paint/write," or to even fill it with a nominalised verb: "how would your own painting/writing begin?" If line 5 is taken to continue from line 4, then it should read "how would your own hand begin to chalk the sun to races that have never seen it?" In this case "hand" could also stand metonymically for the act of painting or writing; in one specific reading, if we consider poetry as an overall theme, this metonymy extends to "handwriting": how could you yourself (as a poet) paint something (with words) that your readers have never seen? The poem here becomes iconic of what it describes: the two ellipses point towards the speaker's inability to find words to express one particular thought and mirror this lack through the syntax.

The last example of ellipsis discussed here is again taken from Dickinson's "A Bird came down the Walk" (J328/Fr359):

(14)   A Bird came down the Walk –
        He did not know I saw –

We set aside a reading of "see" as an intransitive verb for now,[7] and assume that "see" is used transitively and that, hence, the phrase is elliptical. In its transitive use, "see" can either take a noun or a whole clause as its direct object. In the poem, the elided structure after the verb "saw" could, at first glance, either be just the pronoun "him," which would make it a case of argument ellipsis; or it could be that a clause ("him coming down the walk") was elided.

(15)   a. He did not know I saw him.
        b. He did not know I saw him coming down the walk.

---

[7] If "see" is intransitive, we do not require the assumption that some part of the structure was elided. We will return to this when discussing the subcategorisation frame of verbs as a separate phenomenon below.

A number of the bird's actions are described in the following lines, and the resolution of the ellipsis has an impact on how to interpret these lines. If the elided part is assumed to be the argument "him," it might be that the bird is not aware that he is being watched throughout the whole poem. However, if it is the CP that is elided, then the bird might not have known that the speaker saw him coming, yet is aware of being watched after that. Both options are possible since it remains uncertain whether there is any type of recognition of the speaker on the side of the bird. The poems analysed show that ellipsis is used systematically by Dickinson to create interpretative freedom. However, she provides us with a limited number of distinct options (not randomness of interpretation).[8]

So far, we have mainly supplemented Miller's (1987) analysis of structural ambiguities in Dickinson's poetry. The following phenomena will go further in describing how Emily Dickinson not only uses syntactic phenomena, but also semantic and pragmatic ones to create ambiguity. We hence view the following sections in particular as an important extension of Miller's work.

1.3 Semantics

1.3.1 Lexical Ambiguity

Dickinson intentionally uses lexical ambiguity to create interpretative openness. An example of lexical ambiguity is (16): the lexical item comes with several lexical entries (i.e. plausible meanings).

(16) a. $[\![bank_1]\!] = \lambda x.\ x$ is a financial institution
    b. $[\![bank_2]\!] = \lambda x.\ x$ is a riverbank

One example of lexical ambiguity is presented in chapter I.1: in "To pile like Thunder" (J1247/Fr1353), it remains to be specified what it means to "prove" love or poetry in line 6:

(17)   This – would be Poetry –

        Or Love – the two coeval come –
        We both and neither prove –
        Experience either and consume –
        For None see God and live –

---

[8] More examples can be found in the table at the end of this chapter.

The interpretative choice for "prove" makes quite a difference as to the overall interpretation of the poem,[9] since it is not just about the relationship between love and poetry but also about "our" relationship towards both or either of them (see chapter I.1). The two lexical entries are given below:

(18)   ⟦prove₁⟧ = λy. λx. x presents logical reasoning for y

(19)   ⟦prove₂⟧ = λy. λx. x's existence is (implicit) proof of y

In "He fumbles at your Soul" (J315/Fr477), Dickinson resorts to the homophonous word "still" in the last line, which is ambiguous on a structural as well as on a semantic level.[10]

(20)   When Winds take Forests in their Paws –
         The Universe – is still –

Semantically, "still" could be an adjective meaning either "silent" (going together with the homonym "paws"/acoustic "pause" in the previous line) or "motionless," or an adverb meaning "continually," or "up to this point":

(21)   ⟦still₁⟧ = λx. x is silent

(22)   ⟦still₂⟧ = λx. x is motionless

(23)   ⟦still₃⟧ = λt. [λP$_{<i,t>}$: P is true at a time interval immediately preceding t. P is true at time t.]

Structurally, "is" could be either an auxiliary verb that has to be combined with an NP complement ("The Universe is motionless/silent"), going along with the two lexical entries in (21) and (22). Alternatively, "is" could be a full verb complemented by an adverb ("The Universe continually, up to this point exists"), or "is still" could be a case of ellipsis ("The Universe is still ...") where it is not further specified what exactly the universe is. The latter options require the lexical entry in (23).

---

9 For further reading see McIntosh (2000, 109f.), and for a detailed reading of this poem see Miller (1987, 126-30), as well as Bauer et al. (2010).
10 For some other ambiguities in this poem see Leiter (2007, 86f.). For a detailed reading of the poem see Miller (1987, 113-18) and Weisbuch (1975, 98f.).

In "Life, and Death and Giants –" (J706/Fr777), we find the same homophony in interaction with a structural ambiguity:

(24)   Life, and Death, and Giants –
         Such as These – are still
         Minor – Apparatus – Hopper of the Mill –
         Beetle at the Candle –
         Or a Fife's Fame –
         Maintain – by Accident that they proclaim –

"Still" can be interpreted along the lines of (21) or (22). These readings each interact with a structure where "still" ends the first sentence and "minor apparatus" is the subject of a second sentence. In the third case, "still" is interpreted as a particle further modifying "Minor Apparatus," such that "Beetle at the Candle" is the subject of the second sentence. Three possible readings arise from this:

(25)   a. Life, and Death, and Giants are motionless
       b. Life, and Death, and Giants exist continually
       c. Life, and Death, and Giants are still a minor apparatus

Accordingly, the first two readings focus on the nature of life and death and giants, while the third reading sets them in a bigger context.

A special case of lexical ambiguity is the figurative sense words may have in addition to their core or literal meaning. An ambiguity of this sort appears in the first stanza of "My Life had stood" (J754/Fr764)[11] where "carry away" might be understood in the literal sense as transporting something or someone to another location, or in the figurative sense as being emotionally overwhelming (cf. chapter I.6).

(26)   The Owner passed – identified –
         And carried Me away

(27)   ⟦carry away₁⟧ = λx. [λy. [λl. y transports x from l]]

---

[11] For interpretations of this poem, see e.g. Miller (1987, 122-126); Benfrey (2002, 44f.); Weisbuch (1975, 25-39); Vendler (2010, 318-22); and Bauer et al. (2015). Faderman (1998, 203) calls it the "most discussed and debated of all Dickinson poems." Lists of different interpretations can be found in Leiter (2007, 258-72); and Freeman (1998, 271n18).

(28)   ⟦carry away₂⟧ = λx. [λy. y overwhelms x emotionally]

The ambiguity of "carried Me away" in (26) adds to the global ambiguity of the speaker being either human or a gun. When the speaker is understood to be a gun, a literal carrying by the owner is more plausible. However, if the speaker is a person comparing herself to a gun, assuming a figurative meaning of "carry away" becomes more prominent.

A parallel example can also be observed in "Empty my Heart, of Thee –" (J587/Fr393). In this poem, the figurative meaning of "heart" as "the seat or repository of a person's inmost thoughts, feelings, inclinations, etc.; a person's inmost being; the depths of the soul; the soul, the spirit" (*OED* "heart, *n.*" 6.a.) is so conventionalised that it even seems to be preferred at the beginning of the poem. However, as soon as the reader moves on to the second line, the actual physical heart again becomes plausible:

(29)   Empty my Heart, of Thee –
          Its single Artery –
          Begin, and Leave Thee out –
          Simply Extinction's Date –

1.3.2 Reinterpretation

Lexical expressions sometimes have selectional restrictions that determine what kind of arguments they can or cannot combine with. Consider once more the following entries for the first lines of "My Life had stood – a Loaded Gun –" (J754/Fr764):

(30)   My Life had stood – a Loaded Gun –
          In Corners – till a Day

(31)   ⟦stand⟧ = λe. [λx. [λy: y is a physical object that has a vertical dimension. y is in location x in e and y is vertically oriented in e]]

(32)   ⟦my life⟧ = the unique x s.t. x belongs to S and x is a life

As we have seen in detail in chapter I.6, the selectional restriction for "stand in corners" states that the argument has to be a physical object, while a pronoun like "I" or "my" specifies the speaker as human (see (31) and (32)). We have seen that it is necessary to reinterpret either "stand in corners" or "my life," as the combination is undefined.

A similar reinterpretation is necessary in "There's a certain Slant of light," (J258/Fr320):

(33)   When it comes, the landscape listens –
        Shadows – hold their breath –

Both "listen" and "hold one's breath" require a human subject. "Landscape" and "shadow" entail that they are defined as nonhuman (see the lexical entries below):

(34)   ⟦landscape⟧ = λx. x is a landscape

(35)   ⟦shadows⟧ = λx. x is a shadow

(36)   ⟦listen⟧ = λx: x is human. x listens

(37)   ⟦hold one's breath⟧ = λx: x is human. x holds x's breath

The pronoun "it" here most likely refers to "a certain Slant of light": we can either reinterpret "landscape" and "shadow" as personified, such that they have human traits; or we can reinterpret "listen" and "hold one's breath" to cancel the selectional restriction and generalise the meaning of the verbs:

(38)   a. The landscape (with human traits) listens and shadows (with human traits) hold their breaths.
        b. The landscape (in the sense of flora and fauna) is silent, does not give a sound, and shadows do not move.

Again, only a combination of both options seems to capture the intended meaning adequately. Another example is the verb "fumble" in (39) (J315/Fr477):

(39)   He fumbles at your Soul

The presupposition of "fumble" that requires a physical object as argument is encoded in the lexical entry of "fumble," which is given in (40a). Similar to the example taken from "My Life had stood" above, reinterpreting "fumble" depends on the interpretation of "soul": it is either interpreted as an immaterial concept or as a personification. One possibility is to give "fumble" a more general interpretation which allows it to combine with an immaterial interpretation of "soul," as in (40b).

(40) a. ⟦fumble⟧ = λa: a is a physical object. [λb. b clumsily touches a]
b. ⟦fumble⟧ = λa. [λb. b affects a in a sort of roundabout way]

The literal meaning of "fumble," in turn, can combine with an interpretation of a personified "soul." The choice and combination of words create an awareness of the interpretation process itself. Similar to the ambiguity in "My life had stood" of the speaker either being a human being or a gun, the ambiguity of "soul" either being an immaterial concept or a personified entity that can have material traits interacts with the reinterpretation possibilities of "fumble."[12]

1.4 Context-Dependent Expressions

Dickinson also works with ambiguities that are derived from the inherent context-dependency of certain lexical items. These include quantifiers like "some," "no," and "every," modal verbs like "may" and "must," as well as pronouns and presupposition triggers like the definite article "the." In the following, we will consider first how Emily Dickinson uses quantifiers that evoke seeming contradictions which are then resolved through their context-dependent elements. In a second section, we will analyse phenomena that require specific referents within the context, such as pronouns and the definite article.

1.4.1 Resolution of Contradiction

Linguistic theory assumes that the meaning of a modal verb like "may" or a quantifier like "every" is dependent on restrictions further specified by the con-

---

[12] Furthermore, we have seen a radical example of reinterpretation in "I'm Nobody!" (J288/Fr260, see chapter I.3), where the quantifier "nobody" has to be reinterpreted. This reinterpretation is not necessary because of selectional restrictions, but rather because the semantic types of subject and predicate do not match. An overview of additional examples of reinterpretation can be found in the table at the end of the chapter.

text.[13] This dependence in the case of quantifiers is modelled as a silent domain variable C whose value is to be determined by context:

(41) a. No student passed.
b. ⟦No⟧ = λC$_{<e,t>}$. [λP$_{<e,t>}$. [λQ$_{<e,t>}$. it is not the case that there is an x, such that C(x) and P(x) and Q(x)]]
c. ⟦No⟧^{g} (⟦C⟧^{g}) (⟦student⟧^{g}) (⟦passed⟧^{g}) = 1 iff it is not the case that there is an x such that g(C)(x) and x is a student and x passed

The formula does not specify a value for C. C is interpreted by the variable assignment function g which is also responsible for the interpretation of pronouns. Let us assume that Prof. Schmidt utters the sentence in (41a) about the class she teaches. Applying the variable assignment function g to C would be the set of individuals in Prof. Schmidt's class; that is:

(42)   ⟦C⟧^{g} = g(C) = λx. x takes Prof. Schmidt's class

As we have seen in chapter I.1 and I.6 (see also the appendix), modals are inherently context-dependent as well. They are assumed to be quantifiers over possible worlds. Similarly to "no" above, the accessibility relation restricts the quantification:

(43)   ⟦must⟧ = λR$_{<s,<s,t>>}$. [λp$_{<s,t>}$. [λw. ∀w' [(R)(w)(w') → p(w')]]]

(44)   John must be in class.

For example, when uttering (44), we might be talking about an epistemic accessibility relation, where we have evidence in the actual world that John is in class (we know that he is not at home and he usually has class at the time of utterance):

(45)   ⟦R⟧^{g} = g(R) = λw. [λw'. w' adheres to the facts known in w]

The interpretation of (44) is (46).

---

13 We have seen above that contradictions can also be resolved through lexical ambiguity, as e.g. in "To pile like Thunder" (chapter I.1), where only two lexically discrete entries of the verb "prove" solves the contradiction by revealing the syntactic structure of a zeugma.

(46) ∀w' [w' adheres to the facts known in @ → John is in class in w']

The domain restriction is crucial in chapter I.6 in the example from "My Life had stood – a Loaded Gun –" (J754/Fr764). A change of the domain restriction has to be assumed for two different quantifiers in order to make the two sentences non-contradictory:

(47) Though I than He – may longer live
      He longer must – than I –

The interpretation and paraphrase for (47) are given in (48) and (49):

(48) ∃w [R$_1$(@)(w) & lifespan(w)(S) > lifespan(w)(O)] &
      ∀w [R$_2$(@)(w) → lifespan(w)(O) > lifespan(w)(S)]

(49) It is possible that I live longer than he, and it is necessary that he live longer than I.

If the accessibility relation is the same for the two modals "may" and "must," we get a contradiction: it is not possible that all relevant worlds are such that his life extends beyond mine and that there is a world in which my life extends beyond his. However, if we suppose, for example, that the natural facts are that I might live longer than he, but my desires are that he must live longer than I, there is no contradiction anymore. Two different accessibility relations underlie this interpretation option:

(50) a. R$_1$ = λw. [λw'. in w' the same facts hold as in w]
      b. R$_2$ = λw. [λw'. in w', what the speaker desires in w is the case]

The variability of R interacts with the two lines of interpretation that linger in the poem (see a more refined analysis in chapter I.6, section 6.5).

Another example of Dickinson's play with covert contextual restrictions on modals and quantifiers which can resolve an apparent contradiction can be found in "There's a certain Slant of light" (J258/Fr320):[14]

---

[14] For additional comments on this poem see Weisbuch (1975, 81); Leiter (2007, 197-99); Vendler (2010, 126-29); and Spear (1998, 283f.).

(51)   There's a certain Slant of light,
         Winter Afternoons –
         That oppresses, like the Heft
         Of Cathedral Tunes –

         Heavenly Hurt, it gives us –
         We can find no scar,
         But internal difference,
         Where the Meanings, are –

         None may teach it – Any –
         [...]

The use of the quantifiers "none" and "any" in interaction with the modal "may" in line 9 allow for several interpretative options. A plausible structural analysis of line 9 in (51) assumes a second VP to have been elided after "any" (since this version satisfies the identity condition on ellipsis as explained above). The underlying structure with the reconstructed VP is given in (52):

(52)   None may teach it – Any [may teach it].

It is plausible to assume that both quantifiers range over people, due to the verb "teach," whose objects and subjects usually are human.[15] Moreover, the pronoun "it" in the last line in (51) most likely refers to "a certain Slant of light." To discuss possible restrictions for both quantifiers we first look at the interpretation of the two sentences "No one may teach it" and "Anyone may teach it."[16]

(53) a. No one teaches it.
      b. 'There is no x such that x is a person and x is in C and x teaches it'

---

[15] "Teach" can, in principle, also be used to refer to nonhuman subjects (and objects), as in "the accident taught me to be more careful." However, in combination with "none" and "any," which, without further context, we would interpret as referring to people, an interpretation of "teach" as a human activity is most plausible here.

[16] Farr identifies a different reading: "There is probably a characteristic Dickinsonian play on words in her 'Any,' which suggests 'None may teach it – Any[thing]" as well as "None [not any one] may teach it" (Farr 1992, 264), but does not make anything else of the ambiguity; according to McClure Smith, the ambiguity of this line and of one later in the poem "involve[s] the reader in a process of syntactic separation, reconnection, and eventual acceptance of indivisibility" (McClure Smith 1996, 101).

(54) a. Anyone teaches it.
     b. 'For every y such that y is a person and y is in C, y teaches it'

"May" as opposed to "must" is a possibility modal: it existentially quantifies over possible worlds.[17] Different from the epistemic accessibility relation for "must" in (45), we assume a deontic accessibility relation of "may" here, where the evaluation world and the worlds evoked by the modal are similar with regard to the laws in the evaluation world:

(55)   ⟦may⟧ = $\lambda R_{<s,<s,t>}$. [$\lambda p_{<s,t>}$. [λw. $\exists w'$ [(R)(w)(w') & p(w')]]]

(56)   R = λw. [$\lambda w'$. w' adheres to the same laws as w]

With the deontic reading of the modal "may," the interpretation of the two sentences in (51) looks as follows:

(57) a. [no one₁ [may [t₁ teach it]]]
     b. There is no person x such that g(C)(x) and there is a world w' in which the laws of w are observed and in which x teaches it.

(58) a. [anyone₂ [may [t₂ teach it]]]
     b. For every person x such that g(C)(x), there is a world w' in which the laws of w are observed and in which x teaches it.

The paraphrases make it clear that the two sentences are contradictory. The first sentence in (57) states that there is no one for whom it is possible (according to laws and rules) to teach "it," whereas the second sentence in (58) states that it is possible for everyone to teach "it" in some world that is in accordance with laws in the actual world. However, through the domain restriction C, which is not made explicit in the poem, we can avoid the contradiction. It is possible to come to a coherent interpretation of both sentences with a deontic reading of "may" if one considers different restrictions for the two quantifiers. For example, since the poem is about "a certain Slant of light" and the experience of it, one might imagine that one of the quantifiers quantifies over people that have had the experience, whereas the other quantifier quantifies over people that have not had that experience – that is, to assume two different domain restrictions C for

---

17 This is similar to the existential quantifier "some," which existentially quantifies over individuals.

the quantifiers "no one" and "anyone." Moreover, one could assume that the quantifiers quantify over the same people before and after the experience, respectively. A paraphrase of a deontic reading of the two sentences under these assumptions is given in (59).

(59)   No person who has not yet experienced the slant of light is allowed to teach it. Every person who has experienced the slant of light is allowed to teach it.

The superficial contradiction that arises in the two sentences is hence not meant to lead to uninterpretability but is used by Dickinson to make us aware of the inherent context-dependency of quantifiers. It forces the reader to consider two different domain restrictions.

1.4.2 Reference

Another grammatical feature often exploited by Dickinson to create varying interpretations is the use of referential expressions such as pronouns and definite descriptions without proper referents.

As discussed in chapter I.5, the pronoun "it" is used right at the beginning of poem J921/Fr184A and therefore lacks a linguistic referent:[18]

(60)   If it$_1$ had no pencil,
         Would it try mine –

From a grammatical point of view, an appropriate use of these pronouns requires an antecedent that is present in the context (cf. Heim & Kratzer 1998, 243; see also chapters I.4 and I.5 and the appendix). In poetry, there is no immediate context available. The use of referential expressions like pronouns without reference forces the reader to acquire additional information about the referent in order to contemplate options for how to interpret the pronoun, as we have argued in chapters I.4 and I.5. Dickinson exploits this fact. In chapters I.4 and I.5, we made use of a dynamic interpretation system. Accordingly, the meaning of (60) would be the following (ignoring the conditional question for now):

---

[18] The possibility of "it" being used cataphorically is excluded in the poem because, even after the pronoun has been used, no referent is introduced. This is the case also for the following examples.

(61)   λg. g(1) does not have a pencil and g(1) would use S's pencil

In this example, the reader gathers further information about "it" throughout the poem, e.g. that if "it" did not have a pencil, it would use the speaker's; and if "it" had no word, it would make the Daisy almost as big as the speaker and so on. The meaning of the text is the conjunction of all sentence meanings, which are now functions from possible variable assignments to truth values (like (61)). Hence, enough information about the variable can be gathered to restrict the text meaning to plausible variable assignments.

Another example is the poem "He fumbles at your Soul" (J315/Fr477), in which the pronoun "he" is also used at the beginning without a linguistically accessible referent:[19] in the case of (62), the reader has to assume that there is some "he" who has the property of "fumbling at your Soul." In a dynamic framework, the information conveyed by (62) is (63).

(62)   He$_2$ fumbles at your Soul

(63)   λg. g(2) fumbles at A's soul

The reader goes on and accumulates information about "he." The reader could, for example, add the information that "he stuns you by degrees" to her knowledge about the referent of "he" when continuing to read the poem.

(64)   He$_2$ stuns you by degrees –

(65)   λg. g(2) stuns A by degrees

(66)   Combining (63) and (65):
         λg. g(2) fumbles at A's soul & g(2) stuns A by degrees

After having added each sentence given in the poem, the reader's pragmatic interpretation may choose a specific variable assignment that provides a value for the pronoun.

---

[19] Juhasz asks: "Is He lover? Muse? God? Death? It's hard to tell, because the experience described, what the 'He' does to the 'you,' could be sex, creativity, salvation, or dying. An all-powerful force descends upon a subject, whose experience of and with this force appears both terrifying and transcendent" (Juhasz et al. 1993, 53). Some critics, e.g. Small (1990, 108) and Phillips (1988, 180), draw attention to the fact that "He" has been variously read as a reference to Reverend Charles Wadsworth.

For each reader, a different value might fulfil the properties that characterise "he" in the poem. Thus, at a global level, the reader assigns a specific assignment function as an argument of the dynamic text meaning and thus arrives at a specific referent. This could be an individual referent for each reader. However, all referents and variable assignment functions have to fulfil the information given within the text about the referent.

Dickinson also uses plural pronouns in a similar way to the examples above, as can be seen in "I'm ceded – I've stopped being Theirs –" (J508/Fr353A):

(67) I'm ceded – I've stopped being Theirs –
      The name They dropped upon my face
      With water, in the country church
      Is finished using, now,
      And They can put it with my Dolls,
      [...]

Similar to "If it had no pencil" (J921/Fr184A) and "He fumbles at your soul," (J315/Fr477) Dickinson starts out the poem with using the plural pronoun "Theirs." Throughout the poem, the reader can gather information about this group of people. A reader's pragmatic interpretation may depend on the values chosen for the referents. This is another mechanism by which Dickinson creates interpretive freedom.

1.4.3 Presuppositions

Presuppositions (PSPs) are another phenomenon at the semantics-pragmatics interface which Dickinson exploits. As we have discussed in the course of this book, presuppositions are felicity conditions, i.e. conditions that have to be met in the context for a sentence to be interpretable. Presuppositions hence help restrict plausible interpretations, since they narrow down possibilities of what the context is like, but they are also responsible for flexibility in interpretation. If the information conveyed by the presupposition is not explicitly given in the context, the reader has to **accommodate** the missing information. Accommodation is a very complex process, but the general idea behind it is that hearers take the presupposition to hold when it is not explicitly verified or falsified by the context (see, e.g. chapter I.5 for presupposition accommodation in more detail, and especially the appendix). However, accommodation is not freely available and depends on the expression that triggers the presupposition as well as the context.

Similar to the various examples of the uniqueness presupposition of definites (e.g. "the owner" in "My Life had stood," see chapter I.6; or "the robbing" in "This was a Poet," see chapter I.4), the poem "My wheel is in the dark!" (J10/Fr61) has various presuppositions that have to be accommodated: first, the possessive pronoun "my" is used twice; and, second, a definite description is used that does not easily allow for accommodation:

(68)   My wheel is in the dark!
        I cannot see a spoke
        [...]
        My foot is on the Tide!
        An unfrequented road –
        [...]
        Some have resigned the Loom –
        Some in the busy tomb
        Find quaint employ –
        Some with new – stately feet –
        Pass royal through the gate –
        Flinging the problem back
        At you and I!

The possessive definite descriptions "My wheel" and "My foot" both presuppose, respectively, that there is a unique wheel and a unique foot that the speaker possesses. While it is quite straightforward to assume that the speaker has a foot, as long as she is human, it is less straightforward to accommodate the fact that the speaker possesses a wheel. What complicates the accommodation process further is that we could either interpret "wheel" figuratively such that the wheel stands for the speaker's fortune or course of life.

Additionally, several points complicate the search for the unique referent that the definite NP "the problem" in the last stanza requires:

(69)   ⟦the problem⟧ = the unique x such that x is a problem

The verb "flinging" is used in the gerund in the penultimate line, and it hence remains underspecified who "flings the problem." Even though it is the most prominent interpretation to refer "flinging back" to those who "pass royal through the gate" (since it is the nearest VP), it is also possible that "flinging the problem back" refers to all three sets of people mentioned before (those who pass royal through the gate together with those who resign the loom and those who find quaint employ). Even if one decides in favour of one of these options, it remains unclear what exactly "the problem" is. One might consider the people in all three sets mentioned to be at the end of their journey, which, when considering a journey of life, would be equivalent to their death (or, rather, to different fates in death). Further assuming that "you" and "I" are still alive, among other options, "the problem" could be life itself, which is still a problem for those alive but not those who are dead (this raises the question why life itself should be taken to be problematic). It becomes clear that the search for a referent of definite NPs like "the problem," "My wheel" is challenging.

Another example of a definite Noun Phrase is "the lawful Heir"[20] in "Defrauded I a Butterfly" (J730/Fr850):

(70)   Defrauded I a Butterfly –
       The lawful Heir – for Thee –

To find a referent here is also a challenge but for different reasons than in the previous examples. Instead of a lack of presupposed information, the poem, which only contains these two lines, allows for two referents for "The lawful Heir": either the speaker or the butterfly. This is possible because of the interaction of "the lawful Heir" with the ambiguity of the first line as illustrated in (71):

(71)   a.   Defrauded I a butterfly?
       b.   I defrauded a butterfly
       c.   I am a defrauded butterfly

Going along with (71a) and (71b), the heir is most likely the butterfly and the speaker took the inheritance away from the butterfly. With a structure as in (71c), the speaker, who happens to be a butterfly, has been cheated of her inheritance but is "The lawful Heir." Thus, the presupposition triggered by "the" is fulfilled by "butterfly" in both cases. The different readings arise because the

---

20 "Heir" is a relational Noun Phrase as indicated below:
$[\![heir]\!] = \lambda x. [\lambda y.\ x \text{ is the heir of } y]$
In the poem, "Heir" remains semantically underspecified regarding its arguments. The only information about what the inheritance is made of is given through "for Thee": the addressee is the one giving out the inheritance or rather assigning an heir.

butterfly and the speaker can be identical as in (71c) or two different individuals as in (71a) and (71b).

Our examples show that pronouns and presuppositions are used by Dickinson systematically. Both create interpretative flexibility but also narrow down possible interpretations by asking the reader to reconstruct the context. Pronouns without determined referents allow for information about them to be accumulated, but semantics does not fix their referents. Similarly, presuppositions invite inferences about the context which both guides interpretation and leaves some leeway. These phenomena are at the interface between semantics (text meaning) and pragmatics (contextual meaning).

1.5 Conclusion

We have provided a systematic overview of linguistic phenomena that Emily Dickinson uses and exploits often throughout her work. Considering the complex interaction in Dickinson's poetry of all the phenomena just outlined, our claim is confirmed that there is a recurring pattern of how linguistic phenomena from the syntactic, semantic and pragmatic components of linguistic knowledge are used: it is not only the case that Emily Dickinson's poems contain ambiguity, but that this ambiguity is strategic, and establishes a complex structure where a limited number of interpretations arise at the global level of text. This multiplicity of interpretation is achieved through using linguistic mechanisms that are simultaneously restrictive, i.e. determined by grammar to some extent, and flexible. In the pragmatic step these interpretations may be related to each other, for example by disjunction (e.g. "My Life had stood," chapter I.6) or conjunction (e.g. chapters I.1-I.5). The reader not only establishes in which way the interpretations are similar, but also in which relation they stand to the evaluation world of the reader.

In our approach to identifying the semantics of the texts, grammar has taken centre stage. This chapter has shown that our strategy is justified. Emily Dickinson's use of the grammar to create a well-defined interpretive freedom, first at sentence level, then extending to text level, is systematic and pervasive. It occurs at critical junctures in the interpretation of her poems, making it the key to unlocking text meaning. We have not overanalysed the grammatical peculiarities of her poems. Rather, they are the defining property of her poetry. Emily Dickinson as a poet is revealed to be an intuitive linguist: her main tool to convey complex meanings lies within a linguistic analytic approach to language and text. Consequently, in order for readers to understand Emily Dickinson's poetry, it is necessary to also approach her work through linguistic analysis.

Tab. 1: Overview

Phenomena	Examples in II.1	Examples in Part I
Structural Ambiguity	Worn – **now** – and *dull* – sweet, (J921/Fr184; chapter I.5)	We wonder it was not Ourselves **Arrested** it – before – (chapter I.4)
	Like one in danger, **Cautious**, (J328/ Fr359)	To pile like Thunder to its close Then **crumble** grand away (chapter I.1)
	Who never **wanted** – maddest Joy (J1430/Fr1447)	The Owner passed – **identified** – (chapter I.6)
Ellipsis	The **Robbing** – could not harm – (J448/ Fr446; chapter I.4)	Experience either **and consume** – (chapter I.1)
	How would **your own** – begin? (J581/ Fr436)	Tall – like the Stag – **would that?** (chapter I.2)
	He did not know I **saw** – (J328/ Fr359)	He longer must – **than I** – (chapter I.6)
Lexical Ambiguity	We both and neither **prove** – (J1247/Fr1353; chapter I.1)	**Experience** either and **consume** – (chapter I.1)
	The Universe – is **still** – (J315/ Fr477)	
	Such as These – are **still** – (J706/Fr777)	
	The Owner passed – identified – And **carried Me away** – (J754/Fr764; chapter I.6)	
	Empty **my Heart,** of Thee – (J587/Fr393)	
Reinterpretation	**My Life had stood** – a Loaded Gun – (J754/Fr764; chapter I.6)	**Distills** amazing sense (chapter I.4)
	He **fumbles** at your Soul (J315/ Fr477)	[...] I **speak** for Him – (chapter I.6)

Conclusion

Phenomena	Examples in II.1	Examples in Part I
	[...] the Landscape listens – Shadows – hold their breath – (J258/Fr320)	The **Mountains** straight **reply** – (chapter I.6)
Contradiction	Though I than He – **may** longer live He longer **must** – than I – (J754/Fr764; chapter I.6)	We **both and neither** prove – (chapter I.1)
	None may teach it – **Any** – (J258/Fr320)	
Reference	If **it** had no pencil (J921/Fr184; chapter I.5)	**This** was a Poet – It is **That** (chapter I.4)
	He fumbles at your Soul (J315/Fr477)	**This** – would be Poetry – (chapter I.1)
	[...] I've stopped being **Theirs** – (J508/Fr353)	
Presuppositions	**My wheel** is in the dark! (J10/Fr61)	The **Robbing** – could not harm – (chapter I.4)
	Flinging **the problem** back (J10/Fr61)	Would it make **the Daisy,** (chapter I.5)
	The lawful Heir – for Thee – (J730/Fr850)	

II.2 The Linguist as Poet

2.1 Introduction

While in the first part of this book we have been focusing on specific linguistic phenomena and their contribution to the interpretation of the poems in which they occur, the second part serves to synthesize our findings. Thus we could show in chapter II.1 that Emily Dickinson employs the phenomena we identified systematically and strategically, a practice that proves her to be an intuitive linguist. But what is, from a literary perspective, the point of the linguistic awareness that becomes transparent in her poetry? Why does it matter so much for the meaning of her poetry that its author is consciously and wittingly concerned with language? In this chapter, we will try and answer these questions by reading her conscious use of linguistic phenomena as a poetological concept. In other words, we will consider the linguist as a poet who reflects on her own art.

Dickinson systematically uses language and exploits rules of grammar and semantics in a way that results in interpretative flexibility. In this manner, she not only makes evident the flexibility of language but also shows in how far the poet, in using language, is testing it for its possibilities. The range of possibilities itself should therefore be regarded as a feature of Dickinson's poetics. Accordingly, we will give each of the poems discussed in Part 1 another look and see in which way the different linguistic phenomena foregrounded in them contribute to a poetics of possibility. Our conclusions will then be undergirded by the discussion of a poem (J657/Fr466A) in which possibility itself is addressed as the poet's mode of existence. On the basis of our close reading, we will come to broader conclusions concerning the potential of language constituting and changing the worlds described by it.

2.2 Poetics of Possibility: A Brief Review

In Emily Dickinson's poetry, we find a number of examples that foreground linguistic reflection in a way that is hardly possible in other forms of communication. Poetry thus becomes a means to understand language better because to Emily Dickinson poetry is the form of writing in which language can best show its potential. This is one reason why the linguist turns poet. There is another one, closely related to it: **because** language itself is its topic. To make language a topic reflects on Dickinson's apparent conviction that the world – both the inner and the outside world – is accessible through language but also comes into being through language.¹ Dickinson moreover reflects on the relations of meanings; she wonders "where the meanings are" ("There's a certain Slant of light"; J258/Fr320; see chapter II.1) and wishes to "distill sense" ("This was a poet" l. 2; see chapter I.4) in a manner that is probably unique to her (see below in subsection 2.3). The role of semantics is thus to question and foreground meaning – as well as to ask how meaning is actually brought about.

We opened our analyses with "To pile like Thunder" (J1247/Fr1353) in chapter I.1, the central concern of which is a reflection about what poetry **is**. The poet seeks to give a definition of it, but her attempt to liken it to the natural occurrence of thunder piling and crumbling away is thwarted by the realization that poetry appears not by itself, but as a "coeval" companion of love. The poet's attempt at outlining their complex relationship both to each other and to us as human beings proves a logical riddle, as we have seen in our discussion of the line "we both and neither prove." Equally, the speaker's probing at a definition for poetry (and love) is thwarted by lexical underspecification, which helps the poet retain an openness of meaning, and, accordingly, a reflection on linguistic possibilities. This openness appears to be necessary, as poetry is shown to be a constitutive element of the world: not only is it coeval with love, but the final line moreover stipulates that experiencing either of them means seeing God. When the speaker makes the counterfactual statement "This would be Poetry" in a line of poetry, she plays with logic and contradiction in a manner similar to "We both and neither prove." Furthermore, if we assume the last line to mean that the experience of poetry or love has a lethal effect like seeing God, poetry is also characterized in a paradoxical manner. Regarding possibility as the nature of poetry is a way of addressing that paradox. Poetry, in this sense, is not an accessible part of the world but rather the **mode of access** to the world, as we will see later in this chapter as well.

The following poems we discuss, "You said that I 'was Great'" (J738/Fr736) and "I'm Nobody!" (J288/Fr260) in chapters I.2 and I.3 respectively, focus on the question of identity as expressed through language. Both suggest a dialogue between the speaker and an implicit addressee during which the speaker contemplates what it means to be her, either as an individual among many ("I'm Nobody"), or as regards being attributed the adjective "great" ("You said"). Her self-identification in both poems is tightly knit to a playful meditation on the full range, i.e. the possibilities of meaning, a single linguistic expression can

---

1 This statement has a religious dimension implicitly if not explicitly addressed in "If it had no pencil" (see chapter I.5).

have: in "You said," the speaker plays through the possibilities of being "great" by evoking different scales and making salient its context-dependency, as we have shown in our discussion; in "I'm Nobody," the speaker makes use of quantification mechanisms whereby she questions the self-identification of an individual in respect to one's impact in the world. Linguistic mechanisms of context-dependency are elicited through a poetic reflection of their potential but also of their shortcomings. In "I'm Nobody" we have seen that the reinterpretation of the quantifiers "nobody" and "somebody" lead to two overall readings of the text, neither of which can be upheld throughout but which need to be interacting with one another in order to achieve an overall text meaning. The poet as linguist's awareness of the properties of the quantifiers leads to linguist as poet's play on the relation of individual and property in considering possibilities of identity. The poet spins an intricate web of meaning that is steadily examined; poetry, we learn from these two poems, is uniquely capable of addressing the questions a) what language means, and b) how it means – especially when we consider its meaning and the range of possible meanings in relation to us.

In the fourth poem discussed ("This was a Poet"; J448/Fr446A), we have been concerned with the temporary suspension of the Appropriateness Condition that happens because we cannot immediately find a referent for "this" and "that" in the first line of the poem: "This was a Poet – It is That." As has been suggested above, one plausible variable assignment function could map "that" to poetry, and the same variable assignment function could map "this" to the poem itself, or to anything that the speaker regards as the product of a poet's activity. In this way, the specific linguistic awareness of the poet (i.e. how to suspend the Appropriateness Condition without becoming meaningless) serves as a means of expressing what a poet does. The point seems to be that the transformation of something short-lived into something that endures over time is not restricted to any specific item. There are many possibilities of what is being extracted and transformed but whenever amazing sense is distilled from ordinary meanings, this has been a poet's work. Similarly, as the poem goes on, the simultaneous existence of two plausible variable assignments has led us to establish a "Poet Robber" and a "Reader Robber" reading which are not mutually exclusive. In this way, Dickinson can again make a precise point about the possibilities involved in the relationship of poet and reader: each may take from the other without their feeling the loss.

The material act of writing is made a point of concern in the fifth poem in our selection of analyses, "If it had no pencil" (J921/Fr184A). This poem is different in one significant aspect: it is composed in the form of a question. The speaker pointedly asks: "If it had no pencil / Would it try mine"? Though it remains unclear who or what "it" is, the speaker presupposes that "it" does indeed have a pencil (as she does), and a "word" as well. The poem is ostensibly concerned with the creative process of writing poetry and its significance for the life of the speaker, as "it" is shown to be an overwhelming authority in its relation to her. Through the question form of the poem, Dickinson makes the inconclusiveness of her reflection a defining feature: because the poem does not give an answer to its own question, we are asked to reflect alongside the speaker and continue her thoughts even beyond the poem itself. Possibility becomes the mode of existence, one which can be probed by writing poetry, as the speaker is doing herself, and as she is implying "it" is doing, too. The poem's material form, wrapped around a pencil and sent as a gift (see chapter I.5), extralinguistically underlines this invitation to join the poet as a fellow writer, and to explore possibility in her company.

Finally, in our analysis of "My Life had stood" (J754/Fr764) we derived the combination via disjunction of a literal and a figurative reading of the poem in which the speaker is either a gun or a human being (see chapter I.6). These alternatives make us aware of Dickinson's reflecting on the poet's art of combining the literal and the figurative. As a consequence, we have arrived at a third, self-reflexive reading of the poem which intersects the other two: the poem takes note of its being in the world and of the possibilities disclosed by this mode of being. Because coercion and reinterpretation are dominant features of the text, we are alerted to the potential of reading the poem as a meditation about itself, reflecting on the possibilities that arise when language is turned into poetry. Poetry, the immortal agent of the poet, has the potential to change the world when put to work: "For I have but the power to kill, / Without – the power to die –." Language becomes the paramount mode with which to encounter the world, because it is an indissoluble part of it and lends agency to an "Owner" who would not have any without it.

Linguistic reflection, as we have seen, may be explicit in Dickinson's poems – as well as implicit. It is explicit, for instance, in poems such as J1261/Fr1268, "A Word dropped careless on a Page," or, blatantly, J276/Fr333, "Many a phrase has the English language." In J165/Fr1715A, "A Word made Flesh," it is explicit as well as implicit since the speaker reflects on her love of language, "This loved Philology," and speaks of the transformation of the word into a physical thing, flesh.[2] In many of Dickinson's poems language becomes an ontological mode, i.e. when the linguist is a poet and interacts with language as in "Shall I take thee, the Poet said / To the propounded word" (J1126/Fr1243) or the words be-

---

[2] On this poem and its biblical poetics, see Bauer (2006).

come living agents as in "A little overflowing word" (J1467/Fr1501). Overall, Dickinson's attitude as an intuitive linguist towards language is based on the assumption (perhaps even conviction) that language contains and is the world; language creates the link between speaker and world. It is therefore also a means to express relations between elements in the world as well as to try and understand them.³ Moreover, the expressivity that language provides her with enables Dickinson to not only speak of things that are but also to explore and reflect on possible worlds: she does not only write about the (actual) world, but enters a dialogue with it. Similar to the performative power of speech acts – where the utterance of a sentence allows for an alteration of states through language itself (cf. Krifka 2014) – Dickinson's poetry possesses a performative quality that "speaks" things into being. Language hence serves not merely as a means to signify and denote things but also marks difference and identity, and enables the change from one state to another. It opens up possibilities of expression, and it is in poetry that Dickinson as a linguist can best express and experiment with these possibilities.

So far, we have suggested a spectrum of individual cases showing how the mode of possibility figures in Dickinson's poetry. In order to demonstrate how Dickinson defines poetry and herself as a poet, we will analyse a poem which addresses central issues of her poetics of possibility.

2.3 "I dwell in Possibility": Dickinson's Concept of Poetry (as Flexible Use of Language and as Fiction)

The poem that best reflects Dickinson's approach of the linguist as poet is "I dwell in Possibility –" (J657/Fr466A):

1 I dwell in Possibility –
2 A fairer House than Prose –
3 More numerous of windows –
4 Superior – for Doors –

5 Of Chambers as the Cedars –
6 Impregnable of Eye –
7 And for an Everlasting Roof
8 The Gambrels of the Sky –

---

3 Chapter I.6, "My Life had stood," is a case in point: here the relationship between human beings and things is explicitly addressed and negotiated.

9	Of Visitors – the fairest –
10	For Occupation – This –
11	The spreading of my narrow Hands
12	To gather Paradise –

Whereas some critics read this poem mainly in light of Dickinson's biography and gender,[4] our focus is a somewhat different one as we consider it as an example of Dickinson reflecting on poetry as the mode of expression best suited to an author whose foremost concern is the exploration of linguistic phenomena. It offers an answer to the question why Emily Dickinson chooses to be a poet.

The poem is striking in its linguistic makeup from the beginning. The speaker writes that she "dwell[s] in Possibility." The phrase "dwell in" is usually linked to material objects; one dwells in a house or an abode (see *OED*, "dwell, v." 7.[5]). The phrase, however, also allows for other readings that are explored by Dickinson in this context as she links it with the abstract noun "possibility."[6] A full text search in the *OED* for "dwell in" gives a few results that point towards a similar use. Milton has "can envy dwell / In heavenly breasts?" (*Paradise Lost* IX, 729-30); Hooper (1757) writes: "The spirit dwells in ..."; in Southey's poem "Joan of Arc" (1796), one finds the phrase "Rather than dwell in peace"; and in the *Baptist Missionary* (1848), it appears as "the word of God must dwell in us richly." The search results show us that, in combination with a non-material noun, the phrase is ambiguous, as it may refer to 'remaining' (e.g. in peace, or in possibility) or to 'being surrounded' by something, i.e. the speaker in Dickinson's poem either remains in "Possibility" or is surrounded by it. Similar reinterpretation mechanisms are at play in "My Life had stood," where the figurative and literal meanings are equally tightly connected (see chapter I.6). Her phrase thus either means that her state of being is as yet a possible (rather than an actual) one, or that possibility is where she is actually to be found, i.e. it is her mode of existence. This double meaning of "dwell in" is expressive of the speaker's relation to poetry.

---

[4] For biographical and gender-related readings, see, for instance, Juhasz (1977, 106); Doriani (1996, 127); Wohlpart (2001).

[5] "To remain (in a house, country, etc.) as in a permanent residence; to have one's abode; to reside, 'live'. (Now mostly superseded by *live* in spoken use; but still common in literature.)"

[6] See, e.g., *OED* "dwell, v." 4.a. "To abide or continue for a time, in a place, state, or condition" and 5. "to dwell on, upon (†in): to spend time upon or linger over (a thing) in action or thought; to remain with the attention fixed on; now, *esp.* to treat at length or with insistence, in speech or writing; also, to sustain (a note) in music. (The most frequent current use in speech.)"

The relation of a dwelling-place to a linguistic utterance may have been familiar to Dickinson from Thomas Wentworth Higginson's "Letter to a Young Contributor" in the April 1862 issue of *Atlantic Monthly*, where he writes that

> There may be phrases which shall be palaces to dwell in, treasure-houses to explore; a single word may be a window from which one may perceive all the kingdoms of the earth and the glory of them. Oftentimes a word shall speak what accumulated volumes have laboured in vain to utter: there may be years of crowded passion in a word, and half a life in a sentence.[7]

The "Letter" was meant to encourage young poets, whereupon Dickinson wrote a letter of her own to Wentworth Higginson in which she enclosed four of her poems (June 1862).[8] The idea that a single phrase or word may contain a wealth of meaning for the poet to explore was quite congenial to Dickinson (cf. the aforementioned poems J276/Fr333 and J1467/Fr1501); in J657/Fr466A she integrates it into the consideration of "Possibility" as the state and dwelling-place of the poet.

She does so by literalising the metaphor of dwelling in possibility as she identifies "Possibility" with a "House" which is "fairer [...] than Prose." Through the comparison, "Possibility" becomes the antonym of "Prose" – i.e. possibility is poetry.[9] Even though this identification of poetry and possibility is presented here by a surprising inference, it is as old as poetic theory itself. According to Aristotle, it is "not the function of the poet to relate what has happened, but what may happen – what is possible according to the law of probability or necessity" (*Poetics* 1451b, trans. Butcher 1995). Possibility in this sense describes the realm of poetry.

Possibility as such is a guiding principle of Dickinson's method of working as a poet. If one looks at her poems, one finds that she often crossed out words

---

[7] See Miller's (2016) note on "I dwell"; for a full text of the "Letter," see <http://www.theatlantic.com/magazine/archive/1862/04/letter-to-a-young-contributor/305164/>.
[8] For an overview of the influence that the "Letter" had on Dickinson and her writing as well as her ensuing correspondence with Higginson, see the corresponding chapter in Ruth Miller's *The Poetry of Emily Dickinson* (1968).
[9] See Vendler (2010). Kher (1974) writes: "The windows in this fairer house of possibility are in themselves the wide open doors of poetic perception"; he goes on to note the "supernatural quality of the house of poetry" and speaks of its being "haunted" (121), without, however, giving any textual proof. – A similar concept would later appear in Henry James's preface to Portrait of a Lady (1881): "the house of fiction has not one window, but a million – a number of possible windows not to be reckoned, rather" (see Mitchell 2000, 103).

and substituted them with alternatives.[10] Her poems are never presented as fully defined and realised. Her refusal to publish in print goes along with this; critics have noted that she would rather circulate her poems in manuscript, allowing for the presentation of variants as well as autographical subtleties that cannot be achieved in the mechanical representation of print.[11] She plays with language in that she plays with graphic possibilities and semantic as well as lexical variants.

As Dickinson establishes the identity of poetry and possibility by contrasting both with prose, the poem may be read in the context of J613/Fr445: "They shut me up in Prose – / As when a little Girl / They put me in the Closet,"[12] written in the same year as "I dwell" (1862). Poetry is possibility in the sense of freedom and movement, while prose is being shut up and "still" (J613/Fr445, l. 4); Webster even gives the lexical definition "To make a tedious relation" ("Prose, *v. t.*" 2.). Here we can see what, to Dickinson, characterises poetry in comparison to other forms of utterance. At the same time, the second sense of **poetry** indicated above plays a role: poetry is not just contrasted with prose in the sense of verse versus prose but in the sense of a free and flexible rather than a restricted and rigid use of language. In this wider sense Aristotle speaks of the "poet," whom he defines not by the observance of metrical rules but by his or

---

10 See, e.g., Freedman (2011): "Her variants imply a reluctance to make definitive choices about the way in which any poem should be read" (5). It is striking, almost paradoxical, that for "I dwell in Possibility" the only variant seems to be "Gabels" for "Gambrels" (see Miller 2016, 233), probably because "possibility has long been considered part of Dickinson's aesthetic" (Freedman 2011, 5), which she expresses in this poem (i.e. possibility is inherent to it, which is why variants are not necessary). The first comprehensive edition of all poems with textual variants given is Cristanne Miller's *Emily Dickinson's Poems: As She Preserved Them* (2016), which also differs from preceding editions in that she does not suggest a new enumeration, but presents the poems according to fascicle and sheet that they appear on. Similarly, the open access website *Emily Dickinson Archive* (of which Miller is an editor) provides images of all manuscripts and their print counterparts in different editions. For more discussion on variants and the physicality of the fascicles, see especially Heginbotham (2003).
11 See, e.g., Smith (1992), who cautiously speculates: "the reader assumes, therefore, that the particular incident Dickinson describes is representative of her general experience with the world of mechanical literary reproduction and that Dickinson found the printed transformations of her work dissatisfying; most important, the reader concludes that, because of her disappointments, Dickinson chose not to distribute her work in the mass-produced ways to which most unknown authors aspire" (12).
12 J613/Fr445 was found in fascicle 21, displayed on the opposite page to "This was a Poet" (see above, chapter I.1). Heginbotham (2003) reads this as a joke in which prose is visually juxtaposed to poetry (5), "the preferred terrain of the 'little girl' closeted in the wardrobe" (Freedman 2011, 8).

her relation to what happens. If verse as the opposite of prose is defined by the observance of the "rules of prosody" (*OED*, "verse, *n.*" 1.a.), Dickinson has a different idea in mind. Her own fairly free use of verse, which is frequently not restricted by rhyming patterns or established metrical and stanza forms but in fact often rather looks like prose, shows that the contrast between poetry and prose established in J657/Fr466 and other poems is based on a metaphorical sense of the two terms. Even though in J657/Fr466 the pattern of the ballad stanza is predominant (a four-line stanza of which the second and the fourth lines rhyme; alternating lines of four and three stresses), it is not observed with strict regularity. (Cf. line 3, "More numerous of windows," which according to the metrical pattern of the ballad stanza should have four stresses but does not, and the imperfect rhymes "Prose"/"Doors" and "This"/"Paradise".) In this way, Dickinson establishes free relations of sound. The word "Possibility," for example, in this poem allows for a play of sound: it contains "sibil[s]" and evokes "sibilation" (see *OED*, "sibilation, *n.*" 1.a.: "The action of hissing or whistling; a hissing or whistling sound"). The sibyl that is contained in "possibility" is inspired and mysterious. "Sibilation" is furthermore reminiscent of the sound made by snakes and thus creates a link with "Paradise" later in the poem (see below).

If we accept the option that Dickinson is playing with sound and thus integrates some secret wordplay into the opening lines of her poem,[13] the possibilities offered by language are inherent to her utterance – which, in this way, becomes iconic of what it expresses. Accordingly, the "house" which she describes in lines 5–8 is a somewhat enigmatic construction: "Of Chambers as the Cedars." The simile introduces the "wood used to build the House of the Lord in the Old Testament (see 2 Samuel 7:2)."[14] The cedar is a black wood, which is "impregnable of eye" and known for its durability (see Webster 1828, "Cedar, *n.*").

The word "impregnable" appears repeatedly in Dickinson's poems and frequently introduces the double perspective of inside-out and outside-in: in J657/Fr466A, for the speaker who "dwell[s] in Possibility," the windows and doors are openings to the outside world, allowing access to the sky, and allow-

---

13 On the topic of "secret wordplay," see Bauer (2015).
14 See the entry for "cedar" in the online Emily Dickinson Lexicon (http://edl.byu.edu/lexicon/c/14). Leiter (2007) connects the image to a different verse: "The trees of the Lord are full of sap: the cedars of Lebanon which He hath planted" (Psalms 104:16), and points out that, while Dickinson retains the imagery of vitality, she leaves out the praise to God and instead "incorporates it into a 'theology' of her own" (96).

ing the speaker "to gather Paradise"; at the same time, it is not so easy to get in; to the prying eye, possibility is like a black box, just like the one in the wooden drawer in her bedroom, in which Dickinson kept her poems hidden from the public eye.[15] The impregnability of the cedar chambers is a protection against intrusion; she allows for "Visitors – the fairest" only.[16] At the same time, the paradoxical character of the house of poetry as being open and secret at the same time may be evoked by the playful way in which Dickinson uses "Impregnable":[17] apart from the (actual lexical) sense of being proof against attack,[18] Dickinson offers the option to read it as a compound of **impregn** and **-able** (comparable to being **impressible**).[19] Milton in *Paradise Lost* (IX.737-38), for example, speaks of "[Satan's] perswasive words, impregn'd / With Reason." The house of poetry receives impressions from the outside (it has windows), it is impregnated with the outside world, and still it is not transparent for it.

The cedar chambers in the house of possibility thus enable their dweller to look outside but remain undisturbed, except by the fairest visitors. The linguist here expresses that poetry is chosen because of its openness and its adequacy to the flexibility of language. Both poetry and language are open but have fast structures: the "Everlasting Roof" is hence made of "The Gambrels of the Sky." A gambrel (the word is, according to Webster, derived from It. *gamba*, the leg) is

---

15 See Farr (2004), who considers line 5-6 ("Cedars / Impregnable of Eye") as a reference to Dickinson's own "confinement of her poems to the famous cedar chest" (156). However, the wooden drawer in which Dickinson hid her poems from the public "Eye" (l. 6) is listed among the inventory of her room in the online Harvard University Library (http://oasis.lib.harvard.edu/oasis/deliver/~hou01551) and was built principally of cherry wood.
16 Leiter (2007) comments: "If her House is 'fairer,' these visitors are 'fairest.' All we have of them is this assertion; but they resonate with the ethereal 'Hosts' who visit her continually in 'Alone, I cannot be–,' and with the shower of mint that falls ceaselessly into her basket in "I was the slightest in the House–,' poems written during that same year [1862] of astounding poetic productivity. They are her mysterious and endlessly bountiful sources of inspiration, essential to the miraculous process in which she engages" (97).
17 In J642/Fr709, she has "Impregnable my Fortress," in J1525/Fr1571 "Impregnable we are," in J1663/Fr1730 "Impregnable to inquest / However neighborly –" – all uses indicating some sort of shielding against the outside world. The phrase "Impregnable as Light" in J1351/Fr1359 reads like an exception to this usage at first but, in the overall context of the poem, proves to express a similar notion of safeguarding against external influence ("That every man behold / But take away as difficult / As undiscovered Gold").
18 See *OED*, "impregnable, *adj.* and *n.*:" "1. Of a fortress or stronghold: That cannot be taken by arms; [...] 2. *fig.* That cannot be overcome or vanquished; invincible, unconquerable, proof against attack."
19 The *OED*, "impregnate, *adj.*" documents (2.) the erroneous use in the sense of "impregnable."

a hipped roof. The abstract notion of her house's "Everlasting Roof" raises the expectation that a further abstraction is to be made (e.g. eternity), but it is juxtaposed rather tangibly with gambrels, concrete structures in houses as Dickinson knew them.[20] Similar to "Possibility" and "Impregnable," Dickinson is playing with the word and does not use it by chance: gambrel sounds like **gamble**, and this is what she does: she is playing with words and denotations as well as connotations. The word and its sound become another example of what poetry can do better than other kinds of language use: add a playful notion to the utterance and thus make us realise that poetry is where all the possible aspects of language are at home.

If, as Dickinson has it in "Speech is one symptom of Affection" (J1681/Fr1694A), "The perfectest communication [...] Is had within," poetry comes from the inside to the outside (cf. also the movement of the hands that concludes the poem; see below) but does not allow for outside intrusion and is impregnable. Poetry as possibility is very much like a black box as we cannot be entirely sure what will happen. It is also a secret chamber because, as poetry is where the speaker dwells, it becomes identical with herself. The chambers will remain impregnable and become like rooms of the speaker's soul.[21]

The construction in which the prepositions "of" and "for" appear indicate a similar relation of inside and outside. Whereas "of" – in "Of Chambers" and "Of Visitors" – suggests a movement directed at (or towards) the inside (where both "Chambers" as well as "Visitors" are located), "for" – in "For Occupation" – is directed at the outside, the sky and the occupation of "spreading wide" the hands (see below). The poem thus constantly oscillates between these various movements and sometimes is even ambiguous in this respect: are the windows meant for looking out or for getting something in? The house, because of its numerous windows and the roof that opens up towards the sky, becomes the world, and it is from this world that the speaker spreads out her "narrow Hands / To gather Paradise –."[22]

---

[20] "Gambrels are roofs with slopes on each side, of the sort traditionally used in barns. Thus, the image blithely transposes Amherst architecture to the domes of the heavens" (Leiter 2007, 97).

[21] See also Juhasz (1976, 14). Moreover, the image of the soul as both a dwelling as well as the agent who inhabits it is a tradition that goes back to St Teresa's of Avila *Interior Castle*, where the soul is depicted as "both castle and nomadic inhabitant" (Hughes 1997, 379).

[22] Wohlpart (2001) writes: "She moves from narrowness, a symbolic reference to human depravity and sin borrowed from orthodox, Puritan religion, to expansion. The capitalisation of the word 'Hands' suggests a parallel between the poet as creator and God as creator" (65). As

The concluding lines of the poem gesture towards the process of writing: the speaker turns to her hands and to gathering; according to Webster, "gather" may refer to "8. To sweep together. The kingdom of heaven is like a net that was cast into the sea, and gathered of every kind. Matth. xiii.," and the *OED* has "pick up, pluck" (4.c.) but also "To collect (knowledge) by observation and reasoning; to infer, deduce, conclude" (10.). The occupation in the house of possibility/poetry is an action of the hands by means of which a superior world ("Paradise") is collected and grasped, i.e. understood. The (writing) hands of the poet cast out a net and pick up what belongs to it.[23] It is noteworthy in this context that "spreading" and "gather" as well as "dwell" are the only verbs in this poem. They signify the action of the speaker and are connected to poetry (dwell), writing (hands) and putting together/comprehending. These actions seem to be what poetry is about.

At this point it makes sense to return once more to the ambiguity of the first line: the speaker either lives in the house of poetry, i.e. in possible worlds, or she remains in possibility, i.e. has not yet become real (and perhaps will never do so, being merely "possible"). This ambiguity can now be seen as expressing a paradox: what seems to be a limitation (being restricted to what is merely possible) becomes an advantage, as it enables the speaker to grasp a better world, to "gather Paradise." (This goes well with the stress on the "fairer House" of poetry.) We can relate the description of writing poetry as actually grasping what is possible and possibly grasping what is actual to the combination of the literal and the metaphorical in the expression "dwell in Possibility": if "dwell" is meant metaphorically, then "Possibility" has to be literal – and vice versa. This is a structure familiar from other poems by Dickinson as well, most prominently perhaps from "My Life had stood" (J754/Fr764; see chapter I.6 and below section 2.4). The poet as linguist explores this semantic structure, and the linguist as poet makes it expressive of the specific relation of poetry to language and the world: it is not fixed but flexible and at the same time it is clearly structured (literal/metaphorical and metaphorical/literal). This corresponds to Dickinson's description of the house of possibility/poetry, which is both open and well-structured: it is a building with doors and windows (and therefore walls), chambers and a roof structure (gambrels). Thus it is constructed and yet it is natural (its chambers can be compared to cedars) and open (its roof is the sky).

---

much as the poem does provide room for allegorical readings, Wohlpart fails to link his observations back to the text.

23 Here, the poem echoes J921/Fr184 ("If it had no pencil"), in which the notion of "plucking" is also brought in connection with writing poetry; see chapter I.5.

Perhaps for this very reason its roof is "Everlasting" and in this house the speaker is able "To gather Paradise."[24]

At the same time, poetry is always related to the world. This relation becomes most evident in the nature imagery in the poem, e.g. the simile of the cedars. The movement of the speaker's hands is an imitation of the cedars and the gambrels (i.e. the extending, or "spreading," of the roof over the building), and the transition from speaker to house to sky is organic. Hence, the openness as a central image[25] that can be linked back to windows and doors is chosen by the poet to express what possibility, i.e. poetry, means, and linguistic reflection becomes a reflection on the world: poetry is what prose is not, it is not closed (a "closet" as in J613/Fr445) but it is open.[26] We see that the linguist as poet makes a reverse movement from the poet as linguist as she asks in how far language is world. When she gathers Paradise at the conclusion of the poem, she is outgoing and literally gathers all that is outside, that is world: she is looking for those words, "Visitors – the fairest –," that may best express what she wishes to express, that make expression possible. To "dwell in Possibility" means to have a whole reservoir of possibilities at her hands that are based in language, and to exploit these is to write poetry with all its ambiguity, vagueness and semantic openness.[27]

Paradise, the conclusion and climax of the poem, describes possible worlds that Dickinson is able to open up and enter through poetry, i.e. through using language in a way that does not claim to include the actual world (see Bauer and Beck 2014). It is a "golden" world, to use Sir Philip Sidney's (2002, 85) ex-

---

[24] Wohlpart (2001) hence reads the poem as one of "liberation" that "subverts orthodox, religious views on redemption and can most clearly be defined as the establishment of interrelationships with the natural world and with other humans that enable her to transform the quotidian into the sacred" (55). He fails, however, to provide any textual evidence from the poem for this claim but refers mainly to Dickinson's letters and secondary voices (see 76n8).

[25] See Freedman (2011): "'I dwell in Possibility' has often been regarded as a kind of Dickinsonian manifesto precisely because of the way it portrays openness to the beyond as the necessary condition of poetic endeavour" (4). See also Raab (1998, 290), and Morgan (2010) on "the importance of openness" (105). Morgan goes on to write that "to gather paradise" means "gathering or capturing experience in the World." We think that "Paradise" refers to the ability of poetry not just to represent what is actually there but, as it were, the best of all possible worlds.

[26] Pugh (2007) reads the windows and doors as metaphors and regards them as "necessary for the permeability of the poetic stanza (*stanza* translated as 'room,' from the Italian itself)" (15).

[27] See Mitchell (2000): "The point to make, then, is that ambiguity in Dickinson's writing seems to be a fully conscious and deliberate strategy and not simply an accident of the fact of her nonpublication" (100).

pression, which is not restricted by the limitations of the "brazen" world of nature but nevertheless remains relevant to it: poets "may make the too much loved earth more lovely" (Sidney 2002, 85). The relation to the actual world is not determined by the grammar or linguistic convention, nor is the interpretation of poetry established by ordinary assertion. As Dickinson puts it, the house of poetry has more and better doors and windows. The meaning of poetry stands in a much more open relation to the actual world than assertions about reality; Dickinson is thus referring to a set of possible worlds which does not claim to include the actual world but which is relevant to it and which the reader can likewise access by engaging with her poetry. The linguist chooses to be a poet because the absence of any restriction to what happens (to quote Aristotle again) allows her much more freely to realise and put into practice what she has recognised, found, noted in the language.[28]

2.4 Relations of Meaning, Language as World, and the Active Word: The Linguist's Poetic Skill

We have seen by means of one example, "I dwell in Possibility" (J657/Fr466A), how Emily Dickinson consciously exploits the possibilities offered in language and how her linguistic awareness, the basis of poetic creation, becomes the subject of the poem. If we bring together the results from our analysis and read them in the light of other examples from her work, we arrive at a few patterns that can be regarded as further evidence of the way in which Dickinson's linguistic awareness informs her idea of poetry.

This concerns, firstly, her idea of "meaning(s)." As a linguist, even a semanticist, who is looking for "Where the Meanings, are" (J258/Fr320), she mostly finds them in concepts of identity and (internal) "difference." As we have seen, in the poem "I dwell," possibility means poetry – in distinction from prose (see J613/Fr445), which means that, while the speaker says A (possibility), she actually means B (poetry). In other cases, she says A but thus expresses an ambiguity, i.e. she means B **and** C.[29] In "This was a Poet" (J448/Fr446A; see chapter I.4),

---

28 Cf. Freeman (1997), who speaks of Dickinson creating "for us a world of possibilities [...]: a world in which things can happen and be made to happen through the agencies of the self" (25).
29 We discussed one example of this technique in chapter I.2, "If it had no pencil," in which the verb "pluck" echoes its literal meaning by being juxtaposed with "Daisy"; yet in the poem, the verb must be read figuratively and reinterpreted as either "choose (to draw)" or "select (i.e.

she reflects on the notion of meaning in describing how the poet "Distills amazing sense / From ordinary Meanings – / And Attar so Immense." The composition of poetry becomes a quasi-alchemical process of distillation. The poem itself reflects on the difference of meaning in providing us with an unresolved ambiguity as to who is robbed by whom:

(1)   The Robbing – could not harm –

Neither agent nor patient of the "Robbing" are specified; it is thus possible to read the line both as the poet robbing the speakers without harming them, and as the speakers robbing the poet without harming him. Since a final disambiguation is not favoured by the poem as a whole, both readings can be taken conjunctively as one element of the text meaning. The relationship between the two agents is thus dramatised as reciprocal and equitable, since they both rob each other at the same time (and neither comes to harm).

What we find in her poetry is then the linguist's awareness of the tension between linguistic sign (an expression) and what it may mean in a specific context. Frequently the speaker of Dickinson's poems does not just use expressions to convey meaning but reflects on the signs themselves and on how they can be used, as when, in J613/Fr445, she wonders at "still":

(2)   They put me in the Closet –
       Because they liked me "still" –

       Still! Could themselves have peeped –
       And seen my Brain – go round –

The tension between the possible meanings of an expression is moreover often related to metaphor making, e.g. in the context of "I'm Nobody!" (chapter I.5) where the conventional meanings of "nobody" and "somebody" are reversed by playing with quantification and proper names. Similar reinterpretations can be found in "My Life had stood" (chapter I.6), in which two distinct lines of interpretation – i.e. I_{Ind}, where the speaker is a (human) individual, and I_{gun}, where the speaker is a gun – are retained throughout the text, so that the ambiguity of

---

elevate)." Both readings can be retained at the same time, lending the overall text meaning a complexity that is achieved through Dickinson's clever play on possibilities of lexical meaning.

figurative and literal reading creates metaphors for each other.[30] Accordingly, meaning is never simply there but must be established by acts of (re)interpretation in which relations between meanings are considered.

In one example of Dickinson's being a poet as linguist (chapter II.1), "There's a certain Slant of light" (J258/Fr320), the pattern of reinterpretation is analogous to that described above for the relation of the literal and the metaphorical in the expression "dwell in Possibility" and in "My Life had stood" (J754/Fr764):

(3) When it comes, the landscape listens –
     Shadows – hold their breath –

In these lines, the verbs require a human subject, while the subjects linked to them are nonhuman. As the pronoun "it" most likely refers to the "Slant of light" in the opening line of the poem, either the subjects or the verbs have to be reinterpreted: in the first case, "landscape" and "shadows" are personified and thus acquire human traits, in the latter, "listen" and "hold one's breath" are reinterpreted to cancel selectional restrictions and generalise their meanings. Meaning, eventually, resides in the "internal difference."

These reinterpretations, secondly, result in a reality of language that becomes personal: language is part of the world and not separate from it, language and world become interchangeable, and language, the word, becomes real. In "I'm Nobody" (J288/Fr260), the quantifier also denotes a name (see chapter I.3), and they become identical (refer to the same referent) in the poem. There is no longer a tension or a categorical difference between language and world, which becomes also clear to some extent in "My Life had stood" (chapter I.6), when the gun may be both material and immaterial at the same time; the ambiguity is upheld throughout the poem and, hence, the distinction between *res* and *verba* is blurred. In "A Word made Flesh" (J1651/Fr1715A), the speaker stresses that "it is seldom / And tremblingly partook," which implies that "partaking" is regarded as a mode of engaging with words. In the same poem, she speaks of "this consent of Language," regarding it as a decision-making person

---

30 Weisbuch (1998) comments on "My Life had stood" in a vein that is reminiscent of/can be linked with "I dwell": "I don't mean that anything goes interpretively or that the poem is a Rorschach ink blot. I do mean that the poem gets egregiously robbed if you see the gun-to-owner relationship simply as that of a believer to her god or a s a lover to her adored beloved or even (and more interestingly) as language personified in relation to the poet who shoots and masters it. The poem can absorb these meanings, as usual, but it is the play among the possibilities that makes the poem" (206f.).

or institution, and even uses a pleonasm enhancing the expression of her personal involvement with language when she speaks of "this loved Philology."

Language, thirdly, becomes an agent as the poet feels its impact on her and as she works with language and does something with and to it: language is experienced as influencing life; it becomes action and acting.[31] This is particularly true for "If it had no pencil" (J921/Fr184; chapter I.2). Here, the question form of the poem supports the reflection on possible worlds: while we are able to assert the presuppositions of counterfactual conditionals, this is impossible when it comes to the speaker's querying about possible actions by "it" (such as "Would it try mine –"). These queries rather point us to the unlimited number of fictional worlds that are thus to be derived from a set of given presuppositions. The explicit mention of "it" having a "word" contextually links up with the biblical notion of the creative word, and thus emphasises the poem's concern with bringing something into being through speaking and/or writing: language makes the world what it is.[32] Poetic composition is a process which in Dickinson's poems appears as an activity by language itself. In "If it had no pencil," the action expressed by "When it plucked me" may also be seen to originate in language. The poet is chosen by a power that has a "word." And in "Shall I take thee, the Poet said / To the propounded word?" the poet, in the end, is no longer in total control of the words chosen: "The Poet searched Philology / And when about to ring / For the suspended Candidate / There came unsummoned in – / That portion of the Vision / The Word applied to fill" (J1126/Fr1243). While this is a way of describing the process of poetic inspiration, it should be stressed that to Dickinson this process is conceptualised as an activity of language (rather than, say, the Muses).

The examples described so far show that the aspects we have identified in our analysis of Dickinson being a linguist as poet may overlap in some of the poems, i.e. they do not exist in isolation but in combination with each other. This overlap can be found in particular in "To pile like Thunder" (J1247/Fr1353; see chapter I.1) and "You said that I 'was Great'" (J738/Fr736; chapter I.2). In the first case, we have analysed an identification of poetry and love: "this would be Poetry / Or Love" as the two come "coeval." Two different signifiers are linked to one another and thus become identical. This reinterpretation process is intri-

---

[31] This is not primarily meant in the sense of speech acts, which are of course part of the poetic utterances, but mainly in the sense of all aspects of language having an impact on speaker and listener, and on the world.
[32] Another example can be found in chapter I.6, "My Life had stood," where the speaker indicates that she acts for her owner's benefit by "speak[ing] for him."

cately linked to the reality of language becoming personal and *res* and *verba* identical: there is no difference between poetry and love, and, because of this, the internal contradiction of "We both and neither prove" is a seeming paradox only that results from the zeugma (based on the semantic contribution of the verb "prove" as explained in I.1). In this manner, we are made to reflect on the nature of love and poetry, and our relation to each. Accordingly, the line may mean that we cannot by logical argument prove the existence of poetry and love, and, concurrently, it may mean that we give evidence to them because we exist (see I.1, (10) through (22)). The poem has its climax in the concluding lines "Experience either and consume – / For None see God and live –." The action of 'consuming' is evidence for the existence of poetry and love as we experience them and, Phoenix-like, are reduced to ashes in the process (see *OED* "consume v." 3.) – which means that language here becomes an agent and makes something real in the very process of annihilation (a situation also captured by the contradictory "both and neither").

We observe similar patterns in "You said that I 'was Great'" (chapter I.2): the speaker leaves it to the addressee to call her whatever he feels suits best, which means that differences in meaning are cancelled. At the same time, she becomes something other than she is, i.e. the speaker's reality is performatively changed through language and she will become everything the addressee wishes so that "I suit Thee." The metamorphosis that is described in the poem – which is actually going on while it is being described – becomes exemplary of language as an agent that is able to change the world.

The linguist as poet hence does indeed exploit the possibilities that language provides her with. The different linguistic phenomena that we have been able to identify as constitutive of some of her poems (in Part I above) feed into Dickinson's poetics and make her poetry exceptional in that linguistic reflection shows the world and is an intricate part of it (e.g. when *res* and *verba* become identical in her poems). Language and world are structurally related, and this relationship is communicated on a meta-level in her poems, for instance, when reinterpretation takes place. Thus, her poems become expressive of how Dickinson views and imagines the world, and this expression is foregrounded linguistically by means of complex semantic relationships. Language, hence, is not merely an instrument to describe the world but is part of it – as much as the world is part of language.

And yet, we may detect some sort of paradox here: while Emily Dickinson uses language in its common denotative function (which is semantically inconspicuous, although the word is the object of her reflection), she also makes use of implicit linguistic reflections in foregrounding linguistic rules without naming them (see Part I of this book). In this case, what she writes about becomes identical with what she writes. Her awareness of language focusses on structures in language that are, at the same time, structures of world (e.g. when she reflects on the relationship of quantifiers and names in chapter I.5, "I'm Nobody," and of animate and inanimate objects as in chapter I.6, "My Life had stood"). This is what it means, when Dickinson presents us with a speaker who shows to us what language is capable of, and in so doing shows to us the workings of her mind and her soul, of nature and the world: in other words, becomes a poet.

Part III: **Benefits of Interdisciplinary Work**

The purpose of this third and final part of the book is to tie back the empirical findings regarding Emily Dickinson's poetry that we obtained by using the combined methodologies of linguistics and literature in parts one and two to the general research agenda behind them. We want to begin with a discussion of the value that poetic texts have for linguistic theory in III.1, and will then proceed with the perspective of literary studies that use formal linguistics as an analytical tool in the following chapter III.2. The points we make in these chapters are not restricted to Emily Dickinson but of a general nature; her poetry here serves to exemplify these points.

III.1 Poetry as a Data Source for Formal Linguistics

1.1 Introduction

As noted in the Introduction, several subfields of linguistics have already acknowledged poetry and fictional texts as a valuable data source in order to investigate how language works. Formal semantics and pragmatics, however, have hardly ever included poetry as data that is equally interesting as, for instance, experimental, cross-linguistic, diachronic or corpus data. In this chapter, we want to argue that the consideration of poetry as data is worthwhile for formal semantics.[1]

Our line of argument proceeds in two steps. In the next section of this chapter (1.2), we undercut possible counterarguments against the use of lyrical texts as data for investigations of grammar. Specifically, we invalidate the commonly found position that poems are not suitable data because they are not normal or ordinary language. First, we point out similarities to other types of data where linguistic rules are shown to be subject to flexibility which have been proven very fruitful for linguistic investigation, and, second, by showing that certain rules of (universal) grammar[2] cannot be violated and certain types of interpretations are impossible even in poetry.

In section 1.3 of this chapter, we explain why lyrical texts are actually particularly valuable data: because of the specific communicative situation of the text type, speaker and reader do not share a common ground, and thus the context is very limited. Yet, it is precisely this contextual limitation which gives rise to a complex text interpretation where several lines of interpretations intersect (see Part II of this book). Thus, a thorough linguistic analysis of poetry should give further insights especially for context sensitive phenomena. Moreover, poetry is written by a speaker that is especially sensitive to the properties of

---

[1] Some of the material in this chapter has been published in *Linguistische Berichte* (Bade and Beck 2017).
[2] We assume, in the tradition of generative linguistics, that all languages share a common core, UG (see e.g. Matthewson 2012; Pesetsky 1999). Languages differ in those aspects of grammar that are flexible. These can be captured by parameters. Other elements of universal grammar are fixed and all languages adhere to them, e.g. compositional rules like function application. See Beck (forthcoming) for a discussion of semantic parameters and universals.

https://doi.org/10.1515/9783110646825-010

language. Her creative use of language reveals where the grammar permits flexibility. Sections 1.2 and 1.3 put forward the following proposals:

(P1) Lyrical texts follow the rules of UG.
(P2) The high density of creative uses of language by a language expert reveals the potential of language.
(P3) The lack of context creates a special communicative situation that makes poetry particularly fit for investigations of grammar.

We conclude that the investigation of lyrical texts should enrich the range of empirical methods used for the study of the grammar of the human language.

1.2 Validity: Lyrical Texts Do Not Do Things Language in General Cannot Do (P1)

1.2.1 What Might Be Problematic about Lyrical Texts as Evidence

A traditional view on the relation of poetry to the language it is written in defines "poetic language strikingly apart from logical, scientific, historical language" (Miles 1940). Here, poetry is seen as a special case of language that shows significant differences to non-poetic language and can thus provide no insights for the latter. A sentence as in (1), from Emily Dickinson's "My Life had stood – a Loaded Gun –" (J754/Fr764), should, under this view, "resist inclusion in a grammar of English" and "it might prove more illuminating to regard [it] as a sample of a different language" (Thorne 1965, 51).

(1) My Life had stood – a Loaded Gun –
     In Corners – till a Day

Even though, in a broad perspective, linguists by now acknowledge that poetry can give insights into its language of origin, the view of poetry as proposed by Thorne still prevails in most discussions within the field of formal linguistics,[3]

---

[3] This view is not restricted to formal semantics but follows a large tradition as demonstrated in Fries 1952; Thorne 1965; Labov 1972; Fabb 2010. Contrary to that, data of this sort finds some representation in investigations on phonological and phonetic features of language (Hayes 1988; Hayes 1989; Kiparsky 2006; Fabb & Halle 2008). Other current research in this field is related to investigations on the impact of iconic features on interpretation as pursued, for example, by the Iconicity Research Project (Ljungberg 2001; Fischer 2011). Moreover, literary

which becomes evident in the lack of research in formal syntax, semantics, and pragmatics (see the Introduction for more details). However, in order to develop a model of the grammar that includes an understanding of its variable properties vs. its invariant core, lyrical texts provide a valuable data source.

We acknowledge that (1) does not obey all the rules and constraints of Present Day English (PDE). But if (1) were an instance of a language altogether different from PDE, it would be extremely difficult to understand or to retract meaning from it. It is possible to interpret (1) based on the rules of the grammar of PDE. Even though interpretation requires syntactic reanalysis and semantic reinterpretation, the mechanisms used are systematic and generally available as part of our grammatical knowledge, as shown by our analysis of the poem that (1) is part of (see chapter I.6).

Our position is that poetic language is developed from the rules and constraints of non-poetic language (Kuhns 1972; Fabb 2010). Poetic language, as we find it in Emily Dickinson, departs from the grammatical structures of a language in particular, systematic, and limited ways. Let us call the underlying language of our poem L1 and its grammar G. Because of our knowledge of G, which includes knowledge of word meaning, of syntax and of rules of composition, we can identify these departures and we are able to interpret the texts. Our knowledge is implicit but is manifested in the ability to judge certain structures as grammatically acceptable and reject others. Lyrical texts might not be acceptable by the rules of G but might well be acceptable by G' – a grammar close to G. As the poem targets L1 speakers, e.g. native speakers of PDE, it would be impossible for a native speaker of e.g. Mandarin Chinese to understand the poem without any prior knowledge of English. Hence we may consider the language of the poem to be a variety of the same language. The grammar of the poem must be close enough to G to make its language recognisable by G speakers. That is, a speaker with G in mind is able to identify the rules for how G' systematically deviates from G, and she can understand the poem.

1.2.2 Our Position: Poetry as a Language Variety

Poetic language can be especially revealing with regard to the question of how the grammar is structured. It can help us distinguish between universal properties and language specific properties of the grammar. It can also tell us which

---

(narrative) texts have recently been exploited as a data source for studying speaker oriented indexicals (Eckardt 2015).

components of a given grammar are flexible and which are more stable, since the degree of flexibility of the grammar is explored in poetic texts. To study deviances from grammatical form is a common method exploited for the development of linguistic theory. Intuitions and grammaticality judgments mirror native speakers' competence of a language, i.e. its grammar. Studying levels of (un)acceptability is hence taken to be revealing with respect to the structure of the grammar.

As an example, Featherston (2006) compared the degrees of (in)acceptability for relative marker drop in German and English. Whereas in English object marker drop is acceptable (2a) and subject marker drop is not acceptable (2b), both are unacceptable in German ((3a), (3b)). But as seen in (3), (3b) is judged worse than (3a).

(2) a. John saw the girl he liked.
    b. *John saw the girl liked him.

(3) a. * Peter hat das Mädchen gesehen er mag.
         Peter has the girl seen he likes.
    b. ** Peter hat das Mädchen gesehen ihn mag.
         Peter has the girl seen him likes.

The significant difference in acceptability between dropping the subject relative marker versus the object relative marker in German cannot be explained by exposure to these structures or their frequency since both are never used. The fact that the structures in (2b) and (3b) are considerably less acceptable than their counterparts in (2a) and (3a) in both languages, however, should be explained by a cross-linguistically stable property of human language. We can thus see that comparisons of grades of unacceptability are very important for linguistic theory, since they help to identify potentially universal features of human language.[4] The study of literary texts can be seen as parallel to the study of different grades of unacceptability or errors of L2 learners and should as such be equally relevant for the workings of UG.

---

[4] This is further emphasised by the vast study of the deviant grammar of speech errors of second language (L2) learners. Just like the experiment presented above, the ungrammatical structures reveal what the scope of certain linguistic possibilities is, i.e. whether certain structures are unacceptable due to language specific properties or universal properties of human language (e.g. Yamane 2003).

A second argument in favour of considering poetic language as a variant is to compare it to other cases of related grammars which reveal striking similarities to grammatical properties of lyrical texts, e.g. child language as well as diachronic stages of English. Essentially, we argue that all varieties of a language display potential states of that language.

For example, dropping the subject relative marker, which is ungrammatical in PDE adult language, is common in poetry and used by children. Examples (4a) and (5a) are taken from Emily Dickinson's "This was a Poet" (J448/Fr446A). Plausible readings of these lines are given in (4b) and (5b), respectively (see also chapter I.4). They assume that the subject relative markers were elided.

(4) a. We wonder it was not Ourselves
Arrested it – before –
b. 'We wonder it was not ourselves **who** arrested it before'

(5) a. The Poet – it is He –
Entitles Us – by Contrast –
To ceaseless Poverty –
b. 'The poet, it is he, **who** entitles us by contrast to ceaseless poverty'

As Schuele and Tolbert (2001, 258) show, there is a stage just before the age of three where children omit obligatory relative markers and produce sentences like (6a):

(6) a. (there's baby) there's my baby wants to go in train
b. 'There is my baby **who** wants to go in the train.'

They furthermore argue that the same omission is grammatical in English dialects, e.g. Scottish (Schuele and Tolbert 2001, 260). This means that the ungrammatical structures in (4a) and (5a) are commonly accepted in varieties of PDE.[5]

Moreover, historically earlier stages of L1 are also close to the grammar G. Old and Middle English syntax, for example, is extensively studied partly because of its implications for the clause structure of Modern English. The seemingly ungrammatical structures that occur in poetry show tremendous parallels to structures acceptable in earlier stages of English. Therefore, they are equally

---

[5] Bade and Beck (2017) provide further examples of similarities between poetic language and child language (regarding both omission structures and the use of pronouns).

revealing with respect to the syntax of Modern English. One example of structures which are unacceptable in Modern English but were perfectly acceptable in Middle English are Object Verb orders (Biberauer and Roberts 2006). They are also commonly used in poetry as in (7a), taken from Alfred Lord Tennyson's poem "A Farewell," or (8a), taken from Ralph Waldo Emerson's "Give all to love."[6]

(7) a. Flow down, cold rivulet, to the sea,
       Thy tribute wave deliver   (Tennyson 1971, 94)
    b. 'Flow down, cold rivulet, to the sea,
       deliver thy tribute wave'

(8) a. Give all to love;
       Obey thy heart;
       [...]
       Nothing refuse   (Emerson 1918, 90f.)
    b. Give all to love;
       obey thy heart;
       refuse nothing

Not only systematic syntactic changes but also semantic changes are visible in lyrical texts. The origin and development of a word, which is important for how its semantics should be modelled, can sometimes be recovered by looking at its use in verse texts. Quite a number of lexical changes can be observed in Shakespeare's plays, which are partly written in verse. The now common use of "forward" as a verb, for example, was unavailable in Middle English where it was exclusively used as an adjective or adverb. The first written use as a verb is attested in Shakespeare's *Henry IV, Part 1* which was first printed in quarto in 1598 (*OED*):

(9)   [...] Then let me hear
        Of you, my gentle cousin Westmorland,
        What yesternight our Council did decree
        In forwarding this dear expedience.   (Shakespeare 2002, I.1.30-33)

---

6 See Bade and Beck (2017) for other structures that used to be grammatical in Old and Middle English.

Shakespeare enriched the meaning of "forward" by extending its use to another lexical category. It is, of course, possible to observe systematic changes like this in other text types. Poems and verse texts in general, however, draw our attention to examples of unusual and novel structures and the environments they occur in. The unusual way in which certain lexical items like "forward" in (9) are used show under which circumstances an enriched or even completely new meaning is possible and might become conventionalised (see Eckardt 2012 for a recent discussion of this view on language change).

The examples from poems hence illuminate what kind of linguistic structures are subject to change as well as the conditions under which they have the potential to change. These cases of language change also help identify stable properties of grammar as opposed to parts that vary between varieties.

To summarise, we have seen evidence that poetry adheres to a grammar G' close to G, in parallel to child language varieties, dialectal varieties or diachronic stages of language.

1.2.3 (Im)Possibilities

Even though we have seen that structures occur in the grammar of poetry that deviate from G, we now want to briefly discuss cases where logically possible deviances are blocked. These cases reveal the limits of the flexibility of the rule system. It is implausible, for example, to interpret the expression "three person'd God" in (10), from John Donne's "Batter my heart," with a rule that is not Predicate Modification (see the appendix for Predicate Modification).

(10)   Batter my heart, three person'd God; for, you   (Donne 2005, 109)

It seems completely impossible, for example, to assume that "three person'd God" receives a disjunctive interpretation, resulting in a meaning like (11).

(11) $[\![$three person'd God$]\!] = \lambda x.$ three-personed(x) or God(x)
       'x is three-personed or x is God'

Instead, we interpret the Noun Phrase according to Predicate Modification which creates the conjunction of the two elements:

(12) $[\![$three person'd God$]\!] = \lambda x.$ three-personed(x) & God(x)
       'x is three-personed and x is God'

The two lines in (13) taken from Emily Dickinson's "My Life had stood – a Loaded Gun –" (J754/Fr764) can also serve as an illustration for what is an unlikely interpretation, disobeying the rules of composition:

(13)   And every time I speak for Him –
        The mountains straight reply –

A highly implausible interpretation of (13) (which for this very reason was not considered in the analysis of the poem presented in I.6) is the one given in (14) below where the universal quantifier "every time" first combines with its nuclear scope and then with its first argument, the restrictor, thereby violating the order of Functional Application (see the appendix).

(14) $\forall t'$[the mountains reply at t' → I speak at t']
        'Whenever the mountains reply, I speak.'

Instead, we interpret the line according to the order of the elements within the sentence, such that "every time" combines first with its restrictor and then with its nuclear scope:

(15) $\forall t'$[I speak for him at t' → the mountains reply at t']
        'Whenever I speak, the mountains reply.'

The fact that the interpretations in (11) and (14) are unavailable for the structures in (10) and (13) respectively shows that the rules of composition are not to be violated. The mechanisms necessary to interpret poetry hence do not violate hard limits of grammar. The rules of composition constitute one of these hard limits. It seems that all interpretation is driven by compositionality, and that flexibility occurs within its limits.

In sum, we have to distinguish between soft restrictions of the grammar which, if violated or suspended in certain structures (like poetry), still allow for (re)interpretation, and hard restrictions such as, for example, the rules of composition, which are always upheld (also in poetry). The former should not be considered as aiming at obscurity, but as intended by the poet and important for the interpretation of the text. The discussion in Part II has highlighted that Emily Dickinson systematically uses certain mechanisms of grammar – e.g. ambiguity, ellipsis, reference – to yield a certain effect at the global level of the text. A parallel argument could be made for other poets.

1.2.4 Input of Literary Scholarship

Here is a proviso regarding our plot: we acknowledge the fact that there is a wide spectrum of what might be called lyrical uses of language. There are rather trivial lyrical texts which show some of the structural features of poetry but are not characterised by a high complexity of language. Birthday poems like the one in (16) below, for example, have line breaks and show instances of rhyme, but are not characterised by distinctive semantic or syntactic features.

(16) I wish you the
 best birthday ever,
 one that's so
 fantastic that
 it lives in your heart
 forever.
 And I want you
 to know
 that wherever
 you go,
 I'm always
 wishing the best
 for you.[7]

Together with its lack of syntactic and semantic complexity, this type of poetry is also not very interesting from a pragmatic point of view. It is meant for a special occasion. Hence, in the situation they occur, speaker, addressee, and purpose are clearly defined. They are not especially revealing as a data source.

At the other end of the spectrum, there are also highly unconventional lyrical texts, as for example experimental poems, which show that language has some structure but none that will map onto a semantic structure which can then be interpreted according to the rules of composition (e.g. Christian Morgenstern's "Fisches Nachtgesang,"[8] entirely consisting of dashes and bows). We concede that both ends of the spectrum might be unrevealing with regard to the grammatical features of a language. It is, however, important to note that we are looking at lyrical texts that lie in the centre of the spectrum, and argue for those

---

7 Loveliestmoment.blogspot.com/2013/05/birthday-poems.html
8 A facsimile of the original poem can be found here:
https://de.wikipedia.org/wiki/Galgenlieder#/media/Datei:Galgenlieder_025.jpg

texts to be valuable data sources for linguistics. The input of literary scholarship helps identify the poems that are appropriate data since it tells us what types of texts are complex but not uninterpretable. Furthermore, this input is valuable for judging the influence of other, non-compositional features poetic language possesses, and which make it different from ordinary language, besides the variations described above. These features include rhyme, metre and rhythm, for example. It can be considered an advantage of lyrical texts as data source that such non-grammatical features are fairly obvious. Note that not only poetry, but also other data sources for linguistics include factors which make them different from spontaneous language production: in an experimental setting, for example, unnatural tasks tend to put enormous emphasis on aspects of language that are normally much less influential (like word frequency). This means that all data sources require interpretation. The connection to literary studies allows us to consult experts on precisely those features that the linguist does not understand so well.

Summary: P1

As an overall summary of section 1.2, we refine our hypothesis P1 on the basis of the above discussion.

(P1')   Lyrical texts follow the rules of UG. They deviate from the grammar of the language of origin in ways similar to language varieties. They do not allow for violations of universal rules, e.g. fundamental rules of composition.

1.3 Special Value for Semantics and Pragmatics: Lyrical Texts Constitute Particularly Interesting Evidence (P2 and P3)

In this section, we want to give examples of how the creative use of language by an expert makes its limits and its flexibility visible in interesting ways (P2). We then go on to illustrate that the lack of context in poems creates a special discourse situation which makes them especially fit for investigations at the semantics-pragmatics interface (P3). Our discussion shows that linguistic analysis has to be refined or revised in order to deal with data from lyrical texts. This is the basis for our argument that they are a valuable data source.

Contrary to language used by language learners which comes with unintended errors in language production, the poet should be considered a language expert, and her text as a carefully crafted language production. In this case, deviant linguistic structures are used on purpose to yield specific effects. In many cases, a poet reveals through her work that she is engaged in an intuitive linguistic analysis of L1 in order to achieve these effects. This has been discussed and argued for in detail for Emily Dickinson's poetry in chapter II.1. We assume that this very high degree of linguistic awareness and sensitivity to properties of the grammar is frequent among poets. Moreover, poems can be especially revealing for the meaning of context-dependent expressions, since they are presented without surrounding context. The common ground assumed in ordinary linguistic interaction (cf. the appendix and e.g. Stalnaker 1974; Kadmon 2001), which locates speaker and hearer and guides assumptions they make about context-dependent expressions in language, is non-existent when reading a lyrical text. This is due to the fact that the communicative situation the poet found herself in when writing the poem is, in most cases, completely detached from the situation in which the reader is experiencing the poem and that poetry, as a rule, is counterfactually independent, i.e. fictional. Thus, the only information available to the reader is what is given in the text itself.

These considerations are summarised in our hypotheses P2 and P3, repeated below, and will be tested with the help of three examples in the following:

(P2)   The high density of creative uses of language by a language expert reveals the potential of language.
(P3)   The lack of context creates a special communicative situation that makes poetry particularly fit for investigations of grammar.

We consider coercion as a first example in subsection 1.3.1, referential expressions in 1.3.2. and implicatures in 1.3.3.

1.3.1 Creative Use of Language by the Poet: Coercion

Our first example, coercion, relates to (P2). Our data challenge and clarify existing theories of coercion. The examples illustrate what the linguistic and extra-linguistic factors are that promote coercion processes. We show that

   a. conflicts are resolved locally according to the principle of interpretability;
   b. both component parts can be reinterpreted, functor as well as argument;
   c. world knowledge constrains typical interpretations in ordinary contexts.

The full range of grammatically available interpretative options is revealed by lyrical texts, where world knowledge can be suspended.

Coercion is a reinterpretation mechanism that is activated when local semantic mismatches occur in the structure. There are still many unresolved issues regarding the nature of coercion, and how it differs from other reinterpretation mechanisms. In particular, the question what exactly influences coercion operations and at which level of computation it happens is controversial. Some theories see it as a more global repair mechanism that works on a defective semantic structure (Nunberg 1995; Lang and Maienborn 2011). Other theories assume that the coercion process is encoded in the lexical entry of expressions, either via their so called qualia structures (Pustojevsky 1995) or their complex types (Asher 2011). The different theories make different assumptions about the division of labour between the lexicon and the context.

In our view, the debate suffers from the fact that expressions often taken as standard examples of coercion processes seem to be conventionalised and are operative in only very specific contextual settings, as the stereotypical example in (17).

(17)   The ham sandwich wants to pay.

A standard analysis of this example (Nunberg 1995) assumes that a covert transfer function f is inserted into the structure in (17) which maps meals to their consumers to resolve the mismatch between the subject and selectional restrictions of the verb "want," see (18) below:

(18)   f ([[the ham sandwich]]) = the person who had the ham sandwich

What drives this insertion is unclear. In the case of (17), the option is easily available when uttered in a restaurant setting. But it is not the context alone which plays a role: convention seems to be relevant as well – i.e. the mapping function used for (17) is too specialised to be used in other settings. At the same time, it is the only option for resolving the mismatch in (17) when in a restaurant setting.

Examples taken from poetry often display non-conventional, creative uses of figurative language and thereby make visible the full range of interpretative possibilities. Below we repeat the example of a violation of selectional restrictions taken from "My Life had stood – a Loaded Gun –."

(19)   My Life had stood – a Loaded Gun –
         In Corners – till a Day

Our analysis of the poem in chapter I.6 revealed that the mismatch allows for three reinterpretation strategies. All three are valid options in the context of the poem, where it remains unclear throughout the poem whether a gun or a human is the speaker.

(20) a. I stood around in corners. (NP reinterpretation)
         f (⟦my life⟧) = I
     b. My life remained unnoticed. (VP reinterpretation)
         f (⟦stand in corners⟧) = λx. x is neglected
     c. I was neglected. (NP/VP reinterpretation)
         f (⟦my life⟧) = I
         f (⟦stand in corners⟧) = λx. x is neglected

The example shows that the lexicon and syntax alone do not dictate which part of the structure has to be reinterpreted. We can either reinterpret the predicate or its argument, and also both. The latter possibility is the most surprising from the viewpoint of most current theories on coercion, which assume that only local conflicts can trigger coercion processes (cf. Swaart 2011). At the same time, the option is a very prominent one in the context of the poem. Since reinterpreting either the predicate or the argument would be sufficient to resolve the local conflict, it is unclear under existing theories why the option to reinterpret both parts of the structure should be available. It seems to be a question of contextual pressure to reinterpret as in (20c), which poses a challenge to current theories and asks for an appropriate modification of said theories which captures this observation.[9]

The example just discussed shows that the direction of coercion is not fixed. The reinterpretation of both the argument and the functor is possible (as well as both simultaneously), speaking against the **Head Typing Principle**[10] as formulated by Asher (2011), for example, which predicts that the argument is always coerced into a type that fulfils the requirements of the head.

---

9 Further reinterpretation processes of other lines of the poem are analysed in chapter I.6 and in Bade and Beck 2017.
10 Here is a simplified version: If X is a constituent with daughters α and β, (and X is uninterpretable) and α is the syntactic, lexical head, then the typing/interpretive frame of α must be preserved in the composition of α and β

It is crucial that all interpretative options remain available in the poem "My Life had stood" (cf. chapter I.6). The mechanism of resolution is hence not determined according to the local structure, but also by the larger context. Our data reveal an increased range of interpretative possibilities. We see that examples from ordinary contexts are usually constrained by our knowledge of the situation. Through the lack of context in poetry, we find the whole potential of language revealed. Our examples show that existing theories of coercion should allow for more flexibility.

Next, we ask how to constrain a new, more liberal analysis of coercion. Opening the theories of coercion has the danger of forming a theory which is too unrestrictive. Without any limits to inserting a transfer function which changes the referents or shifting the meaning of the verb we might expect the grammar to allow shifts and reinterpretations as in (21a) and (21b), which would lead to a completely arbitrary and impossible interpretation in (21c): Such a reinterpretation needs to be blocked.

(21)   Charlotte smiled.
    a. $f(\llbracket \text{Charlotte} \rrbracket) = \text{Hans}$
    b. $f(\llbracket \text{smile} \rrbracket) = \lambda x.\ x \text{ snores}$
    c. $\llbracket \text{Charlotte smiles} \rrbracket = 1$ iff Hans snores

More research is needed to spell out a revised theory. Here is a first approximation to what we have in mind: we find recurring patterns of what types of reinterpretation strategies are pursued. There are instances in which it is possible to insert a transfer function f which changes the referents of a sentence, e.g. maps the cappuccino to its drinker, the life to its owner. But there must be a contextually well-defined and close relation between the referents which also has some generality to it, e.g. ownership. A function like in (21a) which randomly maps one individual to another is disallowed. Furthermore, the examples from poetry show that we must have good reasons to change the referent: only if a local conflict is involved, arises the need for and possibility of reinterpretation. For instance, changing "my life" to "I" is allowed in the context of a poem because "my life" violates the selectional restrictions of "stand in corners." The second type of reinterpretation mechanism we discussed is shifting the meaning of verbs. In our examples, the meaning of the verb becomes more general and less restrictive in the sense that certain presuppositions are dropped so that the domain set of verbs is widened. For example, "reply" is shifted to a meaning like "make an imitative sound," which will include non-human agents. More research in linguistics is needed to identify in how far grammar restricts why and how we reinterpret. We argue that looking at data from lyrical texts helps develop a theory of coercion which isolates the grammatical factors involved.

Summary: P2

Our discussion leads to the following refinement of P2:

(P2') Creative uses of language in poetry reveal the whole potential of language. A large range of the reinterpretive possibilities that the grammar allows for is laid open. The driving force of reinterpretation is not limited to plain uninterpretability; the direction and pathways of reinterpretation are less fixed than standard coercion theories assume.

1.3.2 Context Dependency in a Dynamic Semantics: Referential Expressions

The second example we discuss explores the role of context or rather the lack thereof in lyrical texts for the interpretation of pronouns. Our findings raise interesting questions on the influence of situations on the interpretation process as a whole. We will see that

a. a genuinely dynamic interpretation is possible.
b. the text type and discourse situation may decide between static and dynamic interpretation, or, more accurately, between the increment size that is operative in a particular context.

The evidence provided by lyrical texts hence has an impact on linguistic theory, specifically the semantics-pragmatics interface.

As discussed in chapters I.4, I.5 and II.1, an utterance like (22) is only appropriate in a context that furnishes a referent for the pronoun.

(22) He sneezed.

Accordingly, if a speaker utters the sentence in (22) out of the blue, a 'Hey wait a minute' effect/challenge will be evoked (von Fintel 2004; Matthewson 2006). The assumption therefore is that checking the context for relevant information happens right away. If no relevant referent is available, sentences will be uninterpretable in the context and challenged by the interlocutors.

Poems behave differently in this respect (for a detailed discussion see chapter I.5). The use of pronouns without an antecedent is common in poetry. Remember (23):

(23)   He fumbles at your Soul (J315/Fr477)

Rather than taking such expressions to be uninterpretable, readers continue to interpret and accumulate information. They build up a compositional interpretation of the whole text. Thus, they arrive at a text meaning and can then try to reconstruct the context.

To model how compositional interpretation proceeds under these circumstances, a dynamic model of interpretation is needed (Kamp 1981; Heim 1982; see also chapters I.4, I.5 and II.1). The semantic value of a sentence in a dynamic framework is its potential to modify and extend information that exists in the context. (24) represents the dynamic meaning of (23).

(24) $\lambda g.\ g(1)$ fumble-at_your_ soul

The result of interpretation is a set of assignment functions, bundling information about the referents in the poem. The application to a context happens after the reader has computed the meaning of the text. Different readers may envision different contexts, i.e. collections of referents that make the text true. Poetry is thus evidence for a dynamic framework. It contributes to an ongoing debate on whether static frameworks are able to describe interpretation processes sufficiently (cf. e.g. Schlenker 2011 for recent discussion).

We have shown that a dynamic system is more appropriate for modelling how interpretation proceeds in lyrical texts. In everyday discourse, the system seems to allow for less flexibility. Our data suggest that it depends on the communicative situation at which level (i.e. size of increment) the context is updated with the information from the text and under which circumstances this pragmatic step of updating the context succeeds or fails. There seem to be two alternatives depending on the situation a speaker is in. First, the whole text is interpreted dynamically and the resulting text interpretation may be then applied to a specific context. Second, smaller units (increment sizes) are interpreted and applied to a specific context immediately. Our data suggest that the pragmatic step always takes place but, given the appropriate communicative setting, can be postponed until text interpretation is completed.

Summary: P3

Our findings result in a refinement of P3:

(P3')   The special communicative situation created in poetry reveals that choosing between static and dynamic interpretation depends on the text type. Dynamic updates are related to the increment size. The pragmatic step can be postponed to text level in lyrical texts and interpretation proceeds dynamically until then.

1.3.3 FictionalAssert and Implicatures

Our last example illustrates the point that lyrical texts are especially well suited for investigations at the semantics-pragmatics interface due to the communicative situation they create (P3). Specifically, we show that, through the special speech act operator they involve, an additional pragmatic mechanism is available in lyrical texts which we call **apparent flouting** (Brockmann et al. 2017).

We have argued in Bauer and Beck (2014) that the pragmatic meaning of fictional texts can be modelled with a special speech act operator FictionalAssert. FictionalAssert relates the fictional worlds described by the text to the evaluation world (the actual world of the reader) via an accessibility relation R. Identifying this relation and thereby specifying what the subjective meaning of the text is for the reader happens after the whole text has been interpreted.

(25) $[\![\text{FictionalAssert}]\!] = \lambda T.\ \forall w\ [T(w)\ \&\ w$ is maximally similar to @ otherwise $\rightarrow R(@)(w)]$

The fact that this operator works at the level of text may explain why certain decisions, like finding a referent for pronouns, can be delayed in lyrical texts (see the preceding subsection). The fact that FictionalAssert establishes an indirect relation to the actual world, via a conditional inference, moreover allows for **apparent flouting**.

Flouting is a term introduced by Grice (1978) and describes the fact that interlocutors can choose to disobey a maxim to create an implicature. An example of disobeying the maxim of quantity is B's utterance in (26).

(26)   A: Did you like the Millers?
        B: I liked Mrs Miller.

B is only giving a partial answer to A's question. Since A assumes B to be cooperative (due to the cooperative principle), she can compute an implicature based on deductive reasoning: B could have said something more informative, i.e. that he liked Mr and Mrs Miller. He did not say that he liked Mr Miller. As a result, A can deduce that B does not like Mr Miller. The reason for B not saying explicitly that he does not like Mr Miller could be based on politeness. People flout maxims for a specific reason and with a specific communicative goal in mind. This is to be contrasted with the possibility that they violate the maxim of quantity, as exemplified by B's utterance in (27).

(27) A: Where are you going?
      B: Out.

Ruling out the option that B does not know where she is going, A can deduce from the answer that B does not want to give an answer and is just being uncooperative. Thus B is not saying less to produce an implicature but simply to withhold information.

At first glance, it seems like Emily Dickinson is violating the maxim of manner with the beginning of "My Life had stood" in saying something ambiguous.

(28) My Life had stood – a Loaded Gun –
      In Corners – till a Day

Let us assume, for the sake of simplicity, that (28) only allows for the two readings in (29a) and (29b) below.

(29) a. I am human and I stand in corners
      b. I am a gun and I stand in corners

The two readings are incompatible and can thus not both be true at the same time. Yet the ambiguity cannot be resolved at this point in the poem and continues to be prominent throughout the whole text (see chapter I.6). Furthermore, given what we know about poems in general and Emily Dickinson in particular, it is unlikely that she is trying to be uncooperative and is thus violating the manner maxim to confuse the reader. So what is her pragmatic intent? As seen in chapter I.6, both readings are relevant. We have argued that they are combined via disjunction (compare also Brockmann et al. 2017):

(30) λw. the speaker is human in w & the speaker stands in corners in w
or
the speaker is a gun in w' & the speaker stands in corners in w

Given that FictionalAssert is a conditional, having a disjunction instead of a conjunction in the antecedent actually makes the statement stronger:

(31) ⟦FictionalAssert⟧ = λT. ∀w [the speaker is human in w & the speaker stands in corners in w **or** the speaker is a gun in w & the speaker stands in corners in w & w is maximally similar to @ otherwise → R(@)(w)]
"For all worlds w where the speaker is human and stands in corners or where the speaker is a gun and stands in corner it holds that w stands in relation R to the actual world."

This disjunction captures that both readings are relevant for the text meaning and even makes the overall assertion stronger, such that for both cases a relation between the text-worlds and the evaluation world of the reader can be established. Both readings contribute to establishing R, the relation of the worlds in which what the text says is true to the actual world. Since both propositions in (30) are part of the text meaning, it forces the reader to reflect upon the relation between human beings and guns to establish R. This reflection mechanism is crucial for the understanding of the poem (see chapter I.6). The ambiguity in (28) is thus not to be considered either a violation or flouting of a maxim. It is a different strategy which seems like flouting/violating conversational maxims at first glance, but, at the level of text, no maxim is violated and the speaker must be considered fully cooperative. The mechanism is thus described as **apparent flouting** (see Brockmann et al. 2017).

Summary: P3

Our observation leads to a second refinement of P3 given below.

(P3") The special communicative situation created by poetry reveals that pragmatic strategies depend on context. The pragmatic step involved in the interpretation of lyrical texts affects the generation of implicatures.

1.4 Conclusion and Outlook

The three main proposals we defended and argued for in this chapter are repeated in their refined versions below:

(P1')   Lyrical texts follow the rules of UG. They deviate from the grammar of the language of origin in ways similar to language varieties. They do not allow for violations of universal rules, e.g. fundamental rules of composition.

(P2')   Creative uses of language in poetry reveal the whole potential of language. A large range of the reinterpretive possibilities that the grammar allows for is laid open. The driving force of reinterpretation is not limited to plain uninterpretability; the direction and pathways of reinterpretation are less fixed than standard coercion theories assume.

(P3')   The special communicative situation created in poetry reveals that choosing between static and dynamic interpretation depends on the text type. Dynamic updates are related to the increment size. The pragmatic step can be postponed to text level in lyrical texts and interpretation proceeds dynamically until then.

(P3")   The special communicative situation created by poetry reveals that pragmatic strategies depend on context. The pragmatic step involved in the interpretation of lyrical texts affects the generation of implicatures.

Given our results, we find that the often made distinction between "ordinary" language and "poetic" language is misleading in that it suggests that poetic language is not ordinary (enough) to be considered as data by formal semanticists and pragmaticists. Our claim is that lyrical texts use a variety of a given language. The grammar of this language variety deviates in certain respects from the grammar of the standard variety. These deviations are not mistakes but are systematic and used by a native speaker to achieve a certain goal. Identifying the system behind these deviations is crucial for understanding the core grammar. Moreover, we have shown that the nature of the pragmatic step in the interpretation of lyrical texts (modelled by FictionalAssert) affects phenomena at the semantics-pragmatics interface. FictionalAssert interacts with dynamic versus static interpretation and with implicature (non-)generation. No doubt further investigation into the scope and the content of the pragmatic step in fiction will reveal further such interactions. Lyrical texts provide a rich data source for future work in semantics and pragmatics.

III.2 Formal Linguistics as a Tool in Literary Studies

If poetry is a data source that helps advance formal linguistic theory, literary studies will be advanced by taking into account the results of formal semantic and pragmatic investigation. Accordingly, this chapter will take up several of the points raised in III.1 but turn around the direction of interest and consider the benefit for literary studies (and not just for Dickinson studies) of exploring the linguistic mechanisms found in Emily Dickinson's poetry. Thus we would like to take up the idea put forward above in III.1.2.4: texts entirely lacking syntactic and semantic complexity are as irrelevant for present purposes as those (few) that cannot be interpreted according to the rules of composition. Emily Dickinson's poems themselves are sometimes closer to one end of the spectrum than the other, but all of them lie within it, i.e. they are complex but not uninterpretable.[1] From the point of view of literary studies, such texts require linguistic explanation in order to reveal their meaning. Accordingly, the nature of the linguistic phenomena will be significant for the literary evaluation of the texts, and an exact, formal description of the semantic and pragmatic mechanisms at work will enable us to address literary questions with greater precision. For example, if we are interested in the notions of identity put forward by Emily Dickinson, it is not just enough to consider such a poem as "I'm Nobody" (J288/Fr260) in a general way. Only by a precise description of her unconventional use of quantifiers in this poem (see chapter I.3) do we arrive at a clear idea of Dickinson's reflection on identity. It is central to this reflection that the same statement refers to what a person is (her properties) and **who** she is (which individual), and that there is an interplay of two persons possibly (and paradoxically) sharing properties and identities.

In particular, we are able to identify three aspects of our linguistic analysis that are especially profitable for literary studies.

---

[1] The poems selected for this study are all challenging but interpretable. In Dickinson's oeuvre, there are a number of poems which present comparatively few difficulties, such a J1763/Fr1788A: "Fame is a bee. / It has a song – / It has a sting – / Ah, too, it has a wing." This is still much more complex than the birthday poem quoted in III.1.2.4 above but easily interpretable as a metaphor (a version of the metaphysical conceit), in which different features of the vehicle all contribute to the overall meaning. Nearer the uninterpretable end of the spectrum, there are utterances such as "'Again' is of a twice" in J1454/Fr1486A ("Those not live yet"), which, considered in isolation, may appear like a line of nonsense poetry.

[1] We have seen that readers of poems and other literary texts are not expected to dismiss them when they come across utterances that appear uninterpretable but to integrate them into a dynamic model of interpretation (see above III.1.3.2). Poetry, because of the delimited context from which to gather information (it is impossible to ask the speaker what she means), is especially suited as evidence for such a dynamic framework. We do not necessarily interpret an utterance immediately but may postpone interpretation to the text level and then establish the relationship between the different utterances. We have seen this, for example, in the case of pronoun resolution in "If it had no pencil" (J921/Fr184A; see chapter I.5) and ambiguity between two equally plausible variable assignment functions in "This was a Poet" (J448/Fr446A; see chapter I.4). Literary studies profit from this analysis as it provides them with a means of explaining the relationship of local and global meanings and of establishing plausible meanings of texts. This relationship will be further discussed below in section III.2.1.

[2] The semantic-pragmatic analysis helps us see why there are not just multiple but sometimes even conflicting interpretations of the same literary texts. It enables us to determine, for example, which combinations of reinterpretations are responsible for the ambiguity of a text, as we have seen in "My Life had stood – a Loaded Gun" (J754/Fr764; see chapter I.6). As a consequence, we can distinguish between meanings that are determined by the way in which the text is composed semantically and, resulting from this compositional meaning, the (pragmatic) meaning a text has for a reader. In a fictional text, this meaning can be modelled with a speech act operator, FictionalAssert (see Bauer and Beck 2014 and above, chapter III.1.3.3), which relates the fictional worlds described by the text to the evaluation world of the reader. Such a linguistic model contributes to literary studies by making it possible to evaluate readings and resolve whether (and in which way) they are based on what the text says. We will consider this gain for literary studies more closely below in section III.2.2.

[3] Literary studies greatly benefit from the linguistic approach pursued by the clarification it provides for the link between language use and fiction. We have seen above in chapter III.1 that a decisive factor in advancing linguistic theory by considering poetic texts is not just the challenge to interpretability they offer but also the opportunity they give us for establishing a dynamic framework of interpretation. The delimited context making this possible is the result of the fictional nature of the texts. What nonfictional texts tell us can always, at least theoretically, be supplemented by further information and therefore corrected, clarified, specified, and disambiguated. This is impossible

in fictional texts, which are counterfactually independent, i.e. cannot be held accountable for their representation of the actual world and therefore cannot be conclusively interpreted by adding information from that world. By our linguistic focus on a framework in which we postpone interpretation to text level and take the pragmatic step needed for establishing the meaning of fictional texts, we have therefore discovered a connection between language use and fictionality that is extremely relevant to literary studies. The connection will be further explained below in section III.2.3.

2.1 Difficulties of Interpretation

In this section, we will take up the linguistic discussion (see above III.1.3.2) of the flexible response to difficulties of interpreting utterances locally and consider its benefit for literary studies. We will discuss its relation to information not provided by the text itself and extend our insight gained by the analysis of Emily Dickinson's poetry to an example from drama (Shakespeare's *Hamlet*). This example will not only show the use of our analysis when it comes to difficulties of interpretation in other fields of literary studies but also indicate what happens if the need for a flexible interpretation arises in a character speech that is part of a fictional text.

2.1.1 Internal and External Information

In the study of literary texts, a model in which we may postpone interpretation to text level is preferable, if not necessary, because of the delimited context. Rather than assert information one by one strictly in the order of reading, a dynamic model of interpretation as it is applied through FictionalAssert allows the reader to collect information on the local level and integrate or revise it at various points during the reading process, and especially after having read the entire text. Unlike everyday discourse, literary texts are self-contained. This does not mean they are disconnected from the culture, time and society in which they were produced. Nor is this to say with Aristotle that each of them is a whole "which has a beginning, a middle and an end" (*Poetics* 1450b); or that every literary text is coherent in itself. But unlike everyday discourse, for which it is potentially possible to provide an infinite amount of additional information, fictional literary texts are self-sufficient units: as a consequence of their counterfactual independence, the texts themselves provide the limited context on which an interpretation of the utterance is based.

Of course, external information may help us understand such texts: in the poem "I found the words to every thought" (J581/Fr436), for example, we may require information about "cochineal" when reading the question "Can Blaze be shown in Cochineal / Or Noon – in Mazarin?" What that question means, however, must still be decided within the context of the poem; we cannot ask the speaker if "shown in Cochineal" means that she asks if a blaze can be painted by using a particular shade of red. We have to decide this on the basis of the poem alone. Furthermore, it may be useful to know what Emily Dickinson means elsewhere when she uses the word. Particular expressions, turns of phrase and grammatical constructions may constitute a poet's idiolect. In the poem "Autumn – overlooked my Knitting –" (J748/Fr786), for example, there is the line "Cochineal – I chose – for deeming"; the context suggests that this is a colour the speaker gets from Autumn for her knitting. Dickinson obviously had a certain liking for the word; nevertheless, we cannot be sure it always means the same.[2] Similarly, even when regarding a text as "fluid" from an editorial point of view (see Bryant 2002), we cannot be sure whether or not an existing variant is to mean the same as the expression included in the text we interpret. In "I found the words to every thought," Johnson's critical edition tells us that there is the variant "done" for "shown" in the line "Can Blaze be shown in Cochineal," which supports, but does not prove, that Cochineal is the colour used to represent a blaze pictorially. A variant can only be part of the context that determines the meaning of the poem if it is part of the poem as it stands in the version we read, rather than an earlier or later state of it, i.e. a different text.[3]

---

[2] She uses the word synesthetically for a tune, for example, in J1059/Fr1083A which begins: "Sang from the Heart, Sire, / Dipped my Beak in it, / If the Tune drip too much / Have a tint too Red // Pardon the Cochineal – / Suffer the Vermillion – / Death is the Wealth / Of the Poorest Bird."

[3] Miller (2016) writes that for Emily Dickinson, "[i]ncluding alternatives in writing out a poem was not a constant practice; well over half of Dickinson's poems contain no alternative words of any kind" (5), and points out that the alternatives noted down in the manuscripts oscillate between "alternative words, revisions, cancellations" (ibid.). Since the purposes are manifold, the mere fact that a variant exists does not immediately tell us something about interpretation. Content-wise, some of the variants can be seen as quasi-synonyms, or expressions of the same (or similar) theme overall; see, for instance, J531/Fr584, in which one line is given alternatively as "And perhaps a **phrase in Egyptian**" or as "And perhaps **latin inscription**" (emphasis added). In other poems, such as J1182/Fr1234, the alternative seems to go in an entirely different direction; two versions of the final two lines of the poem are, firstly, "Leave me not ever there alone / Oh thou Almighty God!," or secondly: "Look to it by its Fathoms / Ourselves be not pursued!" Dickinson's penchant to sometimes note down variants on the same sheet and other times write versions of the same poem on different sheets with significant changes needs

This state of affairs, however, makes fictional literary texts especially suitable for a dynamic model of interpretation: fixed as the contexts are, the relation between the local level, with increment sizes as small as words or phrases, and the global level of the text leads to an overall interpretation of the text. In the case of "I found the words to every thought" the global level of the text suggests that the colour "Cochineal" is meant metaphorically as an example of the word(s) the poet seeks to find. The external information (in particular, other poems by Emily Dickinson) confirms that such a metaphorical reading is plausible but it is the fictional text itself that must warrant it.

2.1.2 Context Information in Character Speech: An Example from *Hamlet*

In the preceding chapters we have seen a variety of linguistic phenomena which are interpreted by means of drawing information from the context. In chapters I.1 and especially I.4, for instance, we discussed **demonstratives**. We have shown that in fictional texts, and poetry in particular, the Appropriateness Condition (cf. Heim and Kratzer 1998), under which the mapping of pronouns – and by extension demonstratives (such as "this") – to a salient referent within the context, needs to be locally (i.e. on the sentence level) suspended, since the available context is (usually) limited to the text itself, and no extralinguistic context is provided where referents may be sought out.

We want to show the benefits of consulting linguistic theory in literary studies beyond the realm of Dickinson's poetry by illustrating the analysis with an example from *Hamlet*. This example likewise provides a challenge to our analysis since it is taken from drama, which means that it occurs in the speech of a character and that performance (real or imaginary) comes into play, i.e. extralinguistic codes such as gestures, movements, dress, etc. (Elam 2002). Though we take these features into account, we regard them as dependent on the linguistic meaning of the text. Consider the referential properties of language in this example:

---

to be taken into account as well for interpretation, for which a one-size-fits-all approach is not helpful. See also Cameron (1992), *Choosing Not Choosing*; Mitchell (2005), Measures of Possibility; and more recently Crumbley and Heginbotham, eds. (2014), *Dickinson's Fascicles*.

(1)   POLONIUS
        Take this from this if this be otherwise.
        If circumstances lead me I will find
        Where truth is hid, though it were hid indeed
        Within the centre.   (*Hamlet* Q2 2.2.153-156)[4]

Elam suggests that the language is self-sufficient and not in need of additional stage directions, though he quotes a slightly different version of the text:

(2)   Thus when Polonius issues his famous triple-decker index 'Take *this* from *these* if *this* be otherwise', the accompanying gestures – absolutely indispensable to the sense of the utterance – are *inscribed* in the language itself, rendering quite redundant the stage directions added by such modern editors as John Dover Wilson ('he points to his head and shoulders').   (Elam 2002, 129)

Modern editions give Polonius' utterance as quoted above, i.e.:

(3)   Take this$_1$ from this$_2$ if this$_3$ be otherwise.
        [indices added for clarification]

In the text version Elam uses, "this$_2$" is rendered as "these" in an effort to clarify the passage; "these" may well refer to his "shoulders," as Dover Wilson suggests.[5] Nevertheless, Elam still glosses over the fact that the various instances of "this" in the passage quoted by him are not all mapped to the same referent but require different indices: while "this$_1$" and "this$_2$" are deictic markers and can ostensibly refer to extralinguistic signs, i.e. possibly indicate gestures to head and torso respectively, "this$_3$" does no such thing. Rather, the context of the conversation between Polonius and the King and Queen suggests that "this$_3$" maps to what was said earlier by Polonius:

---

4 We cite Q2 of *Hamlet* as given in the Arden Shakespeare (2016).
5 Or, as Dawson in the Norton edition indicates, *"indicating his head and torso,"* which solves the numerus issue of "this$_2$" unless rendered as "these"; however, the edition also neglects annotating "this$_3$" in the passage, which is arguably as interesting a question on the textual level as the preceding "this$_1$" and "this$_2$" are with regard to the performance aspect.

(4) [POLONIUS]
And he, repelled, a short tale to make,
Fell into a sadness, then into a fast,
Thence to a watch, thence into a weakness,
Thence to lightness, and by this declension
Into the madness wherein now he raves,
And all we mourn for.

KING
Do you think this?

QUEEN   It may be, very like.

POLONIUS
Hath there been such a time – I would fain know that –
That I have positively said 'tis so
When it proved otherwise?

KING   Not that I know.

POLONIUS
Take this from this if this be otherwise.
If circumstances lead me I will find
Where truth is hid, though it were hid indeed
Within the centre.   (*Hamlet* Q2 2.2.143-156)

We see that there are various instances in this text passage where the demonstrative "this" is used; by the time the reader arrives at "this$_3$" as in (3), a number of possible mappings become clear, depending on which feature of Polonius's previous speech he makes reference to. The most proximal possibility is his avowal that he would not tell a lie ("Hath there been such a time ... When it proved otherwise?"). However, it is equally likely that he wishes to assert once more the information shared earlier – namely that Hamlet's madness stems from his being rejected by Ophelia. The matter is complicated because the multiple repetition of "this" in quick succession marks the demonstrative as conspicuous (see also the King's interjection, "Do you think this?"), alerting the reader to the possibility of multiple referents, and simultaneously asking her to keep track of them. Similar to what we have seen in chapter I.4 on "This was a

Poet," where the reader holds off on interpreting "This" until more information has been gathered by reading on, readers of *Hamlet* may be hesitant to decide for a referent straightaway. Instead of awaiting further information in what immediately follows, however, they will rather go back in the text and revise their state of information in order to assign a possible referent.[6] Either option of identifying a referent for "this$_3$" (paraphrased in (5) and (6) below) interacts with the global level of the text:

(5)   Polonius always tells the truth.

(6)   Hamlet has become mad because Ophelia rejected him.

The reader, of course, knows both (5) and (6) to be untrue: Polonius is not a particularly sincere character, and Hamlet's madness is a ploy. In drama (and in other texts that comprise character speech), dynamic interpretation may therefore involve two stages: taking into account the context of what a character says, and taking into account the context of the whole play. The obfuscation of meaning visible in (3) is characteristic of Polonius, who often does the opposite of what he says he does.[7] As we have seen in chapter I.4, one feature of the demonstrative "this" is that its referent is proximal, as opposed to a relatively more remote referent for the corresponding demonstrative "that." On the one hand, reading (5) is more proximal than (6) as it directly precedes the quoted line; on the other hand, due to the overall length of the text, proximity surely is relative and must remain flexible, in particular because of the afore-mentioned repetition of "this": "this$_3$," which is here under discussion, is separated from the conversational context and potential referents by "this$_1$" and "this$_2$," both of

---

[6] This is easier for a reader than for the spectator of a performance, which confirms views such as Erne's (2003) that Shakespeare's plays were not exclusively written for performance.

[7] See, e.g., earlier in the passage, where Polonius disavows using art (i.e. flourishing speech) in order to communicate relevant information, yet uses curiously stylized speech in doing so:
    Madam, I swear I use no art at all.
    That he's mad, 'tis true, 'tis true 'tis pity,
    And pity 'tis 'tis true: a foolish figure!
    But farewell it, for I will use no art.
    Mad let us grant him then, and now remains
    That we find out the cause of this effect –
    Or rather say the cause of this defect,
    For this effect defective comes by cause.   (*Hamlet* Q2 2.2.96-103)
See also Bross (2017, 171f.).

which point to extralinguistic meaning. Since no referent is available which is not separated by at least two other demonstratives, the reader will need to accommodate different possible referents during the reading in order to make sense of the utterance while acknowledging the peculiarity of the phrasing.

Readers are therefore compelled to adopt a dynamic interpretation to allow them to accumulate (and remember) more information about either Polonius, Hamlet, or the play in general, before they decide on whether there can be a single referent of "this$_3$" – or whether the deliberate lack of clarity as regards the demonstrative contributes to an overall reading of the play in which ambiguity is a meaningful feature.[8] The assigning of a referent may therefore coincide with identifying analogies between the interpretation of the local passage and interpreting the global level of the text. This identification is similar to what we have seen in our analysis of "This was a Poet," where not only the demonstrative "this" contributes to distinguishable readings but other features of the text do so as well, such as the ambiguous line "The Robbing – could not harm –" (see below III.2.2). The interpretation process is further complicated by the communicative situation of literary texts, most noticeable in dramatic discourse: there is the discourse situation on the internal level of communication – i.e. information about the participants, their common ground, conversational goals and their pragmatic use of language etc. – as well as on the external level of communication – i.e. the information conveyed to the reader (or audience) by means of the internal communication. If an ambiguity such as the one in "Take this from this if **this** be otherwise" is considered strategic, is it strategic on behalf of the character within the fiction, or on behalf of the author who tells us something about the character's discourse? The impact on a global text interpretation varies with the answer to this question. Thus, for literary texts, the dynamic model of interpretation that linguistic theory makes available is useful because it allows us to describe how local phenomena interact with each other and with the global level of the text, and how an overall interpretation is made possible through analysing this interaction. At the same time, the perspective of literary studies makes us realize that several of such processes may be connected.

The *Hamlet* example has shown that the local suspension of mapping a demonstrative to a salient referent in the context has consequences for the performance; a linguistically informed interpretation helps decide which "this" requires or suggests a gesture. Furthermore, Polonius's words show that character speeches within works of fiction are also fictional; the referent for the

---
8 See esp. Bross (2017).

demonstrative must be found within the context of the play. At the same time, the author, by making the suspension of mapping the demonstrative to a referent part of a character speech, uses this feature in order to characterize Polonius's way of speaking.

2.2 Literary Interpretation and the Semantics–Pragmatics Interface

In this section, we address several common pitfalls of literary interpretation and show how our method avoids them. In particular, we will consider what adequacy of interpretation means in our approach, and that a text may be dealt with inadequately by either ignoring its ambiguity, by making it mean anything you like, or by adding external information that is not evoked by the text itself.[9] This does not mean that the text meaning is only constituted by what is expressly stated. Accordingly, we will consider the contribution of non-compositional elements (such as the form of a sonnet) to the meaning of a fictional text.

The dynamic model of interpretation allows not only for a closer look at the relation between local phenomena and the text as a whole but also at the interaction of different interpretations and reinterpretations of the same literary text. The semantics-pragmatics interface provides the framework within which adequate interpretation is made possible; it targets the difference between what a text means and what the text means to someone. Within this framework, not only do we find possible readings of a text, but we are also able to make informed statements about the greater plausibility of certain readings over others, which might be possible but not very plausible, especially when considering the interaction between local and global text level (see above 2.1). Ideally, an interpretation that relies on possible and plausible readings alike can be shown to be adequate to the text it references.

---

[9] Expounding assessments of ambiguity from classical antiquity to the present day, Ossa-Richardson (2019) distinguishes between "minimizers" and "maximizers" (9). The former, of whom he cites Rimmon (1977) as an example, speak of ambiguity only when there is the need for a choice between alternative meanings, the latter, represented by Beardsley (1958) and others, aim at "getting as much meaning out of the poem as possible" (Ossa-Richardson 2019, 11). Neither position seems tenable to us in the light of our textual analyses.

2.2.1 Adequacy of Interpretation

Adequacy of interpretation[10] is achieved when the elements of the text and the elements of the interpretation correspond to each other; that is, if there is an element A in the text, there has to be an element A' in the interpretation, and so on. Likewise, if element A translates to ambiguity in interpretation, there will be both A' and A". When text complexity increases, then so must the complexity of interpretation. See, for example, the following line in (7) from "This was a Poet":

(7)   The Robbing – could not harm –

(8)   [[$_{NP}$ the [[robbing *(of)* x] *(by)* y]] [$_{VP}$ not [harm x]]]

There are two contextually available antecedents, the "Poet" and the readers, who are equally plausible candidates for the two variables, though it is not clear which antecedent stands for which variable. The two possible readings come along with two respective sentence structures:

(9) a. [[$_{NP}$ the [[robbing of the_readers] by the_poet]] [$_{VP}$ not [harm the_readers]]]
     b. [[$_{NP}$ the [[robbing of the_poet] by the_readers]] [$_{VP}$ not [harm the_poet]]]

The compositional interpretation provided by formal semantics shows how the semantic ellipsis leads to two discrete readings of the line given in (7), which can be related to the overall text meaning. Since we are dealing with fictional discourse, both readings may persist at the same time; in fact, this may be the very point of the utterance. Since neither agent nor patient of the "Robbing" are specified, the context of the poem allows us to read this line conjunctively in that both the poet robs the readers and the readers rob the poet simultaneously. The relationship between the two agents is thus dramatized as a mutual one through the economic means of a semantic ellipsis, and it becomes reciprocal and equitable with respect to the robbing. Semantic analysis reveals the structures and relations of elements of the sentence in such a way that interpretation emerges directly from the text rather than being arbitrary and indiscriminate.

---

10 This section follows the model for approaching adequacy of interpretation as outlined in more detail in Bauer and Brockmann (2017).

In the case of example (7), the two related interpretations can be represented schematically:

(10)

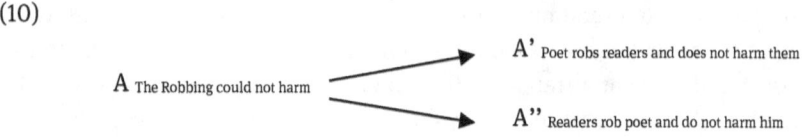

2.2.2 Restriction through Disambiguation

An example from Leiter (2007) shows that the mutual relationship of poet and readers in (7) is not always recognised:

(11)   So sufficient is [the Poet] unto himself, he would scarcely notice should he be robbed. [...] By condemning us 'by Contrast— / To ceaseless Poverty—,' this Poet, far from enhancing his readers, underscores their inadequacy. (208)

Leiter ignores the second reading of the semantic ellipsis; for her, the hierarchy is clearly in favour of the poet. Readings such as Leiter's in (11) neglect essential elements of Dickinson's poetry and do not take into account the complexity of linguistic expression that she achieves, such as the semantic ellipsis above. Leiter's disambiguating the lines restricts the scope of interpretation: instead of presenting a complex and interactive relationship between the poet and the readers, she suggests the poet is presented as superior to the readers, whose "inadequacy" is highlighted. As we have shown in our analysis, however, this does not do the poem justice; since Dickinson exploits a variety of linguistic phenomena, we would miss her point by ignoring them. Analysing Dickinson's poetry linguistically allows for each of these elements to be identified and then reappear in interpretation accordingly. The schema in (10) illustrates the principle: the semantic ellipsis triggers ambiguity, which, since it cannot be resolved but remains global on the level of text, must find its expression in the overall interpretation of the poem as well. Hence, we speak of a mutual relationship between poet and speaker, in which each has an effect of some kind on the other. Deciding for one of the two readings and excluding the other would be detrimental to text interpretation, neglecting, even ignoring that both are expressed in the text. The methodology of formal linguistics proves particularly pertinent here, since this linguistic discipline is concerned with composition, i.e. how meaning in language comes about in combining different parts. Formal linguistics allows a systematic and in-depth approach to the text and reveals how a reader can make sense of these complex units, both within the structures of a sentence or line, as well as in the text of the poem as a whole. As we have seen in chapter II.2, we can then understand the principles that underlie the language of Dickinson's poetry, and arrive at a more rewarding and extensive view of her poetics. Language is the basis of Dickinson's poetry not merely because the poems are linguistic expressions, but because they reflect on language and lend a particular power to linguistic expression.

2.2.3 The "Anything Goes" Approach

Literary criticism sometimes restricts the text meaning, as indicated above. It is also at times doing the opposite by opening what it deems text meaning into the arbitrary. Consider the following example from Robert Smith's (1996) commentary on "You said that I 'was Great'":

(12) The possible affective manipulation of the reader by the poem is facilitated by the poem's exaggerated offering to the reader of the possibility of its **own** manipulation. For example, poem 738 is a poetic offering insofar as it is possible to imagine that the voice is that of the poem as it directly interpellates its reader. [...] **The poem assumes that it will be what its reader chooses to make it, responsive to every whim. This is generally true of Dickinson's canon: her poems can suit the desire of their readers perfectly.** In this case, whether that reader interprets this poem as representing the voice of Dickinson discussing her varied personae ("if Queen it be") or, my own pun-determined choice, a representation of language speaking itself ("Or Page—please Thee"), or anything else at all ("Or other thing—if other thing there be") is ultimately all the same. **The fact that the speaker/poem offers the possibility that she/it can be made absolutely malleable to the desire of its addressee/reader is all that matters.** My own refashioning of the poem—the interpretation of it as a self-reflexive poetic allegory—is simply a "suitable" example of how the speaker's "Stipulus" ensures her poem's successful initial engagement with a reader's interpretive desire. (1996, 139f.; emphasis added)

In our analysis of the poem in chapter I.2, we show that the text offers great flexibility with respect to seemingly conflicting attributes in the context of the notoriously underspecified adjective "great," achieved through the speaker's clever play with scales and lexical meaning. Smith thus reads the poem as "a self-reflexive poetic allegory" and transfers this play to Dickinson's poetics. While it is certainly true that the complexity and richness of her poetry rightfully inspires a great variety of criticism, the claim that it "can be made absolutely malleable to the desire of its addressee/reader is all that matters" – especially if, as Smith suggests, this applies not only to the poem at hand but is valid for Dickinson's canon across the board – has far-reaching implications for the validity of interpretation. If any poem can have any number of meanings and "suit the desire of [its] readers perfectly," does it really have any meaning that we can agree on at all? Or do we only impose readings on the text, irrespective of what it actually says and thus treat it as a completely blank canvas?

The problem with this stance is obvious: if fictional texts did not have semantic meaning specific to the individual text, there would be no point in reading (nor, indeed, writing) them.[11] In the case of "You said," we have shown that, while there is a certain amount of flexibility and freedom, there are restrictions as well, for example in terms of the scales addressed within the poem. The speaker refers to scales such as size, height, and rank; even though the different positions on these scales are juxtaposed paradoxically with each other, none of the speaker's examples leaves the frame altogether (there is no indication that the reader is invited to think about the speaker's wealth, health, looks or age or IQ). The point is hence not, as Smith concludes, that text meaning "can suit the desire of their readers perfectly" without further qualification. The linguistic makeup of the text determines the limitations within which interpretation is to be found. A close linguistic analysis specifies not only where there is flexibility, but also which limitations apply. It adds validity to the resulting interpretations: wholly impossible and implausible readings are circumvented by formal linguistic analysis. What Smith obfuscates in the passage cited is the difference between the text meaning and its significance for an individual reader: the poem does not "assume[s] that it will be what its reader chooses to make it, responsive to every whim." The freedom of interpretation sets in where what the text says is applied by readers to their own evaluation world, in which they may, for example, remember situations in which they have been at the mercy of people like the poem's speaker, who can analyse a well-meant compliment as well as implement it. These situations may be vastly different from each other in

---

11 See also Bauer and Beck (2014).

each reader's case, but this is not the same as saying that the poem may mean anything to any reader. If anything, the relation R between the text worlds and the actual world of the reader leaves a degree of liberty to place emphasis on some parts of the text more than on others, or to read a poem in a specific context.

2.2.4 Reading into the Text: Restricting through Enriching

The last point we would like to make with regard to adequacy of interpretation concerns information that is extraneous to the text itself but is brought into play at the level of text interpretation. The pitfalls connected with this procedure may be avoided by starting with the semantics of the text.

For instance, it is debatable how much scope a particular contextual reference should have across the interpretation of the whole poem. See, for instance, Domnhall Mitchell (2002) on "I'm Nobody":

(13) "I'm Nobody! Who are you?" is often sentimentalized as a kind of apologia for the oppressed and marginal, partly on the grounds that the banishment referred to in the fourth line of the first stanza is traditionally one of the punishments for dissent against tyranny. Such liberal readings of the poem are complicated – though not fully denied – by the inclusion of "Bog" at the end of the poem, for the word was associated derogatively with the Irish in nineteenth-century Massachusetts. Rather than expressing sympathy for the disenfranchised, the speaker expresses both anxiety and contempt for the democratic system that gives "bog-trotters" access to political and cultural influence. (197)

Mitchell gives a thorough analysis of the text in his monograph *Emily Dickinson: Monarch of Perception*, but highlights the point about "Bog" in "I'm Nobody" being a reference to Irish settlers in 19th-century Massachusetts in the essay quoted above. He refers to interpretations that focus on the poem being read as an "apologia for the oppressed and marginalized" as "liberal"; at the same time, his own inclusion of the historical context leads him to present a reading of the poem as a thinly veiled complaint about the Irish having "access to political and cultural influence."

About "A Bird came down the Walk," which we address in chapter II.1, "The Poet as Linguist," Ruth Miller writes: "This poem has no message, no lesson; it has no biographical or historical significance. But for itself we cherish it" (210). For one thing, it is debatable whether the poem truly has "no message" at all (Miller writes that the poem is about "a real bird" (ibid.)); for another, the passage implies that there **should** be "biographical or historical significance." We want to emphasise her assessment at the end: "for itself we cherish it." Paying attention to the biographical and historical context of the poet is often worthwhile and helps to access a poem's subtler references and underlying assumptions, for instance, with regard to the vocabulary and its scope of meaning at a particular period. At the same time, enriching a poem by biographical-historical context may paradoxically lead to a reduction of interpretation: should the fact that "If it had no pencil" was wrapped around a pencil and likely a gift for a specific addressee mean that the poem can be read only with this biographical moment in mind? Likewise: should the fact that "bog-trotters" was a 19th-century slang term for the Irish mean that we consider the message of "I'm Nobody" to be a tongue-in-cheek complaint about the political voice of the marginalized?

It is tempting to award these poems with "historical significance," as Ruth Miller states. But more often than not, the elaboration of a specific context or reference narrows down the possibilities for interpretation and disregards other features of the text, such as the theme of personal identity and belonging, neither of which needs to be necessarily read in a political context. Simply put, "I'm Nobody" is not a poem about Irish settlers – there are no "bog-trotters" mentioned in the poem and it is hard to reconcile such a notion to the "admiring bog" the poem speaks of. If anything, the poem satirizes the frog-like croaking of public speakers. Yet it is possible to read and make sense of the poem with a specific context in mind that is not directly brought up by the poem, as long as its contextual constraints leave intact the interpretative coherence offered by the poem. Through formal linguistic analysis, all possible readings of a poem as far as its language and semantic structure are concerned can be accounted for. Ideally, all elements of the text should be integrated into the interpretation.

2.2.5 The Role of Non-Compositional Meaning

We have outlined the importance of the semantic-pragmatic analysis in our framework in establishing text meaning, and how this analysis helps explain the relation R that the reader draws between the text worlds and the actual world. A challenge is provided by the formalisation of what constitutes non-compositional meaning parts – how to incorporate, for instance, intertextual references, allusions and quotes to other texts into the formal framework we have proposed. Though we have so far not formalised the influence of non-compositional meaning, we argue that every attempt to identify intertextuality is necessarily anchored in the language itself: a quote is only recognizable as a quote if it is a) in some way verbalised in the target text and b) echoes the source text in a way that distinguishes it from other texts, the target text proper included.

Consider the question of identity in "I'm Nobody" as mentioned above. In chapter I.3, we discuss the play with quantifiers and the scope they allow for, but also bring up the issue of possible intertextual references, for instance to the *Odyssey*, and Odysseus' wordplay in calling himself "Nobody" in order to fool the Cyclops. We will assume for the moment that Dickinson's poem does indeed reference the episode, and does not only coincidentally treat the relation between property and name in a way similar to the Odyssey. The Cyclops' name, "Πολύφημος" – or Polyphēmus – can be translated as "many-voiced" or "much spoken of" (*Odyssey* IX.403), allowing for a parallel to the "Somebody" mentioned by Dickinson. Another translation as it is given in *A Greek-English Lexicon* (Liddell-Scott-Jones) is "abounding in songs and legends" – a translation, then, that not only highlights the parallel to "Somebody," but also focuses on the topic of poetry in addition to the play with quantifiers. Readers who have this knowledge of the source text, or who acquire it through e.g. scholarly annotation or research, will accordingly adjust the scope of the relation R to take the added context into account. The pragmatic meaning established for a hypothetical reader may thus focus not only on issues of identity in general but zoom in on the issue of a **poet** and her identity in particular. Yet in either case, the semantic-pragmatic analysis establishes the cornerstones of interpretation which determine R's play as regards pragmatic meaning for a reader.

Similarly, a feature we have often addressed but not formalised in our framework is the question of form or genre. A poem in which the evoking of a fixed generic form is made productive is J315/Fr477, "He fumbles at your Soul" (see chapter II.1). Cristanne Miller (1987) remarks on "its peculiarly tangential coda, or unrhymed concluding couplet" (115) which at first glance appears to be detached from the context of the preceding lines; it lacks "explicit congruence with what preceded" (116). She proposes that the couplet constitute an "analogy for the earlier event" (116); indeed, this is made more salient if we consider the poem's overall structure, which alludes to that of a sonnet: in the English sonnet tradition, the final two lines appear in the form of a rhyming couplet and are set off from the preceding three quatrains; their function is to comment on, summarise, or conclude the poem. In "He fumbles at your soul," we find this structure recalled, though subverted to some degree. While the final two lines first appear separated from the preceding description of the events between "he" and "you" (and "your Soul"), under consideration of the sonnet form, they coincide with the poem's **volta**, "the 'turn' that introduces into the poem a possibility for transformation" (Levin 2001, xxxix). Rather than introduce a change in topic, the final lines provide an analogy by summarising the preceding action through the image of a storm.[12] Yet unlike in a traditional sonnet, the final lines do not constitute a couplet, i.e. are unrhymed; the form is thus recalled and made serviceable to the overall meaning of the text, but not adhered to in the sense that the poem as such would be considered a sonnet. Recognizing the allusion to the form allows for an enriching of the relation R, and of incorporating the knowledge about convention and its function in the pragmatic meaning of the poem.

2.3 The Interface of Linguistic Features and Fictionality

In this section, we will consider some benefits of our approach for the discussion of fictionality. Our analysis has shown that there seem to be particular properties of fictional texts that demand a) a model of interpretation accounting for the interaction of the local and the global level of the text; and b) offer the possibility to generalise from the specific between text worlds and the actual world, retaining semantic types and structures of meaningful text elements.[13] Neither of these are characteristic of non-fictional discourse. Fictional texts therefore doubly contribute to extending semantic concepts; conversely, the semantic conceptualizations of fictional text meaning contribute to advancing literary studies by showing us that fictional and non-fictional texts are, as a rule, interpreted differently. This approach entails new ways of identifying fictionality from a reader-oriented perspective.

In the past, there have been many attempts to distinguish fictional and non-fictional texts by their features. In particular, this has been the concern of narratologists like Cohn:

(14)   Attempting to make up for what she identifies as a general neglect of the distinction between fiction and non-fiction, Cohn suggests three signposts of fictionality that are specific to the fictional domain: the bi-level structure of story and discourse; certain narrative

---

12   See Brockmann et al. (2017).
13   See, for an elaboration, Bauer and Beck (forthcoming).

modes such as the presentation of consciousness; and the doubling of the narrating instance into author and narrator (1999: 130–131). She further argues that the signposts of fictionality point to the 'differential nature of fiction' (131), **reasoning that there are certain semantic elements unique to fiction and which set works of fiction apart from non-fictional works.** (Zetterberg Gjerlevsen 2016, Paragraph 10; emphasis added)

One of the problems that arise from this account is the meaning of "fiction," which Cohn apparently identifies with narrative fiction. Narrative, however, is not identical with fiction: there are non-fictional narratives (i.e. factual accounts) and non-narrative fictional texts (such as Emily Dickinson's poems). All three "signposts of fictionality" are therefore just that: they are characteristic of fictional narratives but do not define fiction logically and are not unique to it. Scholars thus tend to misunderstand each other when it comes to distinguishing fiction from non-fictional works, as can be seen in Cohn's response to Searle:

(15) Among the many theorists of various persuasions who have reiterated the thesis that fictional and nonfictional narratives are lookalikes, it will serve my purpose to single out one who provides an example to prove his point. In his well-known essay "The Logical Status of Fictional Discourse," John Searle writes: "There is no textual property, syntactic or semantic, that will identify a text as a work of fiction" (1975: 325). And again: "The utterance acts in fiction are indistinguishable from the utterance acts in serious discourse, and it is for that reason that there is no textual property that will identify a stretch of discourse as a work of fiction" (ibid.: 327). These statements appear in a speech-act theoretical discussion of the following "stretch of discourse" (ibid.: 322):

> Ten more glorious days without horses! So thought Second Lieutenant Andrew Chase-Smith recently commissioned in the distinguished regiment of King Edwards Horse, as he pottered contentedly in a garden on the outskirts of Dublin on a sunny Sunday afternoon in April nineteen-sixteen.

Searle, who tells us that he picked this passage (the inception of Iris Murdoch's *The Red and the Green*) "at random," seems quite unaware of how effectively it disproves his case. To mention only the most obvious: What "serious" discourse ever quoted the thoughts of a person other than the speaker's own? (Cohn 1990, 784)

Cohn thinks she triumphs over Searle by turning his example against him. Indeed, she is quite correct in pointing out that quoting the thoughts of another person is much more typical of fictional texts than any other form of discourse. But she seems to misunderstand Searle, who only speaks of syntactic and semantic properties of the text. And, in this respect, he is right. An exclamation like "Ten more glorious days without horses!" is not phrased any differently in fictional and non-fictional contexts. Furthermore, Cohn's claim as regards the restrictions for the non-fictional quotation of thoughts is problematic, as even a random example from the internet shows: "Electric cars are the future, or so think many car manufacturers."[14]

This is why we think it makes much more sense to define fictional texts logically as being independent from the actual world, i.e. not asserted in the ordinary sense, and then differentiate their meaning from non-fictional texts by considering the dynamic framework of interpretation and the pragmatic meaning derived from the text meaning by the speech act operator FictionalAssert. In other words: the main difference between fictional and non-fictional texts lies in the way in which their meaning is established. Theoretically, it is thus possible to interpret any non-fictional text as fiction and vice versa, although in practice this is unlikely. Cohn's "signposts of fictionality," even though they do not indicate necessary and defining features of fiction, invite us to read a text as fiction. Furthermore, there are, as a rule, unambiguous paratextual instructions, such as the word "novel" on the cover of a book or authorial statements such as the following by Emily Dickinson, which clearly show that a text is written as fiction: "When I state myself, as the Representative of the Verse—it does not mean—me—but a supposed person" (L268). The word "Representative" is instructive since it shows that Dickinson addresses the specific way in which the meaning of fiction is brought about: the individual that speaks is not the author making a factual statement but "a supposed person" that acts as a "Representative" of what the poem says.[15] The first-person speaker can be seen as one indi-

---

14 https://www.techadvisor.co.uk/feature/digital-home/best-electric-cars-for-2017-3653671/
15 See also Herrnstein Smith, who emphasizes the representative character of poetry, and in whose view "what a poem distinctively and characteristically represents is not images, ideas, feelings, characters, scenes, or worlds, but discourse. Poetry does, like drama, represent actions and events, but exclusively verbal ones. And, as a verbal composition, a poem is distinctively and characteristically not a natural utterance, but the representation of one" (Herrnstein Smith 1971, 269). Dickinson provides a direct counter-example to Käte Hamburger, who considers poetry non-fictional; in *Die Logik der Dichtung*, Hamburger postulates: "Das Erlebnis kann 'fiktiv' im Sinne von erfunden sein, aber das Erlebnis – und mit ihm das Aussagesubjekt, das lyrische Ich, kann nur als ein reales und niemals ein fiktives vorgefunden werden" (Hamburger

vidual instantiation of what the poem fictionally asserts. This representativeness enables its readers to put themselves in the position of the speaker and/or addressee, i.e. interpret the poem as having a meaning **for them**.

Paradoxically, the specific openness of a fictional text, its having a meaning for its readers which is as different as their lives but still not arbitrary, is brought about by a limitation: its restriction to the contexts which it includes.[16] We cannot ask the speaker who says "This was a Poet" to whom or what she refers by "this"; we have to evaluate the poem as a whole for the options it may give us and then consider those options and their relation to each other as the intended meaning of the utterance. This process of interpretation is a hallmark of the fictional text. We notice the ambiguity of "My Life had stood – a Loaded Gun –" and cannot ask if the speaker imagines what a gun's life is like or if she wants to make a statement about her life. We must read on and realize that both options are maintained throughout the poem so that its meaning lies in their very co-presence and not in the discarding of the one in favour of the other. But if this mode of interpretation characterizes fictional poems, stories and plays, it is no coincidence that we interpret them pragmatically in a specific way. If interpretation is not concluded locally, we are invited to reflect on the meaning itself and ask pragmatically about what the text may mean for us. A formal linguistic analysis of the relationship between textual interpretation and the pragmatic step remains a challenge, just as Emily Dickinson's poetry will have many more challenges in store for linguists and literary scholars alike.

1957, 246). Why the speaker of a poem should not be considered fictive – as indeed we do, and as Dickinson's "supposed person" suggests likewise – remains unclear; see also Zipfel 2001, 300f.

16 This point is related to what Beardsley considers the "prime mark of fictionality in poetry," i.e. "'address without access.' I mean that the ostensible speaker evidently wishes to communicate with someone directly and immediately – there is an ostensible someone whom he is addressing – but the *author* has cut his text loose from any particular occasion that might afford access to such an addressee" (Beardsley 1981, 304f.). Like Herrnstein Smith, Beardsley considers poetry *"representation* of an illocutionary action" (307), and, therefore, "[o]ur task is rather to *construct* appropriate actions by filling in the gaps of the text in a reasonable way" (307). While we find the notion of "gaps" somewhat misleading (the text is deliberately constructed that way and does not lack anything; its context is deliberately delimited), we share the view that the reader will do something with the communication and relate it to her evaluation world.

Appendix

In this appendix, we will give a brief introduction into the linguistic theory we assume as the background for our analyses throughout this book. Readers who are familiar with formal linguistics will not need to consult the appendix. We will look at three components of linguistic analysis: syntax, semantics, and pragmatics. We will introduce basic concepts from each of the three components in turn, starting with syntax in section 1.1, proceeding with semantics in section 1.2, and finishing with pragmatics in section 1.3.

For the purposes of this book, we generally use the simplest possible framework that can help us analyse the data. This framework is only extended if necessary. For a general introduction to modern linguistic theory, see e.g. Beck and Gergel (2014, chapter 1).

1.1 Syntax

1.1.1 Phrase Structure Grammar

In the tradition of Generative Grammar (Chomsky 1981; Haegeman 1994; Haegeman and Guéron 1999), we analyse all sentences of natural language as hierarchical structures generated by a set of recursive rules, constrained by general principles. On the basis of these rules and principles, we can define what kind of structures are well-formed sentences (cf. e.g. Beck and Gergel 2014, 8).[1] The structure of a sentence is made up by component parts, called "constituents." The individual constituents are phrases that are constructed in a systematic way, endocentrically: each phrase has a lexical head which determines the category of the phrase. Other elements are built around this head and occupy different hierarchical positions. The Noun Phrase (NP) "the actress," for example, is headed by the noun "actress" and has in its specifier position the determiner "the." It can be further modified, for example with the Prepositional Phrase (PP) "with long hair," which is an adjunct. The whole NP can occupy a certain position in the sentence (Inflectional Phrase, IP),[2] for example be in its specifier position if it is the subject. The resulting structure of a sentence, for

---

[1] A detailed follow-up to this very simplistic introduction here can be found e.g. in Haegeman (1994); Haegeman and Guéron (1999); and Beck and Gergel (2014).
[2] The assumption is that sentences are headed by the position which carries inflection or modals. For details and arguments for this assumption see Haegeman & Guéron (1999).

https://doi.org/10.1515/9783110646825-012

example the one given in (1), is represented either in the form of a tree (see (2)) or equivalently as a labelled bracketing (see (3)).

(1)   The actress gave a marvellous performance.

(2)
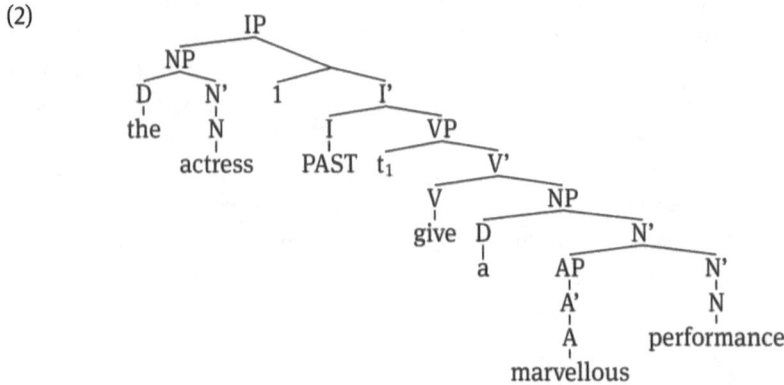

(3)   [$_{IP}$ [$_{NP}$ the$_D$ [$_{N'}$ actress$_N$]] [1 [$_{I'}$ PAST [$_{VP}$ t$_1$ [$_{V'}$ give$_V$ [$_{NP}$ a$_D$ [$_{N'}$ [$_{AP}$ [$_{A'}$ marvellous$_A$]] [$_{N'}$ performance$_N$]]]]]]]]

(2) and (3) are equivalent in that these are possible representations of the structure associated with the sentence in (1). Both encode the same hierarchical relations between the constituents of the sentence. In the course of this book, we will often simplify representations for the benefit of the reader and thus will not always be very detailed in labelling each node in the tree. For the purposes of a formal semantic analysis, the hierarchical structure as indicated by (2) or (3) is the required input.

1.1.2 Syntactic Ambiguities

There is a close relationship between the structure of a sentence and its interpretation. The structure serves as the input to semantic analysis and thus determines it. One kind of example where this becomes obvious is ambiguity. A sentence can receive multiple interpretations if there are multiple structural analyses for it. Consider the example in (4).

(4)   The woman looked at the man with the binoculars.

In (4), the PP constituent "with the binoculars" is either an adjunct of the VP modifying the looking action of the woman, or it is an adjunct to the NP, modifying "man." The two available structures are given in (5) and (6) below, both in tree and bracketed form.

(5) a. [IP [NP The woman] [1 [I' PAST [VP t₁ [V' **look** [PP at [NP the man]] [PP **with the binoculars**]]]]]]

b.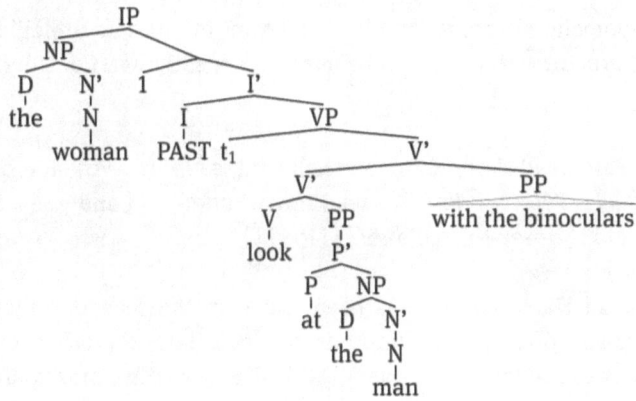

(6) a. [IP [NP The woman] [1 [I' PAST [VP t₁ [V' look [PP at [NP the [N' man [PP **with the binoculars**]]]]]]]]]

b.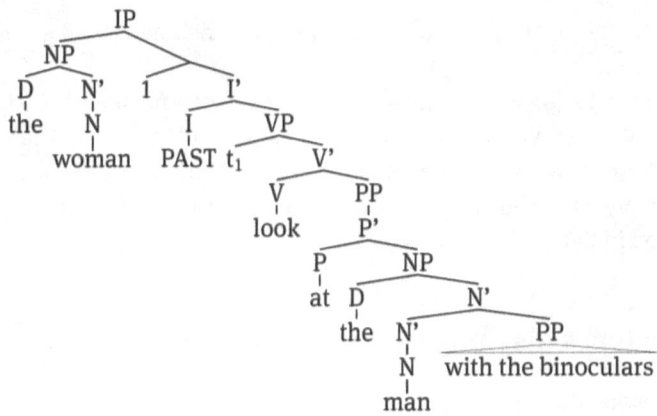

The structure in (5) has the interpretation that the woman used binoculars in order to look at the man. The structure in (6) means that the woman looks at the man who has binoculars. The meaning of the PP does not change – it is only its position that triggers this difference in meaning. We observe examples of this structure-to-meaning mapping throughout the book and thus oftentimes first provide the reader with a structural analysis of the sentences we interpret.

1.1.3 Ellipsis

Another syntactic phenomenon that is relevant in our data are elliptical structures, i.e. structures that seem to be missing a constituent. Consider the following example:

(7) a. Peter read Harry Potter and Sally did ~~read Harry Potter~~, too.
 b. [IP [NP Peter] [I' PAST [VP read Harry Potter]]] [and [IP2 [NP Sally] [I' [I did] [VP ~~read Harry Potter~~]] [too]]]

The VP "read Harry Potter" has been elided in the second conjunct, yet its meaning is still present. The Verb Phrase "read Harry Potter" in the first conjunct serves as its antecedent; as a result the two Verb Phrases are identical. This is usually considered a requirement for ellipsis, i.e. the sentence in (7) cannot be understood as Peter having read *Harry Potter* and Sally having watched *Lord of the Rings*. There is a certain flexibility in interpreting ellipsis, however, when pronouns are involved, see (8).

(8) Sally$_1$ visited her$_1$ mother and Mary$_2$ did ~~visit her$_{1/2}$ mother~~, too.

The example in (8) is ambiguous due to the different referents available for "her" in the elided VP: Either Mary visited Sally's mother, or she visited her own mother. Here, ellipsis and the reference for "her" interact to create ambiguity. We see many examples of structural ambiguity and ellipsis entering a complex interaction in Emily Dickinson's poems.

1.2 Sentence Meaning in Formal Semantics

1.2.1 Compositionality

Formal semantics assumes that interpretation follows the principle of compositionality (Frege 1892) according to which the meaning of a sentence is determined by the meanings of its parts.

The hierarchical structure determined by syntax is the input to a set of interpretive rules. The rules combine the meanings of the sentence parts to derive the meaning of the sentence. We adopt a referential theory of meaning, i.e. meanings are actual objects. For example, proper names like "Bob" refer to individuals in the real world, i.e. in this case the individual Bob. Most nouns, verbs, and PPs like "dog," "smoke" or "in Texas" denote the set of things that have the property, i.e. the set of dogs, the set of smoking individuals, the set of things in Texas. Semantic types make precise what kind of meaning an expression has. The semantic type of individuals is <e> (for 'entity'). The type of sentences is <t> for truth value. Properties are functions from individuals to truth values <e,t>, see Heim and Kratzer (1998). Language can furthermore refer to more abstract notions like times (type <i>), e.g. "5 pm," or degrees (type <d>), e.g. "5 cm," or events (type <v>) like "running". Our discussion throughout the book makes use of this type theory and follows a Heim and Kratzer style notation.

Language is used to describe possible states of affairs in addition to stating facts about the actual world. To capture this, semanticists employ the notion of **possible worlds**: possible worlds make reference to possible ways things could alternatively have turned out to be. For example, there is an alternative world where Donald Trump never became president of the United States. This is not true in the world we live in, called the 'actual world' or the 'evaluation world,' but we can still talk about this alternative state of affairs, by e.g. expressing our wish that he never had become president. In order to capture this ability to talk about the here and now as well as other alternative worlds, we will treat sentence meanings as propositions (cf. Heim and Kratzer 1998; Heim and von Fintel 2011). A sentence denotes a set of possible worlds, the worlds in which it is true.

Given these basic assumptions, let's look at how interpretation proceeds for the simple example in (9a). Meanings are accessed via the **interpretation function**, represented as double brackets, i.e. (9c) reads as "the meaning of 'Klaus smokes.'"

(9) a. Klaus smokes.
 b. [s [NP Klaus$_{<e>}$] [VP smokes$_{<e,<s,t>>}$]]
 c. ⟦ [s [NP Klaus$_{<e>}$] [VP smokes$_{<e,<s,t>>}$]] ⟧

A simplified syntactic structure of the sentence in (9a) is given in (9b). The meaning of the leaves in the tree are specified in the lexicon. "Smokes," for example, is a property of type <e,<s,t>>, i.e. a function from individuals of type <e> to a proposition, which in turn is a function from worlds of type <s> to truth values of type <t>. In other words, it is the function that returns the truth value 1 for its arguments if the individual which is its first argument smokes in the world which is its second argument. Its lexical entry is given below:

(10) $[\![smokes_{<e,<s,t>>}]\!] = \lambda x: x \in D_e. [\lambda w: w \in D_s. \text{ x smokes in w}]$[3]
"the meaning of 'smoke' is the function which maps an individual x and a world w to the truth-value 1 iff the individual x smokes in world w"

In the notation defined in Heim and Kratzer (1998) this function is represented in (10). "λx" says that this is a function whose domain is individuals. The information provided after the colon is called the 'domain description': it describes what the arguments fed into the function are.[4] In this case, they have to be individuals and worlds.[5] The information provided after the full stop is the value description of the function. It tells us what a given argument is mapped to. In the example, x and w are mapped to true if x smokes in w. Semantic types determine how constituents can be combined to form the meaning of a sentence. A few rules of composition allow us to combine meanings.

One basic combinatory rule suggested in Heim and Kratzer 1998, among others that we will not discuss here, is **Functional Application:**

(11) Functional Application (FA):
If α is a branching node and $\{\beta,\gamma\}$ is the set of α's daughters, then α is in the domain of $[\![\ ]\!]$ if both β and γ are and $[\![\beta]\!]$ is a function whose domain contains $[\![\gamma]\!]$. In this case, $[\![\alpha]\!] = [\![\beta]\!]([\![\gamma]\!])$.
(Heim and Kratzer 1998, 49)

We can apply Functional Application to example (9) above: the meaning of the NP "Klaus," which is the individual Klaus (type <e>), fits the meaning of the VP "smokes," because "smokes" is a function looking for an individual as an argument. Thus, we can apply the function "smokes" to the argument "Klaus" via

---

[3] Throughout this book, we adopt the notational shorthand of omitting the outermost brackets if the result does not lead to an ambiguous interpretation (see Heim & Kratzer 1998, 38).
[4] A notational shorthand that we have adopted throughout the book is to omit the domain description (cf. Heim and Kratzer 1998). Thus, the lexical entry of "smokes" can also be written as '$\lambda x. [\lambda w. \text{ x smokes in w}]$.'
[5] But there could be further restrictions on the argument, e.g. presuppositions, see the section on presuppositions below.

FA. (12) presents a compositional interpretation of (9) with the resulting proposition.

(12) a. ⟦Klaus smokes⟧ iff (FA)
 b. ⟦smokes_{<e<s,t>>}⟧ (⟦⟦Klaus_{<e>}⟧⟧) iff (Lexicon)
 c. [λx. [λw. x smokes in w]] (K) iff (Simplification)
 d. λw. K smokes in w

In (12a), we apply FA. In (12b), we insert the lexical entries for both elements. K stands for the person "Klaus." We can simplify (12c) by replacing the variable x with the argument "Klaus." The result is the proposition Klaus smokes. Note that all steps are equivalence transformations.

1.2.2 Quantification

The type system is recursive, and language has higher type expressions. Examples of higher-type functions are **quantifiers** like "no" or "every." They denote a relation between two sets of individuals. For example, the quantifier "every" in (13) below relates the property of being a runner to the property of stretching. In this case the relation is a subset relation, the set of runners is included in the set of stretchers. In functional terms, "every" takes two properties of type <e,<s,t>> and says that all individuals which have the property described by the NP "runner," also have the property described by the VP "stretches" in the world of evaluation. This is formally described in (14) and (15) below. Quantifiers are usually understood to be contextually restricted. The technical implementation can be seen in chapter II.1, but we have left it out here for simplicity.

(13) Every runner stretches.

(14) ⟦every_{<<e<s,t>>,<<e,<s,t>>,t>>}⟧ = λP_{<e<s,t>>}. [λQ_{<e,<s,t>>}. [λw. ∀x [P(x)(w) → Q(x)(w)]]]
 "every denotes the function from properties P, properties Q and worlds w to truth values which returns true iff for all individuals x, if P is true of x in w, Q is true for x in w"

(15) ⟦every⟧(⟦runner⟧)(⟦stretches⟧) = λw. ∀x [x is a runner in w → x stretches in w]

"Every" is called a universal quantifier since it makes a universal statement (formalized as '∀'). There are also existential quantifiers like the indefinites "some" and "a" (formalized as '∃'). They claim the existence of an individual with the described properties. Their negative counterparts are quantifiers like "no" which state the non-existence of individuals with both properties they combine with. These are examples of nominal quantifiers, quantifying over individuals. Natural language can quantify over different semantic types, e.g. also over times ("sometimes," "often"), over degrees ("biggEST"), or over worlds. One way to quantify over possible worlds is by using **modals** such as 'may' in (16).

(16)   Klaus may smoke.

(16) does not state that the property of smoking is currently true of Klaus in the actual world. Rather we are talking about the possibility of Klaus smoking. This could describe a scenario where we are in a designated smoking area where Klaus is allowed to smoke. This interpretation of (16) is given informally in (17).

(17)   According to the law, it is possible for Klaus to smoke.

Parallel to nominal quantifiers like "every" or "some," which relate sets of individuals, modals like "may" and "must" (of type <<s,<s,t>>,<<s,t>,<s,t>>>) relate possible worlds: those worlds which satisfy certain restrictions, e.g. where the laws of the actual world hold, to the worlds where the proposition they combine with is true. The restriction is sometimes referred to as the **accessibility relation R** of the modal, since it relates the worlds quantified over to the actual world by accessing certain salient information from it, e.g. the laws of the actual world. A lexical entry of 'may' capturing this is given in (18).

(18)   ⟦may⟧ = $\lambda R_{<s,<s,t>>}. [\lambda p_{<s,t>}. [\lambda w_{<s>}. \exists w' [R(w)(w') \& p(w')]]]$
"the meaning of 'may' is such that it takes an accessibility relation R, a proposition p and a world w, and says that there is a world w' s.t. R(w)(w') holds and p(w') holds."

For example in (16) above, the first argument of "may" is the relation that holds between worlds in which the same laws are obeyed, see (19a) below. "May" combines with that proposition and the proposition "Klaus smokes," see (19b). The result is a set of worlds w such that there is a world w' in which all the worlds of w are obeyed and Klaus smokes in w'.

(19) a. λw. [λw". the laws of w are obeyed in w"]
 b. ⟦may⟧(λw. [λw". the laws of w are obeyed in w"])(λw'''. Klaus smokes in w''')
 c. λw. ∃w' [the laws of w are obeyed in w' & Klaus smokes in w']

Just like nominal quantifiers, modals vary in their quantificational force. 'May' above has existential force, i.e. it says there exists a possible world which is accessible from w in which the proposition it combines with is true. The interpretation of the sentence in (16) is thus that there exists a possible world where Klaus smokes and all the laws of the actual world are obeyed. That does not mean that it is a necessity that Klaus smokes, but rather that it is a possibility. Modals that express necessity, like "must," have universal force, i.e. they make claims about all possible worlds that are relevant in the context of the sentence. The context determines which aspect of the actual world is relevant for the meaning of the modal statement, i.e. it need not be laws that we are referencing to, but could also be facts or wishes that hold in the actual world. In other words, the **accessibility relation** of the modal may vary and lead to different readings. Modals are thus inherently context dependent, as all quantifiers are. The context dependency is the contextual specification of what exactly is quantified over. For modals, this is the accessible worlds. A closer look at nominal quantifiers reveals that we usually quantify over a relevant set of individuals rather than every individual in the whole world. At several points in the book the context dependency of quantifiers becomes relevant.

Another construction which is relevant for the purpose of this book closely related to modals is **conditionals** like the one in (20).

(20)   If it rains, I take the bus.

Conditionals are treated as expressing a necessity, i.e. what **must** hold given a certain state of affairs. The sentence in (20), for example, expresses that in all worlds in which it rains, I take the bus. Accordingly, conditionals are considered to involve a covert universal modal like "must" (e.g. Kratzer 1991). In contrast to the modal statements discussed above, the conditions under which the proposition holds are given explicitly. In (20), quantification is over worlds in which it rains. In addition, we only consider those worlds that are compatible with the normal course of events in the actual world. This is due to the covert assumption that nothing unusual happens, e.g. that I win the lottery and buy a car. So what (20) expresses is that in all worlds in which it rains and in which nothing unusual happens I take the bus. For a more in depth introduction to modality and possible world semantics, see von Fintel and Heim (2011).

1.2.3 Reference to the Context

We next consider linguistic expressions which require contextual information in order to be interpretable. These include pronouns, demonstratives and presuppositions. We extend our system in order to capture this context sensitivity.

Assignment Functions and Pronouns

Pronouns are considered variables. They can only be assigned a meaning relative to a given context. (21) below without any context cannot be judged true or false. Let us assume a context for (21), however, where three referents have been introduced in the conversation: Sally, Tina and Klaus. Tina and Klaus are talking to each other and Tina utters (21). In this case, the pronoun "she" refers to Sally. In a different context, "she" would not refer to Sally.

(21)   She always laughs a lot.

A variable assignment function g is the formal tool that models the identification of the pronoun's referent (cf. Heim and Kratzer 1998, 239). The interpretation function is relative to that assignment function, see the interpretation of "she" in (22a).

(22)   a. $[\![she_1]\!]^g = g(1) =$ Sally
       b. $g(1)$ is only defined if $g(1)$ is female

Pronouns carry an index which serves as an argument for the variable assignment function. It returns an individual as a referent. g is thus a function from indices to individuals; it "stores" the individuals in a given context under numbers. Variables can be of type <e>, as in (22), but also of type <e,t> and <s,<s,t>>. Furthermore, Heim and Kratzer (1998) introduce a condition that the context must provide an appropriate referent for any given pronoun, which they call the **Appropriateness Condition:**

(23)   **Appropriateness Condition:**
         A context c is appropriate for an LF [**a sentence structure**] φ only if c determines a variable assignment g_c, whose domain includes every index which has a free occurrence in φ (Heim and Kratzer 1998: 243).

The context specified above is appropriate since there is a salient referent for the pronoun "she," or, more technically, the assignment function g has in its domain the index 1 which returns an appropriate referent, Sally. As mentioned above, using a pronoun is inappropriate in the absence of such a referent, e.g. if (21) were uttered out of the blue. The pronoun also comes with certain presuppositions, for the case above that the referent must be singular and female, see (22b). We will turn to presuppositions below.

Demonstratives
The system of variables introduced above can be extended to **demonstratives** (see Büring 2011). Similar to pronouns, the referent of demonstratives is established by context, i.e. in our model by the variable assignment function, see (24b). In addition to the index, demonstratives carry presuppositions regarding the relative position of the referent to the speaker, see (24c):

(24) a. I want this.
 b. $[\![this_3]\!]^g = g(3)$
 c. $g(3)$ is only defined if $g(3)$ is proximal to the speaker

Presuppositions
Restrictions imposed on the context, such as the requirement that the referent of "this" be proximal, are called presuppositions in semantic theory. Presuppositions are requirements that have to be met in order for the sentence to be felicitously uttered. Words that introduce presuppositions are called triggers. In addition to pronominal forms, the definite article "the" is an example of such a presupposition trigger. It introduces the presupposition that the noun it combines with denotes a property which exactly one individual possesses. One property of presuppositions is that they, in contrast to other types of inferences, are stable under embedding, e.g. negation, i.e. both sentences in (25) share the presupposition that there is a unique king of France.

(25) a. The king of France is bald.
 b. The king of France isn't bald.

Presuppositions are modelled as definedness conditions. A sentence will lack a truth-value, be undefined, if its presuppositions are not met. Formally, presupposition triggers denote partial functions. The arguments for which the function is defined are given after the colon, just like the domain restrictions introduced above, see (26).

(26)   ⟦the⟧ = $\lambda f_{<e,t>}$: there is a unique x s.t. f(x) =1. the unique x s.t. f(x) =1.
"the meaning of 'the' is the function from properties to individuals whose domain is properties f which are true of exactly one individual, and which maps such properties f to the unique individual they are true of."

"The" is a partial function of type <<e,t>,e>. If the presupposition triggered by "the" is not met, the meaning of the sentence containing "the" will be undefined. Semantic undefinedness is mapped onto pragmatic oddness via Stalnaker's bridge (von Fintel 2004). As a result, sentences with unfulfilled presuppositions will be judged inappropriate.

Selectional restrictions are a special kind of presupposition. Like other presuppositions they are lexically encoded restrictions on suitable arguments. For example, "reply" in (27a) below requires the individual it combines with to be animate. If selectional restrictions are violated there is a semantic mismatch in the sentence. See for example the personification in (27a). Since "reply" denotes a partial function, see (27b), the meaning of (27a) is undefined, see (27c).

(27) a. The mountains reply.
      b. ⟦reply⟧ = λx: x is human. [λw. x replies in w]
          "the meaning of 'reply' is a partial function that maps an individual x and a world w onto true only if x is human."
      c. ⟦reply⟧(x)(w) = 1 if x is human and replied in w, 0 if x is human and did not reply in w, undefined otherwise.

The selectional restriction of "reply" does not match the properties of "the mountains," which are inanimate. The sentence is undefined due to an unmet presupposition and would lead to pragmatic oddness under normal circumstances. The mismatch, however, can be resolved by reinterpretation or coercion. For example, a looser interpretation of "reply" is conceivable for (27a) which fits the property of the subject, e.g. as "producing an echo." See chapter I.6.

1.3 From Semantics to Pragmatics

1.3.1 The Pragmatic Step

The preceding section has provided an introduction to the grammatical mechanisms that derive the semantics of an utterance. Its linguistic structure (the syntax) is mapped to a propositional meaning by a system of rules that combine the meanings of the parts, from the lexicon up, to the meaning of the whole structure.

In this section, we investigate what happens when such a meaning is uttered in a context. A connection has to be made between the semantics (a proposition) and the context, resulting in the pragmatic meaning of the utterance. We refer to this connection – the mapping of the semantics and the context to the pragmatics – as the **pragmatic step**.

First, let's take a closer look at the linguistic notion of context. We follow Stalnaker (1978), who models the accumulation of information in a conversation. Participants in a conversation share a set of assumptions. This set of assumptions is called the **common ground**: a set of propositions assumed to be true for the purposes of the conversation by the participants. In a conversation about the organization of a soccer practice, for example, the common ground might contain the propositions that there will be a soccer practice, that it will be at the usual time and place, that it will aim at practicing soccer skills etc. The **context set** is the intersection of the propositions in the common ground. In the example, this would be (28).

(28) $\cap\{\lambda w.$ there will be practice in w, $\lambda w.$ practice will be at 7pm in w, ...}
        = $\lambda w.$ there will be practice in w & practice will be at 7pm in w & ...

The context set is the information shared by the participants in the conversation at a given time. When a sentence is uttered against this context, it is added to the information that was available before the utterance. For example, if I utter (29) in the context of (28) (and the other participants accept it), the proposition denoted by (29) is added to the common ground and consequently to the context set, as in (30).

(29)   Pirjo has put together a warm-up programme.

(30) $\cap\{\lambda w.$ there will be practice in w, $\lambda w.$ practice will be at 7pm in w, ...} $\cap$ {$\lambda w.$ Pirjo has put together a warm-up in w} =
        $\lambda w.$ there will be practice in w & practice will be at 7pm in w & Pirjo has put together a warm-up in w & ...

Formally, we assume that the pragmatic step of adding a proposition to a context is performed by a speech act operator (see Krifka 2014 for a recent theory).

In the example, the speech act is an assertion. A simplified version of the corresponding operator Assert is defined in (31), where c is the context set. We assume that the utterance (29) comes with this operator. If c is as in (28), the result is (30) as desired, cf. (32).

(31)   ⟦Assert⟧ = λp. [λc. [λw. c(w) & p(w)]]

(32)   ⟦Assert⟧ ([λw. Pirjo has put together a warm-up in w])(c) =
        λw. there will be practice in w & practice will be at 7pm in w & Pirjo has put together a warm-up in w & ...

The application of the speech act operator results in an updated context set. More generally, speech acts change the context. This does not have to be in terms of assertion and an updated information state. There are other speech acts, for example those indicated by a question, e.g. (33), or promises, like potentially (34).

(33)   Can Pirjo put together a warm-up programme?

(34)   I will take care of the goal keeper training.

The theory of speech acts and speech act operators models how the pragmatic meaning of an utterance is derived from its semantics and the context. In this book, we discuss the semantics as well as the pragmatics of fictional utterances. Hence we ask what the pragmatic step is in fiction. Our answer to this question follows Bauer & Beck (2014): the pragmatic meaning of a fictional utterance is an inference that the reader draws from the semantics of the text, which allows her to relate the text to her own context. Bauer & Beck's proposal is modelled with the speech act operator FictionalAssert given once more in (35) (see the Introduction for more discussion).

(35)   ⟦FictionalAssert⟧ = λT. [λc. [λw. ∀w' [T(w') → R(w)(w') & c(w)]]]

In the main parts of the book, we mostly leave out the context c because it does not contribute to our discussion. But this sketch shows how our analysis of the pragmatic meaning of fictional texts fits into a larger theory of pragmatic interpretation.

1.3.2 Implicatures

Linguists have observed that hearers frequently draw inferences that go beyond what is literally said. Such inferences are called **conversational implicatures**. We follow a Gricean view of implicatures according to which implicatures arise as a result of reasoning based on the four **conversational maxims**: quantity ("say as much as needed, not more or less"), quality ("say only what you know to be true"), relevance ("make your contribution relevant"), and "manner" ("say something that is not obscure, avoid ambiguity")(cf. Grice 1975). A basic assumption is that participants of a conversation generally try to follow these maxims because the **cooperative principle** holds, which says that all speakers are cooperative, rational agents who seek information exchange. To illustrate how pragmatic reasoning based on these assumptions proceeds, we offer the example of a scalar implicature in (36).

(36)   Peter invited Mary or Sue.

The sentence is logically entailed by "Peter invited Mary and Sue," which is called the scalar alternative of the sentence with "or," and is something stronger the speaker could have said. By hearing (36) the hearer assumes that the speaker uttered the most informative sentence they could have, following the cooperative principle and obeying the maxim of quantity. The hearer reasons that the speaker must believe the stronger alternative to be false and infer that Peter did not invite both. This is how the stronger, exclusive reading of "or" is derived via pragmatic reasoning on part of the hearer. One property of implicatures is that they, as opposed to presuppositions, disappear under negation, or, in the case of scalar implicatures, reverse their pattern, consider (37).

(37)   Peter did not invite Mary or Sue.

The sentence means that Peter did not invite either of the two. It does not mean that it is not the case that he invited one but not the other. There is thus no exclusive reading of "or" below negation. This follows from Gricean reasoning as introduced above since now the alternative (38) is logically entailed and thus weaker than (37):

(38)   Peter did not invite Mary and Sue.

Thus, the speaker could not have said anything stronger, and there is an implicature based on the maxim of quantity. Implicatures in fictional contexts are an interesting phenomenon discussed in chapter II.1.

1.4 Glossary of Abbreviations and Notations

Tab. 1: Glossary

Symbol	Meaning
@	actual world
λ	lambda operator
⟦ ... ⟧	meaning brackets
⟦ ... ⟧^{g}	interpretation relative to assignment function g
[ ]	function brackets within a formula; scopal relations within a tree; variable assignment function
≤	ordering of a scale
*	before sentence: ungrammaticality marker; in a formula: plural operator
**	plural operator
λx: PSP. φ(x)	presupposition (PSP) introduced by a colon and ended by a period.
FA	Functional Application
PM	Predicate Modification
∀	universal quantifier
∃	existential quantifier
<e>	the type of individuals
<t>	the type of truth-values
<v>	the type of eventualities
<i>	the type of time intervals
<s>	the type of worlds
<a,b>	a function from a to b

Bibliography

Aesop. (n.d.) 2012. *Aesop's Fables*. Translated by George Fyler Townsend. http://www.literature.org/authors/aesop/fables.
Anonymous. 2013. "Birthday Poems." loveliestmoment.blogspot.com/2013/05/birthday-poems.html.
Aristotle. (n.d.) 1995. *Poetics*. Translated by S. H. Butcher. http://www.gutenberg.org/files/1974/1974-h/1974-h.htm.
Asher, Nicholas. 2011. *Lexical Meaning in Context*: A Web of Words. Cambridge: Cambridge University Press.
Bade, Nadine, and Sigrid Beck. 2017. "Lyrical Texts as a Data Source." *Linguistische Berichte* (251): 317-56.
Barker, Wendy. 2002. *Poems' Progress*. Writers & Young Writers Series 3. Texas: Absey & Co.
Bauer, Markus, Matthias Bauer, Sigrid Beck, Carmen Dörge, Burkhard von Eckartsberg, Michaela Meder, Katja Riedel, Janina Zimmermann and Angelika Zirker. 2010. "'The Two Coeval Come': Emily Dickinson and Ambiguity." *LiLi* 40 (158): 98-124.
Bauer, Matthias. 1995/1996. "The Language of Dogs: *Mythos* and *Logos* in Emily Dickinson." In *Connotations* 5 (2-3): 208-27.
Bauer, Matthias. 2006. "'A Word Made Flesh': Anmerkungen zum lebendigen Wort bei Emily Dickinson." In *Bibeldichtung*, edited by Volker Kapp and Dorothea Scholl, 373-92. Berlin: Duncker & Humblot.
Bauer, Matthias. 2015. "Secret Wordplay and What It May Tell Us." In *Wordplay and Metalinguistic / Metadiscursive Reflection: Authors, Contexts, Techniques, and Meta-Reflection*, edited by Angelika Zirker and Esme Winter-Froemel, 269-88. Berlin: De Gruyter.
Bauer, Matthias, Nadine Bade, Sigrid Beck, Carmen Dörge, Burkhard von Eckartsberg, Janina Niefer, Saskia Ottschofski and Angelika Zirker. 2015. "Emily Dickinson's 'My life had stood a loaded gun' – An interdisciplinary analysis." *Journal of Literary Semantics* 44 (2): 115-40.
Bauer, Matthias, and Sigrid Beck. 2009. "Interpretation: Local Composition and Textual Meaning." In *Dimensionen der Zweisprachenforschung / Dimensions of Second Language Research: Festschrift für Kurt Kohn*, edited by Michaela Albl-Mikasa, Sabine Braun, and Sylvia Kalina, 289-300. Tübingen: Narr.
Bauer, Matthias, and Sigrid Beck. 2014. "On the Meaning of Fictional Texts." In *Approaches to Meaning: Composition, Values, and Interpretation*, edited by Daniel Gutzmann, Jan Köpping, and Cécile Meier, 250-75. Leiden: Brill.
Bauer, Matthias, and Sigrid Beck. Forthcoming. "Isomorphic Mapping in Fictional Interpretation."
Bauer, Matthias, and Saskia Brockmann. 2017. "The Iconicity of Literary Analysis: The Case of Logical Form." In *Dimensions of Iconicity*, edited by Angelika Zirker, Matthias Bauer, Olga Fischer, and Christina Ljungberg, 331-44. Amsterdam: Benjamins. https://doi.org/10.1075/ill.15.19bau.
Bauer, Matthias, Joachim Knape and Susanne Winkler. 2009. "Disarmed: Ein interdisziplinäres Gespräch über Ambiguität am Beispiel des kausativen Verbs." In *Dimensionen der Zweisprachenforschung / Dimensions of Second Language Research: Festschrift für Kurt*

Kohn, edited by Michaela Albl-Mikasa, Sabine Braun, and Sylvia Kalina, 153-276. Tübingen: Narr.
Beardsley, Monroe C. (1958) 1981. *Aesthetics: Problems in the Philosophy of Criticism*. Indianapolis: Hackett Publishing Company.
Beardsley, Monroe C. 1981. "Fiction as Representation." *Synthese* 46: 291-313.
Beck, Sigrid. 2011. "Comparison Constructions." In *Semantics: An International Handbook of Natural Language Meaning* 2, edited by Klaus von Heusinger, Claudia Maienborn and Paul Portner, 1341-89. Berlin: De Gruyter Mouton.
Beck, Sigrid. Forthcoming. "Semantic Parameters and Universals." In *Blackwell Companion to Semantics*, edited by Lisa Matthewson, Cécile Meier, Hotze Rullmann, and Thomas Ede Zimmermann. Hoboken: Wiley.
Beck, Sigrid, and Remus Gergel. 2014. *Contrasting English and German Grammar*. An Introduction to Syntax and Semantics. Berlin: de Gruyter Mouton.
Beck, Sigrid, and Uli Sauerland. 2000. "Cumulation is Needed: A Reply to Winter." *Natural Language Semantics* 8 (4): 349-71. doi:10.1023/A:1011240827230.
Beck, Sigrid, and Arnim von Stechow. 2006. "Dog after Dog Revisited." In *Proceedings of the Sinn und Bedeutung* 10, edited by Christian Ebert and Cornelia Endriss, 43-54. http://www.sfs.uni-tuebingen.de/~cebert/papers/.
Benfrey, Christopher. 2002. "Emily Dickinson and the American South." In *The Cambridge Introduction to Emily Dickinson*, edited by Wendy Martin, 30-50. Cambridge: Cambridge University Press.
Benvenuto, Richard. 1983. "Words Within Words: Dickinson's Use of the Dictionary." *ESQ: A Journal of the American Renaissance* 29 (1): 46-55.
The Bible: Authorized King James Version. 2008. Edited by Robert P. Carroll, and Stephen Prickett. The World's Classics. Oxford: Oxford University Press.
Biberauer, Theresa, and Ian Roberts. 2006. "The Loss of Residual 'Head-final' Orders and Remnant Fronting in Late Middle English: Causes and Consequences." In *Comparative Studies in Germanic Syntax*, edited by Jutta Hartmann and Laszlo Molnárfi, 263-98. Amsterdam: Benjamins.
Brockmann, Saskia, Susanne Riecker, Nadine Bade, Matthias Bauer, Sigrid Beck, and Angelika Zirker. 2017. "FictionalAssert and Implicatures." In *Proceedings of Linguistic Evidence 2016. Empirical, Theoretical, and Computational Perspectives*, edited by Sam Featherston, Robin Hörnig, Reinhild Steinberg, Birgit Umbreit, and Jenni Wallis. University of Tübingen, online publication system. http://dx.doi.org/10.15496/publikation-19038.
Bross, Martina. 2017. *Versions of* Hamlet: *Poetic Economy on Page and Stage*. Paderborn: Schöningh.
Bryant, John. 2002. *The Fluid Text: A Theory of Revision and Editing for Book and Screen*. Ann Arbor: University of Michigan Press.
Budick, Emily Miller. 1985. *Emily Dickinson and the Life of Language: A Study in Symbolic Poetics*. Baton Rouge: Louisiana State University Press.
Burke, Edmund. 1990. *A Philosophical Enquiry into the Origin of our Ideas of the Sublime and Beautiful*. Oxford: Oxford University Press.
Büring, Daniel. 2011. "Pronouns." In *Semantics: An International Handbook of Natural Language Meaning* 2, edited by Klaus von Heusinger, Claudia Maienborn, and Paul Portner, 971-96. Berlin: De Gruyter Mouton.
Cameron, Sharon. 1992. *Choosing Not Choosing: Dickinson's Fascicles*. Chicago: University of Chicago Press.

Cameron, Sharon. 1979. *Lyric Time: Dickinson and the Limits of Genre*. Baltimore: Johns Hopkins University Press.
Carroll, Lewis. 1998. *Alice's Adventures in Wonderland and Through the Looking-Glass and What Alice Found There*. Edited by Roger Lancelyn Green. Oxford: Oxford English Novels.
Chomsky, Noam. 1957. *Syntactic Structures*. 's-Gravenhage: Mouton.
Coseriu, Eugeniu. 1988. "Thesen zum Thema 'Sprache und Dichtung.'" In *Energeia und Ergon, Band 1: Schriften von Eugenio Coseriu (1965-1987)*, edited by Jörn Albrecht, 291-94. München: Wilhelm Fink Verlag.
Cohn, Dorrit. 1990. "Signposts of Fictionality: A Narratological Perspective." *Poetics Today* 11 (4): 775-804.
Crane, Stephen. 1897. "Flanagan and His Short Filibustering Adventure." *McClure's Magazine* 9: 1045-52.
Crumbley, Paul, and Eleanor E. Heginbotham, eds. 2014. *Dickinson's Fascicles: A Spectrum of Possibilities*. Columbus, OH: Ohio State University Press.
Cuddy, Lois A. 1978. "The Latin Imprint on Emily Dickinson's Poetry: Theory and Practice." *American Literature* 50 (1): 74-84. doi: 10.2307/2925522.
Deppman, Jed. 2008. *Trying to Think with Emily Dickinson*. Amherst: University of Massachusetts Press.
Deppman, Jed, ed. 2013. *Emily Dickinson and Philosophy*. New York, NY: Cambridge University Press.
Dickens, Charles. (1852-53) 1977. *Bleak House*. Edited by George Ford and Sylvère Monod. New York: Norton.
Dickens, Charles. (1864-65) 1997. *Our Mutual Friend*. Edited by Adrian Poole. London: Penguin Books.
Dickinson, Emily. 1955. *The Poems of Emily Dickinson*. Edited by Thomas H. Johnson. Cambridge, MA: Belknap Press.
Dickinson, Emily. 1958. *The Letters of Emily Dickinson*. Edited by Thomas H. Johnson. Cambridge, MA: Belknap Press of Harvard University Press.
Dickinson, Emily. 1961. *The Complete Poems of Emily Dickinson*. Edited by Thomas H. Johnson. New York: Back Bay Books.
Dickinson, Emily. 1998. *The Poems of Emily Dickinson. Variorum Edition*. Edited by Ralph W. Franklin. Harvard: Harvard University Press.
Donne, John. 2005. *The Variorum Edition of the Poetry of John Donne*. Edited by Gary A. Stringer. Bloomington: Indiana University Press.
Doriani, Beth M. 1996. *Emily Dickinson: Daughter of Prophecy*. Amherst, Massachusetts: University of Massachusetts Press.
Eberwein, Jane D. 1983. "Dickinson's Nobody and Ulysses' Noman: 'Then there's a pair of us?'" *Dickinson Studies: Emily Dickinson (1830-86), U.S. Poet* 46: 9-14.
Eberwein, Jane D., ed. 1998. *An Emily Dickinson Encyclopedia*. London: Greenwood Press.
Eberwein, Jane D. 2013. "Outgrowing Genesis? Dickinson, Darwin, and the Higher Criticism." In *Emily Dickinson and Philosophy*, edited by Jed Deppman, 47-67. Cambridge: Cambridge University Press.
Eckardt, Regine. 2012. "Grammaticalization and Semantic Reanalysis." In *Semantics: An International Handbook of Natural Language Meaning* 3, edited by Klaus von Heusinger, Claudia Maienborn and Paul Portner, 2675-701. Berlin: de Gruyter.
Eckardt, Regine. 2015. *The Semantics of Free Indirect Discourse. How Texts Allow Us to Mind-read and Eavesdrop*. Boston/Leiden: Brill.

Elam, Keir. 2002. *The Semiotics of Theatre and Drama*. London: Routledge.
Emerson, Ralph Waldo. (1867) 1918. *Poems*. New York: Houghton Mifflin.
Erfani, Farhang. 2013. "Dickinson and Sartre on Facing the Brutality of Brute Existence." In *Emily Dickinson and Philosophy*, edited by Jed Deppman, 175-87. New York: Cambridge University Press.
Erne, Lukas. 2003. *Shakespeare as a Literary Dramatist*. Cambridge: Cambridge University Press.
Fabb, Nigel. 2010. "Is Literary Language a Development of Ordinary Language?" *Lingua* 120 (5): 1219-32.
Fabb, Nigel, and Morris Halle. 2008. *Meter in Poetry: A New Theory*. Cambridge: Cambridge University Press.
Faderman, Lillian. 1998. "'My Life had stood – a Loaded Gun –.'" In *An Emily Dickinson Encyclopedia*, edited by Jane Donahue Eberwein, 203-04. London: Greenwood Press.
Farr, Judith. 1992. *The Passion of Emily Dickinson*. Cambridge, MA: Harvard University Press.
Farr, Judith. 2004. *The Gardens of Emily Dickinson*. Cambridge, Mass. Harvard University Press.
Featherston, Sam. 2006. "Experimentell erhobene Grammatikalitätsurteile und ihre Bedeutung für die Syntaxtheorie." In *Sprachkorpora – Datenmengen und Erkenntnisfortschritt*, edited by Werner Kallmeyer and Gisela Zifonun, 49-69. Berlin: De Gruyter.
Ferlazzo, Paul J. 1976. *Emily Dickinson*. Boston: Twayne.
Fintel, Kai von. 2004. "Would you believe it? The King of France is Back! Presuppositions and Truth-Value Intuitions." In *Descriptions and Beyond*, edited by Marga Reimer and Anne Bezuidenhout, 315-41. Oxford: Oxford University Press.
Fischer, Olga. 2011. "Cognitive Iconic Grounding of Reduplication in Language." In *Semblance and Signification*, edited by Pascal Michelucci, Olga Fischer and Christina Ljungberg, 55-81. Amsterdam: Benjamins.
Fludernik, Monika, and Daniel Jacob, eds. 2014. *Linguistics and Literary Studies / Linguistik und Literaturwissenschaft. Interfaces, Encounters, Transfers / Begegnungen, Interferenzen und Kooperationen*. Berlin: De Gruyter.
Ford, Karen Jackson. 1997. *Gender and the Poetics of Excess: Moments of Brocade*. Jackson: University of Mississippi Press.
Franklin, Ralph W. 1986. *The Master Letters of Emily Dickinson*. Amherst: Amherst College Press.
Freedman, Linda. 2011. *Emily Dickinson and the Religious Imagination*. Cambridge: Cambridge University Press.
Freeman, Margaret H. 1972. "Emily Dickinson's Prosody: A Study in Metrics." University of Massachusetts, Ph.D. diss.
Freeman, Margaret H. 1997. "Grounded Spaces: Deictic -self Anaphors in the Poetry of Emily Dickinson." *Language and Literature* 6 (1): 7-28. doi:10.1177/096394709700600101.
Freeman, Margaret H. 1998. "A Cognitive Approach to Dickinson's Metaphors." In *The Emily Dickinson Handbook*, edited by Gudrun Grabher, 258-72. Amherst: University of Massachusetts Press.
Frege, Gottlob. 1892. "Über Sinn und Bedeutung." *Zeitschrift für Philosophie und philosophische Kritik* 100: 25-50.
Fries, Charles C. 1952. *The Structure of English: An Introduction to the Construction of English Sentences*. New York: Harcourt, Brace, and Company.
Grabher, Gudrun, Roland Hagenbüchle, and Cristanne Miller, eds. 1998. *The Emily Dickinson Handbook*. Amherst: University of Massachusetts Press.

Grice, Herbert P. 1978. "Further Notes on Logic and Conversation." In *Syntax and Semantics* 9, edited by Peter Cole, 41-57. Academic Press.
Groenendijk, Jeroen, and Martin Stokhof. 1991. "Dynamic Predicate Logic." *Linguistics and Philosophy* 14 (1): 39-100.
Hacquard, Valentine. 2011. "Modality." In *Semantics: An International Handbook of Natural Language Meaning* 2, edited by Klaus von Heusinger, Claudia Maienborn, and Paul Portner, 1484-515. Berlin: De Gruyter Mouton.
Haegeman, Liliane M. V. 1994. *Introduction to Government and Binding Theory*. Oxford: Blackwell.
Haegeman, Liliane M. V., and Jacqueline Guéron. 1999. *English Grammar: A Generative Perspective*. Oxford: Blackwell.
Hagenbüchle, Roland. 1988. *Emily Dickinson: Wagnis der Selbstbegegnung*. Tübingen: Stauffenburg.
Hallen, Cynthia L., and Laura M. Harvey. 1993. "Translation and the Emily Dickinson Lexicon." *Emily Dickinson Journal* 2 (2): 130-46. https://muse.jhu.edu/article/245262.
Hamblin, Charles L. 1973. "Questions in Montague English." *Foundations of Language* 10: 41-53.
Hamburger, Käte. (1957) 1977. *Die Logik der Dichtung*. Stuttgart: Klett.
Hayes, Bruce. 1988. "Metrics and Phonological Theory." In *Linguistics: The Cambridge Survey*, edited by Frederick Newmeyer, 220-49. Cambridge: Cambridge University Press.
Hayes, Bruce. 1989. "The Prosodic Hierarchy in Meter." In *Rhythm and Meter*, edited by Paul Kiparsky and Gilbert Youmans, 201-60. Orlando: Academic Press.
Heginbotham, Eleanor E. 1998. "'This was a Poet—It is That' (P448)." In *An Emily Dickinson Encyclopedia*, edited by Jane D. Eberwein, 285-86. Westport, Conn: Greenwood Press.
Heginbotham, Eleanor E. 2003. *Reading the Fascicles of Emily Dickinson: Dwelling in Possibilities*. Columbus, OH: Ohio State University Press.
Heim, Irene. 1982. *The Semantics of Definite and Indefinite Noun Phrases*. University of Massachusetts, Ph.D. diss.
Heim, Irene, and Kai von Fintel. 2011. *Intensional Semantics*. Cambridge, MA: Massachusetts Institute of Technology.
Heim, Irene, and Angelika Kratzer. 1998. *Semantics in Generative Grammar*. Oxford: Blackwell.
Herrnstein Smith, Barbara. 1971. "Poetry as Fiction." *New Literary History* 2 (2): 259-81.
Higginson, Thomas Wentworth. 1862. "Letter to a Young Contributor." *Atlantic Monthly* (9): 401-11. http://www.theatlantic.com/magazine/archive/1862/04/letter-to-a-youngcontributor/305164/.
Homer. (n.d.) 1953. *The Odyssey*. Translated by Augustus T. Murray. Cambridge, MA: Harvard University Press.
Horace. (n.d.) 2004. *Odes and Epodes*. Translated by Niall Rudd. Harvard: Harvard University Press.
Horace. (n.d.) 2005. *Ars Poetica*. Translated by A. S. Kline. http://www.poetryintranslation.com/PITBR/Latin/HoraceArsPoetica.htm.
Hughes, Sheila Hassell. 1997. "A Woman's Soul Is Her Castle: Place and Space in St Teresa's Interior Castle." *Literature and Theology* 11 (4): 376-84.
Jackson, Virginia. 2005. *Dickinson's Misery: A Theory of Lyric Reading*. Princeton: Princeton University Press.
Jakobson, Roman. 1960. "Closing Statement: Linguistics and Poetics." In *Style in Language*, edited by Thomas A. Sebeok, 350-77.

Johnson, Kyle. 2001. "What VP Ellipsis Can Do, and What it Can't, but not Why." In *The Handbook of Contemporary Syntactic Theory*, edited by Mark R. Baltin 439-79. Malden, MA: Blackwell.

Juhasz, Suzanne. 1976. *Naked and Fiery Forms: Modern American Poetry by Women, A New Tradition*. New York, Hagerstown, San Francisco, London: Harper & Row.

Juhasz, Suzanne. 1977. "'I Dwell in Possibility': ED in the Subjunctive Mood." *Dickinson Studies: Emily Dickinson (1830-86), U.S. Poet* 32: 105-09.

Juhasz, Suzanne, Cristanne Miller, and Martha N. Smith, eds. 1993. *Comic Power in Emily Dickinson*. Austin: University of Texas Press.

Jüngel, Eberhard. 1993. *Tod*. Gütersloh: Gütersloher Verlagshaus Mohn.

Kadmon, Nirit. 2001. *Formal Pragmatics*. Oxford: Blackwell.

Kamp, Hans. 1981. "A Theory of Truth and Semantic Representation." In *Formal Methods in the Study of Language*, edited by Jeroen Groenendijk and Theo M. V. Janssen, 277-322. Amsterdam: Mathematisches Centrum.

Karttunen, Lauri. 1973. "Presuppositions of Compound Sentences." *Linguistic Inquiry* 4 (2): 169-93. http://www.jstor.org/stable/4177763.

Karttunen, Lauri. 1977. "Syntax and Semantics of Questions." *Linguistics and Philosophy* 1: 3-44.

Kher, Inder Nath. 1974. *The Landscape of Absence: Emily Dickinson's Poetry*. New Haven: Yale University Press.

Kiparsky, Paul. 2006. "A Modular Metrics for Folk Verse." In *Formal Approaches to Poetry*, edited by B. Elan Dresher and Nila Friedberg, 7-49. Berlin: De Gruyter.

Konietzko, Andreas, and Susanne Winkler. 2010. "Contrastive Ellipsis: Mapping between Syntax and Information Structure." *Lingua* 120: 1436-57.

König, Ekkehard, and Manfred Pfister. 2017. *Literary Analysis and Linguistics*. Berlin: Erich Schmidt Verlag.

Kratzer, Angelika. 1991. "Modality." In *Semantics: An International Handbook of Contemporary Research*, edited by Arnim von Stechow and Dieter Wunderlich, 639-50. Berlin: De Gruyter.

Kratzer, Angelika. 2009. "Making a Pronoun: Fake Indexicals as Windows into the Properties of Pronouns." *Linguistic Inquiry* 40 (2): 187-237.

Krifka, Manfred. 1995. "The Semantics and Pragmatics of Polarity Items." *Linguistic Analysis* 25: 1-49.

Krifka, Manfred. 2014. "Embedding Illocutionary Acts." In *Recursion: Complexity in Cognition*, edited by M. Speas and T. Roeper, 59-87. Berlin: Springer.

Kuhns, Richard. 1972. "Semantics for Literary Languages." *New Literary History* 4 (1): 91–105.

Labov, William. 1972. "Some Principles of Linguistic Methodology." *Language in Society* 1 (1): 97-120.

Lang, Ewald, and Claudia Maienborn. 2011. "Two-level Semantics: Semantic Form and Conceptual Structure." In *Semantics: An International Handbook of Natural Language Meaning* 1, edited by Klaus von Heusinger, Claudia Maienborn, and Paul Portner, 709-40. Berlin: De Gruyter.

Leech, Geoffrey. 1969. *A Linguistic Guide to English Poetry*. New York: Longman.

Leiter, Sharon. 2007. *Critical Companion to Emily Dickinson: A Literary Reference to her Life and Work*. New York: Facts On File.

Levin, Phillis. 2001. *The Penguin Book of the Sonnet. 500 Years of a Classic Tradition in English*. London: Penguin.

Lindberg-Seyersted, Brita. 1968. *The Voice of the Poet: Aspects of Style in the Poetry of Emily Dickinson*. Cambridge, Mass: Harvard University Press.
Link, Godehard. 1991. "Plural." In *Semantik/Semantics: Ein internationales Handbuch zeitgenössischer Forschung*, edited by Arnim von Stechow and Dieter Wunderlich, 418-40. Berlin: De Gruyter.
Ljungberg, Christina. 2001. "Iconic Dimensions in Margaret Atwood's Poetry and Prose." In *The Motivated Sign: Iconicity in Language and Literature* 2, edited by Max Nänny and Olga Fischer, 351-66. Amsterdam: Benjamins.
Maier, Emar. 2014. "Language Shifts in Free Indirect Discourse." *Journal of Literary Semantics* 43 (2): 143-67.
Maier, Emar. 2017. "Fictional Names in Psychologistic Semantics." *Theoretical Linguistics* 43 (1-2): 1-45.
Matthewson, Lisa. 2006. "Presuppositions and Crosslinguistic Variation." In *Proceedings of the NELS 26 Sentence Processing Workshop*, edited by Carson T. Schütz, 63-76.
Matthewson, Lisa. 2012. "Methods in Cross-Linguistic Semantics." In *Semantics: An International Handbook of Natural Language Meaning* 1, edited by Klaus von Heusinger, Claudia Maienborn, and Paul Portner, 268-84. Berlin: De Gruyter.
McGregor, Elizabeth Johnson. 1987. *The Poet's Bible: Biblical Elements in the Poetry of Emily Dickinson, Stephen Crane, Edwin Arlington Robinson, and Robert Frost*. Brown University, PhD. diss.
McIntosh, James. 2000. *Nimble Believing: Dickinson and the Unknown*. Michigan: University of Michigan Press.
Miles, Josephin. 1940. "More Semantics of Poetry." *The Kenyon Review* 2 (4): 502-07.
Miller, Cristanne. 1987. *Emily Dickinson: A Poet's Grammar*. Cambridge, MA: Harvard University Press.
Miller, Cristanne. 2016. *Emily Dickinson's Poems: As She Preserved Them*. Cambridge, MA: Belknap Press.
Miller, Ruth. 1968. *The Poetry of Emily Dickinson*. Middletown, CT: Wesleyan University Press.
Milton, John. (1667) 1981. *Paradise Lost*. Edited by Alastair Fowler. London: Longman Annotated English Poets.
Mitchell, Domhnall. 2000. *Emily Dickinson: Monarch of Perception*. Amherst: University of Massachusetts Press.
Mitchell, Domhnall. 2002. "Emily Dickinson and Class." In *The Cambridge Companion to Emily Dickinson*, edited by Wendy Martin, 191-214. Cambridge: Cambridge University Press. Amherst: University of Massachusetts Press.
Mitchell, Domhnall. 2005. *Measures of Possibility: Emily Dickinson's Manuscripts*.
Montague, Richard. 1970. "English as a Formal Language." In *Linguaggi nella Società e nella Tecnica*, edited by Bruno Visentini, 189-223. Milano: Ed. di Comunità.
Moore, Colin H. 2012. "Zeugma." In *The Princeton Encyclopedia of Poetry and Poetics*, edited by Roland Greene, Stephen Cushman, Clare Cavanagh, Jahan Ramazani and Paul Rouzer, 1533. Princeton: Princeton University Press.
Morgan, Victoria N. 2010. *Emily Dickinson and Hymn Culture: Tradition and Experience*. Farnham, England, Burlington, VT: Ashgate.
Mudge, Jean M. 1975. *Emily Dickinson and the Image of Home*. Amherst: University of Massachusetts Press.
Nunberg, Geoffrey. 1995. "Transfers of Meaning." *Journal of Semantics* 12: 109-32.
Ossa-Richardson, Anthony. 2019. *A History of Ambiguity*. Princeton: Princeton University Press.

Ouida. 1871. *Under Two Flags*. 2 vols. Leipzig: Bernhard Tauchnitz.
Ovid. (n.d.) 1980. *The Metamorphoses of Ovid*. Translated and edited by Mary M. Innes. London: Penguin.
The Oxford English Dictionary Online. Oxford: Oxford University Press. http://www.oed.com/.
Pesetsky, David. 1999. "Linguistic Universals and Universal Grammar." In *The MIT Encyclopedia of the Cognitive Sciences*, edited by Robert A. Wilson and Frank C. Keil, 476-78. Cambridge, MA: MIT Press.
Phillips, Elizabeth. 1988. *Emily Dickinson: Personae and Performance*. University Park, PA: Pennsylvania State University Press.
Poesio, Massimo. 1996. "Semantic Ambiguity and Perceived Ambiguity. In *Semantic Ambiguity and Underspecification*, edited by Kees van Deemter and Stanley Peters, 159-203. Stanford: CSLI.
Pollack, Vivian R. 1974. "Emily Dickinson's Literary Allusions." *Essays in Literature* 1: 54-68.
Pollack, Vivian R, ed. 2004. *A Historical Guide to Emily Dickinson*. Oxford: Oxford University Press.
Porter, David T. 1966. *The Art of Emily Dickinson's Early Poetry*. Cambridge, MA: Harvard University Press.
Pugh, Christina. 2007. "Ghosts of Meter: Dickinson, After Long Silence." *The Emily Dickinson Journal* 16 (2): 1-24. doi:10.1353/edj.2007.0011.
Pustejovsky, James. 1995. *The Generative Lexicon*. Boston: MIT Press.
Raab, Josef. 1998. "The Metapoetic Element in Dickinson." In *The Emily Dickinson Handbook*, edited by Gudrun Grabher, Roland Hagenbüchle, and Cristanne Miller, 273-98. Amherst: University of Massachusetts Press.
Richards, Eliza, ed. 2013. *Emily Dickinson in Context*. New York: Cambridge University Press.
Rimmon, Shlomith. 1977. *The Concept of Ambiguity: The Example of James*. Chicago: University of Chicago Press.
Schlenker, Philippe. 2011. "Quantifiers and Variables: Insights from Sign Language (ASL and LSF)." *Baltic International Yearbook of Cognition, Logic and Communication*: Vol. 6.
Schöpp, J. C. 1997. "'Amazing sense distilled from ordinary meanings': the Power of the Word in Emily Dickinson's Poems on Poetry." In *Poetics in the Poem: Critical Essays on American Self-Reflexive Poetry*, edited by D. Z. Baker, 90-103. New York: Peter Lang.
Schuele, Melanie, and Leslie Tolbert. 2001. "Omissions of Obligatory Relative Markers in Children with Specific Language Impairment." *Clinical Linguistics and Phonetics* 15 (4): 257-74.
Seaton, Beverly. 1995. *The Language of Flowers: A History*. Virginia: University of Virginia Press.
Searle, John R. 1975. "The Logical Status of Fictional Discourse." *New Literary History* 6 (2): 319-32.
Sewall, Richard B. 1975. *The Life of Emily Dickinson*. New York: Farrar Straus and Giroux.
Shakespeare, William. (1609) 2000. *The Sonnets*. Edited by Stephen Booth. New Haven: Yale University Press.
Shakespeare, William. (1597) 2002. *King Henry IV, Part 1*. The Arden Shakespeare. Edited by David Scott Kastan. London: Thomson Learning.
Shakespeare, William. (1595) 2003. *Romeo and Juliet*. Edited by G. Blakemore Evans. Cambridge: Cambridge University Press.
Shakespeare, William. (1600) 2016. *Hamlet*. Edited by Anthony B. Dawson. New York: Norton.

Shakespeare, William. (1600) 2016. *Hamlet*. The Arden Shakespeare. Revised edition. Edited by Ann Thompson and Neil Taylor. London: Bloomsbury.
Sharvit, Yael. 2008. "The Puzzle of Free Indirect Discourse." *Linguistics and Philosophy* 31 (3): 353-95.
Sherwood, William R. 1968. *Circumference and Circumstance: Stages in the Mind and Art of Emily Dickinson*. New York: Columbia University Press.
Sidney, Sir Philip. (1595) 2002. *An Apology for Poetry*. Edited by R. W. Maslen. Manchester: Manchester University Press.
Small, Judy Jo. 1990. *Positive as Sound: Emily Dickinson's Rhyme*. Athens and London: The University of Georgia Press.
Smith, Martha Nell. 1992. *Rowing in Eden: Rereading Emily Dickinson*. Austin, TX: University of Texas Press.
Smith, Robert N. 1996. *The Seductions of Emily Dickinson*. Tuscaloosa: Alabama University Press.
Sparks, Elisa Kay. 2011. "Chronological List of Criticism on Emily Dickinson's 'My Life had Stood, a Loaded Gun.'" *Clemson University*.
Spear, Lynne E. F. M. 1998. "'There's a certain Slant of light.'" In *An Emily Dickinson Encyclopedia*, edited by Jane Donahue Eberwein, 283-84. London: Greenwood Press.
Spenser, Edmund. (n.d.) 1958. *The Works of Edmund Spenser. The Minor Poems*. Vol. 2. Edited by Edwin Greenlaw. Baltimore: Johns Hopkins Press.
Staines, David. 1982. *Tennyson's Camelot: The Idylls of the King and Its Medieval Sources*. Waterloo, Ontario: Wilfrid Laurier University Press.
Stalnaker, Robert. 1974. "Pragmatic Presuppositions." In *Semantics and Philosophy*, edited by Milton Munitz and Peter Unger, 197-213. New York: New York University Press.
Stalnaker, Robert. 1978. "Assertion." In *Syntax and Semantics 9*, 315-32.
Stechow, Arnim von. 1984. "Comparing Semantic Theories of Comparison." *Journal of Semantics* 3: 1-77.
Stechow, Arnim von. 1996. "The Different Readings of Wieder 'Again': A Structural Account." *Journal of Semantics* 13: 87-138.
Stechow, Arnim von. 2009. "Tenses in Compositional Semantics." In *The Expression of Time*, edited by Wolfgang Klein and Ping Li, 129-66. Berlin: De Gruyter.
Swaart, Henriette de. 2011. "Mismatches and Coercion." In *Semantics: An international Handbook of Natural Language Meaning* 1, edited by Claudia Maienborn, Klaus von Heusinger, and Paul Portner, 547-97. Berlin: De Gruyter.
Tennyson, Alfred. (1895) 1908. *Idylls of the King*. Edited by Hallam Tennyson. London: Macmillan.
Tennyson, Alfred. 1971. *Tennyson's Poetry: Authoritative Texts, Juvenilia and Early Responses, Criticism*. Edited by Robert W. Hill Jr. London: Norton.
Thackrey, Donald E. 1963. "The Communication of the Word." In *Emily Dickinson: A Collection of Critical Essays*, edited by Richard B. Sewall, 51-69. Englewood Cliffs: Prentice-Hall.
Thorne, James Peter. 1965. "Stylistics and Generative Grammars." *Journal of Linguistics* 1 (1): 49-59.
Vendler, Helen. 2010. *Dickinson: Selected Poems and Commentaries*. Cambridge, MA: Harvard University Press.
Wardrop, Daneen. 1996. *Emily Dickinson's Gothic: Goblin with a Gauge*. Iowa City: University of Iowa Press.

Waugh, Linda R. 1980. "The Poetic Function in the Theory of Roman Jakobson." *Poetics Today* 2 (1a): 57-82.
Webster, Noah. (1828) 1970. *An American Dictionary of the English Language*. New York: Johnson Reprint.
Weisbuch, Robert. 1975. *Emily Dickinson's Poetry*. Chicago: University of Chicago Press.
Weisbuch, Robert. 1998. "Prisming Dickinson; or, Gathering Paradise by Letting Go." In *The Emily Dickinson Handbook*, edited by Gudrun Grabher, Roland Hagenbüchle, and Cristanne Miller, 197-223. Amherst: University of Massachusetts Press.
Winkler, Susanne. 2005. *Ellipsis and Focus in Generative Grammar*. Berlin: De Gruyter.
Winter-Froemel, Esme, and Angelika Zirker. 2010. "Ambiguität in der Sprecher-Hörer-Interaktion: Linguistische und literaturwissenschaftliche Perspektiven / Ambiguity in Speaker-Hearer-Interaction: Linguistic and Literary Perspectives." *LiLi* 40.158: 76-97.
Wohlpart, A. J. 2001. "A New Redemption: Emily Dickinson's Poetic in Fascicle 22 and 'I Dwell in Possibility.'" *South Atlantic Review* 66 (1): 50. doi:10.2307/3202029.
Wyatt, Thomas. (n.d.) 1981. *The Complete Poems*. Edited by R. A. Rebholz. New Haven: Yale University Press.
Yamane, Maki. 2003. *On Interaction of First-Language Transfer and Universal Grammar in Adult Second Language Acquisition: Wh-Movement in L1-Japanese/L2-English Interlanguage*. University of Connecticut, Ph.D. diss.
Zetterberg Gjerlevsen, Simona. 2016. "Fictionality." In *The Living Handbook of Narratology*, edited by Peter Hühn et al. Hamburg: Hamburg University. http://www.lhn.uni-hamburg.de/article/fictionality.
Zipfel, Frank. 2001. *Fiktion, Fiktivität, Fiktionalität. Analysen zur Fiktion in der Literatur und zum Fiktionsbegriff in der Literaturwissenschaft*. Berlin: Erich Schmidt Verlag.

Index

acceptability 182
accessibility relation 116, 146f.
accommodation 18, 60, 70, 84, 88, 92, 94, 104, 152f., 207
active 106, 115
additive particle *see* presupposition
Aesop
– "The Crow and the Pitcher" 6
agent 21, 66f., 85, 87, 112, 115, 118, 161f., 168, 172, 175, 192, 209
allegory 212
ambiguity 7f., 31, 51, 67, 69, 71, 73, 88, 100, 105, 107, 116f., 135, 137f., 140ff., 145, 148, 154f., 163, 168ff., 186, 196f., 200, 207ff., 219
– global ambiguity 67, 74, 143
– lexical ambiguity 10, 20ff., 24, 27, 32, 34, 133, 140
– local ambiguity 23, 55, 69, 76
– logical ambiguity 73
– referential ambiguity 74
– structural ambiguity 10, 30, 74, 93, 103, 133, 136, 140, 142
– syntactic ambiguity 60, 62, 90, 134f.
anaphora 76
antecedent 18, 80, 82, 137, 150, 194, 197, 209
antonym 164
apparent flouting 195
apposition 69, 88, 100, 102, 104, 111
Appropriateness Condition 56f., 160, 203
Aristotle 164f., 171
– *Poetics* 164, 201
assertion 5, 18, 31, 61, 80, 93f., 171, 197
– Assert 5
Atlantic Monthly 164

Carroll, Lewis
– *Through the Looking-Glass* 43
cataphora 150
cleft-structure 58, 61, 73
coercion 8, 100, 161, 189ff.
common ground 5, 179, 189, 207

communication 2, 7, 37ff., 76, 158, 179, 189, 194, 207, 219
– non-fictional communication 80
comparison 15, 23, 36, 90ff., 102, 112, 115f., 164f.
– comparative construction 111
compositional interpretation 44, 57, 194, 209
– rules of composition 179, 181, 185ff., 199
conditional 6, 18, 29, 84, 122, 197
conjunction 47f., 61f., 69, 71, 76, 94, 100, 115, 118, 151, 155, 172, 185, 197, 209
connotation 4, 22, 36, 39, 168
– ambiguous connotation 86
consequent 18, 84
context 4, 17, 29f., 33f., 37, 45, 56ff., 62, 68, 79f., 83ff., 88ff., 104, 113, 121ff., 135, 142, 145f., 148, 150, 152, 155, 163, 165, 169, 174, 179, 188, 190, 192ff., 200ff., 206f., 209, 214
– biographical context 84
– context-dependency 27, 55, 133, 145f., 150, 160, 189
– contextual information 27, 31, 34, 49, 57
– contextual parameters 27
– contextual restriction 147
– fictional context 105
– fixed context 27
– intratextual context 92
– local context 81
contradiction 20f., 24, 32, 117, 120, 122, 133, 145, 147, 149f., 159, 175
cooperation 57, 106, 196
coordination 104
counterfactuality 22, 159, 189
– counterfactual conditional 18, 79f., 82, 86f., 93, 174
– counterfactual independence 201
– counterfactual question 84
Crane, Stephen
– "Flanagan and His Short Filibustering Adventure" 114

definite article *see* presupposition
definiteness 84, 94, 103, 150, 153

- covert definite 17
- definite article 103, 145
degree 27, 29, 39, 85, 116
- degree semantics 28f., 33
demonstrative 10, 17, 54ff., 66, 72, 74, 81, 203, 206, 208
- demonstrative resolution 76
- that 54ff., 60, 63, 68, 72, 90
- this 17, 19, 54ff., 68, 72, 90, 203
denotation 57, 80f., 103, 162, 168
Dickens, Charles
- *Bleak House* 43
- *Our Mutual Friend* 86
Dickinson, Emily – Letters 4, 170
- L243 119
- L261 4
- L268 218
- L320 119
- L353 119
- L486 119
- L506 119
- Master Letters (L187, L248, L233) 84, 91, 112
Dickinson, Emily – Poems 4
- J10/Fr61, "My wheel is in the dark!" 153
- J1059/Fr1083A, "Sang from the Heart, Sire" 202
- J106/Fr161, "The Daisy follows soft the Sun –" 91, 112
- J1126/Fr1243, "Shall I take thee, the Poet said" 1, 161, 174
- J1130/Fr1156, "That odd old man is dead a year –" 89
- J118/Fr103, "My friend attacks my friend!" 124
- J1182/Fr1234, "Remembrance has a Rear and Front –" 202
- J1185/Fr1236, "A little Dog that wags his tail" 87
- J1212/Fr278, "A word is dead" 124
- J124/Fr108, "In lands I never saw – they say" 91
- J1247/Fr1353, "To pile like Thunder to its close" 140, 159, 174
- J1261/Fr1268, "A Word dropped careless on a Page" 161
- J1351/Fr1359, "You cannot take itself" 167
- J1454/Fr1486A, "Those not live yet" 199
- J1467/Fr1501, "A little overflowing word" 162, 164
- J1525/Fr1571, "He lived the Life of Ambush" 167
- J1651/Fr1715A, "A Word made Flesh is seldom" 86, 121, 123, 161, 173
- J1663/Fr1730, "His mind of man, a secret makes" 167
- J1681/Fr1694A, "Speech is one symptom of Affection" 168
- J1763/Fr1788A, "Fame is a bee" 199
- J186/Fr237, "What shall I do – it whimpers so –" 87
- J258/Fr320, "There's a certain Slant of light" 144, 147, 159, 171, 173
- J276/Fr333, "Many a phrase has the English language –" 161, 164
- J288/Fr260, "I'm Nobody! Who are you?" 27, 32, 41, 43, 52, 145, 159, 172f., 176, 199, 213
- J315/Fr477, "He fumbles at your Soul" 141, 144, 151f., 215
- J328/Fr359, "A Bird came down the Walk –" 87, 135, 139, 213
- J339/Fr367, "I tend my flowers for thee –" 91, 112
- J448/Fr446A, "This was a Poet" 42, 54, 58f., 73, 76, 137, 153, 159f., 171, 183, 200, 206, 209, 219
- J462/Fr697A, "Why make it doubt – it hurts it so" 87
- J479/Fr458A, "She dealt her pretty words like Blades" 125
- J481/Fr460, "The Himmaleh was known to stoop" 91, 112
- J488/Fr446A, "This was a Poet" 17
- J499/Fr369A, "Those fair – fictitious People –" 86
- J500/Fr370, "Within my Garden, rides a Bird" 87
- J501/Fr373A, "This World is not Conclusion" 59
- J508/Fr353A, "I'm ceded – I've stopped being Theirs –" 152
- J531/Fr584, "We dream – it is good we are dreaming –" 202

- J565/Fr527, "One Anguish – in a Crowd –" 106
- J581/Fr436, "I found the words to every thought" 138, 202
- J587/Fr393, "Empty my Heart, of Thee –" 143
- J590/Fr619, "Did you ever stand in a Cavern's Mouth –" 113
- J613/Fr445A, "They shut me up in Prose –" 54, 165, 170f.
- J636/Fr700A, "The Way I read a Letter's" 36
- J642/Fr709, "Me from Myself – to banish –" 167
- J657/Fr466A, "I dwell in Possibility –" 64, 158, 162, 164, 166, 171
- J704/Fr734, "No matter – now – Sweet –" 89
- J706/Fr777, "Life, and Death and Giants –" 142
- J730/Fr850, "Defrauded I a Butterfly –" 154
- J738/Fr736, "You said that I 'was Great'" 26, 36, 159, 174, 211
- J748/Fr786, "Autumn – overlooked my Knitting –" 202
- J754/Fr764, "My Life had stood – a Loaded Gun –" 42, 99, 125, 142ff., 153, 155, 161ff., 169, 172, 176, 180, 185, 190, 192, 196, 200, 219
- J793/Fr753A, "Grief is a Mouse" 36
- J8/Fr42B, "There is a word" 83
- J85/Fr87A, "'They have not chosen me,' he said," 91, 112
- J921/Fr184A, "If it had no pencil" 19, 79, 84, 90, 134, 150, 152, 159f., 169, 174, 200

Dickinson, Emily – Poetics 8, 16, 1, 158, 161f., 175, 211f.
Dickinson, Emily –Letters
- Master Letters (L187, L248, L233) 110
disambiguation 73, 118, 172, 200, 210
disjunction 19, 29, 122, 155, 161, 185, 196f.
Donne, John 8
- "Batter my heart" 185
- "La Corona" 83
drama 203, 206, 218
Dynamic Function Application 81

dynamic interpretation 57, 62, 66, 81, 95, 150f., 194, 200f., 203, 206, 208

ellipsis 8f., 20, 30f., 55, 61, 65, 70, 76, 88, 115, 133, 137, 139, 141, 148, 186
- identity condition 137, 148
- noun ellipsis 138
- semantic ellipsis 66, 69, 209
Emerson, Ralph Waldo
- "Give all to love" 184
- "The Poet" 55
Emily Dickinson Archive 165
Emily Dickinson Lexicon 166
existential *see* modal force

feature 82, 87
felicity 56, 104, 152
FictionalAssert 5ff., 23, 37, 48, 74, 93f., 122, 195, 197f., 200f., 218
- mapping 38, 49f.
- relation R 6, 38f., 49f., 74f., 96, 122, 126, 195, 213
fictionality 2, 4, 7, 27, 37, 80, 93, 105, 174, 179, 189, 195, 200f., 203, 207ff., 212, 216, 219
figurative meaning 86, 91, 100, 105, 142f., 153, 161, 163, 173
formal semantics 1f., 101, 179, 209
Functional Application 186

Generative Grammar 3
generative linguistics 179
God *see* religion
gradable *see* degree
grammar 3, 7f., 127, 133, 136, 150, 155, 179, 181f., 185f., 189, 192, 198
- rules of grammar 94, 133, 158, 181
- ungrammaticality 9, 85
- universal grammar, UG 179, 182

Head Typing Principle 191
Herbert, George 8
Higginson, Thomas Wentworth
- "Letter to a Young Contributor" 164
Homer
- *Odyssey* 43, 215
homonymy 141

homophony 141f.
Horace
– *Ars Poetica* 123f.
– Ode IV.9 123

iconicity 139, 180
identity 39, 41f., 44ff., 49ff., 96, 114, 159f., 162, 171, 199, 214f.
idiolect 4, 202
imperative 31, 33
implicature 32f., 38, 90, 103, 105, 189, 195, 198
– conversational implicature 89
indeterminacy 50
– referential indeterminacy 55
– structural indeterminacy 65
index 56f., 66, 81
indexical 90, 97, 107, 180
– I 107
– thee 90
inference 6, 35, 86, 155, 164
infinitive 17, 46
inflection 108
interdependency 55
interrogative *see* question
inversion 9, 108
irony 63, 109, 114, 124

Jesus Christ *see* religion
Jonson, Ben
– *Timber* 123

lexical entry 63, 103, 140f., 144, 190
lexicon 190f.
linguistics-literary scholarship 1
literal meaning 7, 36, 59, 63, 86, 88, 91, 100, 103, 105f., 109f., 113, 118, 120, 123, 125, 142, 145, 161, 163, 169, 173

Mackay, Charles
– *Little Nobody* 43
metaphor 59, 82, 86, 90, 92, 107ff., 114, 123, 125f., 164, 169, 172f., 199, 203
metaphysical poetry 8
metonymy 102, 111, 139
Middle English 183
Milton, John

– *Paradise Lost* 163, 167
mismatch 42, 58, 82, 84, 88, 100f., 109, 113, 115, 145, 190
– type mismatch 45
modal 6, 30, 68f., 115, 117, 145, 147, 149
– may 145, 147f.
– modal force 116
– must 145, 147
– would 18, 22
Morgenstern, Christian
– "Fisches Nachtgesang" 187
morphology 69
– inflection 108
Murdoch, Iris
– *The Red and the Green* 217

negation 68

Old English 183
omission 183
Ouida
– *Under Two Flags* 109
Ovid
– *Metamorphoses* 123

paradox 159, 165, 167, 169, 175
partial function 58
passive 106, 112
past perfect 101
patient 66f., 87, 172, 209
Pelegromius, Simon
– *Silva Synonymorum* 123
performance 203, 206f.
performative analysis 92f.
performative interpretation 94, 97
performative quality 162
personification 82, 115, 125, 144f., 173
pleonasm 174
plurality 33, 101, 106, 152
poet-reader relationship 55, 73, 76, 138, 160
possessive 88
pragmatic step 7, 155, 194, 198
pragmatics 3, 5, 198
Predicate Modification 185
Present Day English (PDE) 181

presupposition 10, 18, 27, 35, 44, 58, 60f., 68, 70, 76, 79ff., 87ff., 91ff., 101, 104, 107, 133, 144f., 152ff., 161, 174, 192
- accommodated presupposition 94
- counterfactual presupposition 80
- existence presupposition 154
- presupposition accommodation 97, 152
- presupposition failure 101, 107f.
- uniqueness presupposition 18, 65, 103
pronoun 10, 56, 63, 66, 68, 72, 74, 79, 81ff., 87f., 90, 97, 106, 114, 139, 143ff., 148, 150, 152f., 155, 173, 193ff., 200, 203
- covert pronoun 66, 72
- elided relative pronoun 88
- he 151
- him 139
- I 143
- it 57, 61f., 72, 79ff., 84ff., 90, 144, 148, 173
- my 143
- pronoun resolution 57, 76, 200
- relative pronoun 55
- thee 90
- Theirs 152

qualia structure 190
quantifier 10, 41, 43, 46, 49, 51, 113, 145, 147f., 150, 160, 173, 176, 186, 199, 215
- any 148
- every 145
- no 41, 145
- nobody 41f., 44ff., 49, 51, 160
- none 148
- nuclear scope 186
- restrictor 186
- some 145, 149
- somebody 41, 43, 46, 49, 51, 160
question 31, 44ff., 50, 79f., 82, 90f., 93, 97, 150, 160f., 174
- polar question 93f.

reference 8, 34, 36, 41ff., 45f., 50, 59, 80, 107, 123, 150, 186, 205, 213
- non-referential 41
- referent 56ff., 66, 74, 79, 81ff., 87, 90, 94, 138, 145, 150f., 153f., 160, 192f., 195, 203, 206f.
- referential expression 133

- self-referentiality 55, 90
- temporal reference 69
- underspecified reference 97
reflexivity 68
reinterpretation 10, 20, 32, 41ff., 51, 63f., 82ff., 92, 100ff., 107ff., 112, 119f., 126f., 133, 144f., 160f., 163, 172ff., 181, 190f., 200, 208
- metaphoric reinterpretation 16
- referential reinterpretation 44, 46
relative clause 88
relative marker drop 182
religion 16, 22, 60, 83, 85ff., 91f., 95f., 121, 123, 135, 159, 170
- Bible 4, 16, 22, 83, 86, 161, 166, 169, 174
resultative construction 85

salience 33, 56, 68, 160, 203, 207, 215
scale *see* degree semantics
scope 29, 68, 88, 115, 215
selectional restriction 58, 143ff., 173, 190, 192
semantic composition 51f.
semantic openness 170
semantic violation 56
semantics-pragmatics interface 11, 133, 152, 155, 188, 193, 195, 198, 208
Shakespeare, William 184
- *Hamlet* 201, 203
- *Henry IV* 184
- *Romeo and Juliet* 114
- sonnet 18 123
Sidney, Sir Philip 170
Southey, Robert
- "Joan of Arc" 163
speech act 2, 162
- speech act operator 5ff., 23, 195, 200, 218
speech act operator *see* FictionalAssert
Spenser, Edmund
- *Amoretti* 106
St Teresa of Avila
- *Interior Castle* 168
Statius
- *Silvae* 123
subcategorisation frame 139
subject auxiliary inversion 80
symbol 37

syntax 3, 9, 16, 19, 54f., 60, 73, 100, 104, 139f., 148, 155, 183, 191
– syntactic reanalysis 181

Tennyson, Alfred 8
– "A Farewell" 184
– "The Coming of Arthur" 9
– "Tithonus" 119
– *Idylls of the King* 9
tense 101
topic time 101
trigger *see* presupposition

undefinedness 102, 144
underspecification 7, 11, 15f., 24, 28f., 39, 85, 103, 139, 153f., 212
– lexical underspecification 19, 90, 159
– structural underspecification 55
uninterpretability 82, 133, 150, 188, 191, 194, 199f.
uniqueness-condition 60
utterance time 89

vagueness 133, 135, 170
variable 56, 90, 151
– domain variable C 146
– free variable 17
variable assignment function 56ff., 60, 62f., 66f., 72, 74, 81, 84, 95, 146, 160, 194, 200
– mapping 56, 60, 63, 67, 160
variant 165, 182, 202
– lexical variant 165
variation 188
variety 181, 185, 198

Webster's *Dictionary* 4, 16, 28, 39, 89f., 109, 114, 165, 167, 169
Wyatt, Thomas
– "Whoso list to hunt, I know where is an hind" 106

zeugma 20, 175

www.ingramcontent.com/pod-product-compliance
Lightning Source LLC
Chambersburg PA
CBHW031806220426
43662CB00007B/540